H ERE, with the compliments of the Commonwealth Club of California, is your copy of the new book "Powers of the President in Foreign Affairs"—the result of a three-year research project commissioned by the Board of Governors of this Club and financed from the Club's permanent fund, held by Commonwealth Club, Inc. Authors of this book are four distinguished scholars under the general direction and editorship of Dr. Edgar E. Robinson, Margaret Byrne Professor of American History, Emeritus, Stanford University. The developing power in international relations under Presidents Truman, Eisenhower, Kennedy, and Johnson is here related to our nation's historic standards, the national needs in a nuclear age, and the Constitution.

Commonwealth Club-financed research studies have included such diverse topics as the impact of occupational restrictions; the equity of compensation to automobile accident victims; the Legislature of California (a study led by a distinguished former Governor) ; California social welfare (the first definitive examination). These research projects differ from the well-known reports of Commonwealth Club Study Sections (published in the Club's *Transactions*) in that they are the work of paid professional researchers instead of, as in the latter case, studies by volunteer Club members based on the testimony of experts pro and con.

If you would like additional copies of "Powers of the President in Foreign Affairs," a limited number are available at $5 each postpaid. Send order with remittance to the Commonwealth Club of California, Hotel St. Francis, San Francisco, California 94119.

Powers of the President in Foreign Affairs

POWERS *of the* PRESIDENT
in FOREIGN AFFAIRS

1945   1965

HARRY S. TRUMAN, DWIGHT D. EISENHOWER
JOHN F. KENNEDY, LYNDON B. JOHNSON

by

EDGAR E. ROBINSON

and

ALEXANDER DE CONDE, RAYMOND G. O'CONNOR
MARTIN B. TRAVIS, JR.

A RESEARCH STUDY COMMISSIONED BY
THE COMMONWEALTH CLUB OF CALIFORNIA
FOUNDED 1903

A RESEARCH STUDY
COMMISSIONED BY THE BOARD OF GOVERNORS OF
THE COMMONWEALTH CLUB OF CALIFORNIA
AND FINANCED BY THE FUNDS OF
THE COMMONWEALTH CLUB, INC.

THE AUTHORS

Alexander De Conde, Professor of American History,
    University of California, Santa Barbara.

Raymond G. O'Connor, Professor of American History,
    Temple University.

Edgar E. Robinson, Margaret Byrne Professor of American History,
    Emeritus, Stanford University.

Martin B. Travis, Jr., Professor of Political Science,
    State University of New York at Stony Brook, Long Island.

Limousines Line the White House as the National Security Council, the Cabinet, and Congressional Leaders Meet the Day of President's Cuba Missile Crisis Address

FOREWORD

We are traveling at a feverish pace through kaleidoscopic times. The past half century has witnessed such fantastic technological advances that previously formidable barriers of time and distance have been largely obliterated.

That earlier dream of journeying "Around the World in 80 Days" has given way to the realization that man can now cover that distance by aircraft in less than two days; and also to the realization that man can now orbit the earth by spacecraft in less than two hours. Again, that earlier amazement during World War I concerning the relatively ineffective shelling of Paris from a distance of 75 miles, has given way to the disturbing realization that man can now accurately fire guided missiles, which are capable of completely devastating vast areas, several thousand miles away.

Many factors, including the development of nuclear energy, have combined during the past fifty years to bring about awesome changes in man's capabilities and in the pattern of his existence. Regardless of the relative contributions made by these various factors, it seems clear that as a result all segments of the human race have been brought into close contact, and that man's horizons, both physical and sociological, have inevitably widened.

In this exciting and often bewildering maelstrom of development, the people of many nations have looked to the United States for leadership in international affairs; and in turn, the people of the United States have generally looked to their President to furnish the inspiration and direction for that leadership.

In this setting, two questions are of transcendent importance and interest: (1) What is the extent of the power that has been conferred upon the President of the United States, and (2) What is the extent to which our recent presidents have exercised that power?

These questions are of the type which the Commonwealth Club of California studies in view of its avowed purpose to "investigate and discuss problems affecting the welfare of the Commonwealth and to aid in their solution." The present investigation was conducted by authority of the Board of Governors under the supervision of the Research Committee. The research on this subject and the development of the analysis were entrusted to the direction of Edgar E. Robinson, Margaret Byrne Professor of American History Emeritus at Stanford University, and a past President of the Commonwealth Club. As Director of Research, he was authorized to seek the assistance of Alexander De Conde, Raymond G. O'Connor, and Martin B. Travis, Jr., in preparing this presentation. Its publication completes the first stage in the Commonwealth Club's customary procedure of finding and considering the facts basic to "problems affecting the welfare of the Commonwealth."

Only a subsequent vote of the entire Club on specific questions may be deemed to reflect the official position of the Commonwealth Club of California.

HOMER R. SPENCE
Chairman, Research Committee
Commonwealth Club of California

CONTENTS

ILLUSTRATIONS

PREFACE

In the tradition of the Commonwealth Club of California, that "association with scholars in the universities" may provide citizens with information vital to their function, this volume has been prepared for the members of the Commonwealth Club.

A time of crisis in the nation coincided with the outpouring of studies (1961-1965) upon various aspects of the foreign relations of the United States. Yet inquiry in a dozen universities revealed that the subject of pressing public concern visualized in this study had not been given adequate attention.

The participants in this undertaking have sought to examine the decisions and actions that each of the four most recent presidents of the United States have brought to bear upon the conduct of American relations with other nations in the period 1945-1965. The exercise of their powers, constitutional and otherwise, in the new age of nuclear potentiality has been the great problem of each of these presidents.

The story of these years is well known. Each day brings additions to our information. Countless facets of the story have already been revealed by participants. It has seemed necessary, however, to review the activities of each administration in considerable detail in order to provide a framework for analysis of the stupendous problem that now confronts the American people. How does the increase of presidential power in foreign affairs affect the future of our republican form of government and our democratic society in the United States?

Edgar E. Robinson

March 1, 1966

A President of the United States Addresses the Commonwealth Club of California

(Every President from Theodore Roosevelt to Dwight D. Eisenhower has accepted the Commonwealth Club's invitation to address its forum.)

I. Precedents: Powerful Presidents, 1789-1945

★ I ★

Precedents: POWERFUL

PRESIDENTS

1789 - 1945

by EDGAR E. ROBINSON

A CHANGING CONCEPT of presidential power in foreign affairs developed during the years 1945-1965, a concept allied with the appearance of hitherto unknown elements in the foreign relations of the United States. The government of this nation, through its President, was confronted with an unprecedented task and demanded of the people a new outlook upon their responsibilities.

The constitutional basis for the President's power in foreign relations is found in Article II of the Constitution of the United States:

> "The President shall be Commander-in-Chief of the army and navy of the United States. . . . He shall have power, by and with the advice and consent of the Senate, to make treaties, provided two-thirds of the Senators present concur; and he shall nominate, and by and with the advice and consent of the Senate, shall appoint ambassadors, other public ministers and consuls . . . . he shall receive ambassadors and other public ministers. . . ."

The actions of the President in foreign relations today go far beyond this brief enumeration of powers. How did this come about? How has this constitutional power of the President in relations with other nations emerged as we know it today? Just how does this power operate in heat of conflict, either in negotiation or in battle?

Until 1914 most of the interpretation of what was transpiring in the world outside the United States was left to public officials—of whom the President was foremost—and to specialists in foreign relations. In the ensuing fifty years the entire picture of the world in the mind of the citizen has changed. Unofficial interpretation of what has been and of what ought to be by the commentator, in the press or on radio and television, has created an image of the world desired by a few speakers or writers. The man in the street thus formulates his basic ideas of foreign "problems" and foreign policy from television, radio, and press correspondents.

The years since 1945 have been filled with reports of armed conflict somewhere in the world. The term Cold War is understood by every citizen. The outbreak of violence in furtherance of political programs within the United States may at times give concern to the President, although as a rule the officials of cities, of counties, and of states are herein responsible. But events outside the United States are the special concern of the President, whether it be the terror in Poland, 1945-1947; the Philippine Civil War, 1946-1950; guerrilla war in Greece, 1946-1949; the Indo-China War, 1946-1954; the Korean War, 1950-1953; the Guatemalan rebellion in 1954; the Hungarian repression in 1956; the bombardment of Quemoy and Matsu in 1958; the Cuban Civil War in 1958-1959; unheavals in the Congo in 1961; or civil war in Santo Domingo and South Vietnam.

In this rapidly changing world, analogy is dangerous to truth, and logic is often a vain resource. But in seeking a judgment upon the value of the President as agent of the public will, the individual American citizen may well ask himself whether the present objective of the United States is peace in an orderly world, or "cold war" in a world of continuous struggle among nations for international domination.

In the Kennedy administration, a new development gave importance to a group of young advisers the President had assembled. By 1963, and especially after the assassination of the President, came a flood of books that reflect the appearance of power in foreign affairs that supplements personal presidential power.

Concern on the part of scholars and journalists with the concentration, diffusion, and extension of executive power has been matched by concern in the Congress and in the press with the overwhelming influence of the Central Intelligence Agency in foreign relations. Yet it is evident today that the President's power as Commander-in-Chief of the armed forces not only transcends all the other powers prescribed for him in the Constitution, but supersedes all other elements that enter into the foreign relations of the United States.

In a world of independent nations convulsed by revolution, this nation finds it necessary to be constantly in a position of defense as well as in an attitude of helpfulness. We must do our part no less to protect ourselves and our way of life, than to make possible on the planet a future compatible with our own aspirations. In furtherance of these purposes, the governmental structure erected by the United States Constitution at the end of the 18th century, and altered in practice by necessity many times in the 19th and 20th centuries, appears now to be inadequate. The basic source of presidential power, for Johnson in the age of nuclear weapons, as for Washington in the age of the flint-lock musket, is still the document of 1787.

The twenty years following the end of World War II have witnessed the creation of a *modus vivendi* to meet the need, as we shall see, that the events of the Truman, Eisenhower, Kennedy, and Johnson administrations have forced upon the President in his new role in international affairs. A pragmatic attitude on the part of these presidents is not without precedent. For the exercise of presidential power in the stream of our history has not rested alone in law. In considering the powers of the President, numerous students have examined the acts, declarations, and decisions of each Executive and settled each "case." The facts have been established. Such undertakings form an important contribution for the use of scholars. But for the citizen, the "facts" are of little value unless they find place in the great stream of developments that make up the story of the American people.

The power to act—rather than power to negotiate, as this was understood in the 18th century—has become crucial in our national life. Yet this kind of power has been exercised by conquerors since the beginning of time. The absolute ruler was the man who *acted*. Our long struggle in the past two centuries has been to substitute for the will of the conqueror, the will of the people. In the nuclear age this widespread authority is possessed by millions of people in the United States. Yet the power of the President to *act* in the crises of the nuclear age must be immediate or it may be useless. It is thus the basic problem of our democracy that is under examination at the present time.

The framers of the Constitution were concerned with a different problem in 1787—the possibility of a movement against the new government of the United States when and if it came into being. Revolution was in the air, and allegiance to a King had been given up. Accordingly, the framers, in creating an Executive, gave him the power of "Commander-in-Chief of the Army and Navy of the United States."

Not until they reached the second article of their great document did the Founding Fathers deal with this Executive. In making certain that the fruits of their struggle for independence of a monarch should not be lost in lack of protection for the *citizen,* they gave their first attention in Article I to the legislative branch of government, the Congress, which was to represent in its two houses both the states and the *citizens.*

There was at the time no such ruler in the world as a president. In the new United States he was to have power "by and with the consent of the Senate" to make treaties. And "by and with the advice and consent of the Senate" he might appoint ambassadors and other ministers and consuls, and receive those from other countries.

From these words we can see that presidential power in foreign relations is technically a shared power, shared mainly with the Senate.[1] Nothing in the Constitution itself suggests who shall have a final or decisive voice in determining American foreign policy. The President's powers, even as Commander-in-Chief, appear to be limited, and his action, as we shall see, may always be checked by the other two branches of government, the legislative and the judicial.

Yet despite the vague language of the Constitution, giving the President powers that are implied rather than stated, the history of presidential power in foreign relations has been that of steady, apparently inevitable growth.[2] With a few exceptions, the President himself has exercised most of the power that the makers of the Constitution had divided between him and Congress. Power over foreign relations under the Constitution, in other words, became much more a personal function of the presidency than did the President's other constitutional duties.[3]

Nothing so clearly reveals the extension of the powers of the President in foreign relations as the "executive agreement." Although the State Department inaugurated the separate Executive Agreement series as late as 1929, more than 1,300 agreements with foreign governments were made by the President without the participation of the Senate, between the date of the inauguration of President Washington in 1789 and the beginnings of President Roosevelt's "revised" policy in 1939.[4]

As the President is the sole representative of the nation in its relations with other nations, diplomacy and communication with foreign governments are conducted in his name. He can delegate many of these duties, but diplomatic and foreign policy obligations take up so much of the President's official time, that many wonder how he can fulfill his other duties. In the twentieth century some of these obligations became virtually unavoidable, because increasing danger in foreign affairs called for increasing concentration of power in the presidency.[5]

In the beginning of the national government under the Constitution, it was natural that the power of the President in foreign relations should be personified in the leadership of General Washington. George Washington was widely known as the soldier who had led the forces of the Revolution to a successful conclusion of a seven-year war. The power he now acquired as Commander-in-Chief, subordinate as was thought to his civil powers, was scarcely notable in his own conception of his high office. There was neither army nor navy worthy of the name under the new government. Without diplomatic experience or knowledge of the legislative process, Washington felt that the Senate of the newly established Congress might control the new government. He was without reputation as an executive.

Throughout his eight years in office it was indeed the Congress that dominated the government and Washington emerged—as his Farewell Address showed—only the first among equals in his nation. Yet his influence has been incalculable, especially in the warning to his countrymen to steer clear of permanent alliances with any portion of the foreign world of competing and potentially hostile nations— a gesture not so much of isolationism as of prudence.

In action, Washington was scarcely successful in asserting his influence in foreign affairs. For example, in proposing the Jay Treaty with England, President Washington hoped to have the Senate "advise" him in formulation of the terms. The Senate set a precedent, however, by refusing to "advise" in advance, and debated the provisions of the treaty in secret before giving reluctant "consent" by a close vote.

It would be a mistake to limit our consideration of presidential power to the enunciation of powers set down in the Constitution or implied in Court decisions and legislative enactments since 1789. Power is, in its basic definition, "ability to act," or "authority to act or speak for others," or "possession of controlling influence over others." Few presidents have lacked ability to act; none have lacked authority to speak; and some, like Washington, Wilson, and Franklin Roosevelt, have found their greatest power in their influence over the American people.

Circumstances supplemented the "power" of the three presidents who were chiefly responsible for the present continental dimensions of the United States and its appendages in the Caribbean and the Pacific. Thomas Jefferson was fortunate in his exercise of power in diplomacy which brought about the purchase of Louisiana from Napoleon in 1803. Jefferson knew that he had no constitutional power to acquire the vast territory of Louisiana and considered calling for a constitutional amendment. But he did not take this course, feeling that the Congress would approve of his bold transaction. The Congress did approve, and voted to pay the bill of $15,000,000, or about three cents an acre for 828,000 square miles of the richest land in the world.

Another strong-willed President brought a yet greater area than Louisiana into the national domain as a result of the Mexican War. Faced with a long-existent boundary disagreement with Mexico in the area between the Nueces River and the Rio Grande, President James K. Polk ordered the disputed territory occupied by American troops. He then informed Congress that war had been forced upon the United States by the advance of Mexican troops into the disputed area. With the approval of his Cabinet for strong measures, Polk asked of Congress on May 11, 1846, a declaration of war. This was forthcoming in a sweeping vote supported by the necessary funds. Polk had used both his power as Commander-in Chief and his prestige as President to good effect.

This was not true of William McKinley who, as President of the United States in 1898 was a reluctant actor in the drama of the Spanish-American War. The second half of the nineteenth century had been marked by a growing belief that the United States was arbiter of the destinies of the Western Hemisphere. Although increasing numbers of Americans favored the independence of Cuba, President McKinley was unwilling to recognize rebellious Cuba as a state independent of Spain. When destruction of the U.S. Battleship *Maine* in Havana harbor demanded action, the President temporized, handing the matter over to Congress. The Congress, in accord with public sentiment in this country, promptly declared war, the means and ends of which were hotly debated not only by political party leaders but within parties as well.

Meanwhile, the decision on what came to be discussed as "colonialism" was found in passage by the Congress of a joint resolution by which the "Republic" of Hawaii was annexed to the United States in the summer of 1898. The war to "liberate" Cuba had given us, as well, military possession of Puerto Rico and of the Islands of the Philippines.

With the treaty of peace signed in December of 1898 and subsequently ratified by the Senate, President McKinley in peace as in war had been *led* to the decision. His basic attitude was never clear. He merely permitted himself to be swept into the strong current of world politics. At the time, however, there was no general belief among the American people that the President had the power in law and in precedent to make *his* policy the policy of the United States.

This attitude reflected the spirit of a pioneering people who in the nineteenth century had conquered the continent. In the middle of the century, nevertheless, a president brought the executive office to full stature, not only in the view of his countrymen, but in the eyes of the world. The extent of the power of the presidency in time of crisis, was still an undecided question when Abraham Lincoln assumed office in the greatest crisis the nation has yet faced. So far, notably, had American power symbolized by the President developed by mid-century, that the Civil War within our borders became a primary concern of the nations of Western Europe. Although Lincoln at once proceeded with all the prestige of his office in his effort to save the Union, it was only after four years of armed conflict that the extent of his power was clearly seen. He had forced the issue. Had he not done so, the principle of federal union would have died with the demise of the Constitution.

Lincoln demonstrated that within the provisions of the Constitution there could be an Executive who might exercise the powers of a Dictator—for a time and for a cause supported by the people. Despite his capacity in meeting the mounting catastrophes of those trying years of Civil War—and despite the good fortune of a "moral" cause—it is clear that Lincoln's success is attributable to his basic power as Commander-in-Chief of the military forces of the nation. This made possible his issuance of the Emancipation Proclamation as a war measure in areas in rebellion. It made possible as well his suspension of the writ of *habeas corpus,* together with his crucial choice and control of military commanders. If the nation reveres Lincoln for saving the Union, it is because his power as Commander-in-Chief established the prestige of the presidency and became an example to later executives.

With the mounting presidential power of the twentieth century, Theodore Roosevelt was at once identified. No one could doubt that President Roosevelt was in fact the head of the dominant branch of the government when he was in office. "My belief," Roosevelt wrote, "was that it was not only his (the President's) right, but his duty, to do anything that the needs of the Nation demanded, unless such action was forbidden by the Constitution or by the laws."[6]

Roosevelt, his long-range vision projecting presidential power beyond limits hitherto conceived of as possible, entered upon the international stage with the intention of playing a major role. Unlike any of his predecessors since John Quincy Adams, Roosevelt was keenly aware of the importance of the United States in a world of competing nations. He was convinced that this nation should lead all of the others and that the President himself should personalize this leadership. He was prepared to strengthen the armed forces, and in the civil branches of the government in Washington he established a group of aides devoted to realization of his American dream. In address and in action, he increased the power of the Executive at the expense of all other divisions of the government.

In his decision on Panama, for example, he showed what the Executive could do despite congressional delay. To encourage revolution where an independent state would then negotiate a settlement favorable to the United States would bring benefit, he believed, to mankind; and he proceeded accordingly. Sending the fleet around the world was a gesture introducing a newly active element in world politics.

Woodrow Wilson came reluctantly to the exercise of his power in foreign relations. Foreign policy was not discussed in the presidential campaign of 1912. Entering upon his term of office with minority support, as a result of a three-cornered poll, President Wilson did not visualize expansion of American interests beyond our borders. Events at the outset forced his hand.

With or without congressional approval, and often without consultation with his chosen advisers in the executive branch of the government, Wilson formulated a definitive foreign policy for the United States between 1913 and 1921. Prior to the declaration of war by Congress in April, 1917, the President had issued ninety important pronouncements, addresses, and appeals in which he spoke to the people of the problems in foreign relations that confronted the United States. His faith in democracy was so great that he did not exclude from the knowledge of the people any facts of international relations that were compatible with the public interest.

It was widely believed that Wilson had "kept us out of war" when he was re-elected to the presidency in 1916. Those words in an age of slogans presently changed to "making the world safe for democracy," and Wilson as Commander-in-Chief carried the nation through the First World War, refusing to make American policy a program of nationalism. This led to his inclusion of the program for a League of Nations in the peace negotiations.

Wilson's influence in international relations rested in his skill as protagonist of plans for *international* peace as distinguished from peace *between* nations, and his words were weapons in the international arena. His power as spokesman for the American people (as he thought) might have made over the world. This power, however, was subject to the approval of another constituent part of the American constitutional system. The Senate refused to ratify the proposed treaty of peace including membership in Wilson's own creation of the League of Nations.

While waging war, Wilson as Commander-in-Chief succeeded in bringing crucial aid to his Allies. When he had formulated the "peace without victory" prior to our entrance into the war, he believed he was speaking for the people of the United States. But he was vetoed by the people, as well as by Congress. A strong President, Wilson was nevertheless unable to establish his cherished design for the United States and the world.

Herbert Hoover's unprecedented knowledge of the world economic situation was reflected in his attempt to avert disaster in war-ravaged Europe by a moratorium on war debts; by his support of conferences on limitation of armament; and by his plan for an international economic conference which was to have taken place in London in 1933. Always mindful of the limitations upon his presidential powers implicit in the Constitution, President Hoover adhered strictly to the constitutional interpretation of his office.

Accepting at once the need of vigorous action in economic matters abroad, as well as at home, President Franklin Roosevelt promptly gave recognition to the Soviet Union in 1933. This was an indication that he would use every means at his disposal to assert the role of the United States in world politics. As war clouds gathered over Europe, Roosevelt's so-called "quarantine" speech in Chicago on October 5, 1937, signalized a change in the "neutrality" of the United States proclaimed by the Congress in 1935, and a new and positive assertion of American strength in a world at war in Europe and Asia. His message to Congress on January 4, 1939, advocated the boycotting of "aggressive governments." In September, 1940, by executive agreement, President Roosevelt turned over fifty destroyers to Great Britain, remarking in the following December, "We must be the arsenal of democracy." In January, 1941, a lend-lease bill was introduced in the Congress and passed to aid governments "whose defense the President deems vital to the defense of the United States." In July, 1941, when the Second World War was gathering fury, Roosevelt froze Japanese assets in the United States and placed an embargo on shipment of aviation fuel, gasoline, and oil to Japan. And in August of 1941, The Atlantic Charter, a declaration of common purpose, was agreed upon by President Roosevelt and Prime Minister Winston Churchill of Great Britain.

Thus, Roosevelt had dexterously led the nation from the posture of aloofness in which he had found it in 1933, to a position of involvement with Britain and France against Germany, Italy, and Japan. This personal conduct of American foreign policy by a vigorous executive exercising his constitutional power eventually produced a result not unanticipated. Japan, Far Eastern wing of the Axis powers, attacked American bases in the Pacific, and the United States Congress declared war upon the Axis nations. Franklin Roosevelt had not only led the American people out of their deeply-felt absorption in their own concerns, but had also maneuvered them into an acceptance of their duty, as he saw it, to come to the aid of the Allies in World War II. From this acceptance of duty in the world the nation has thus far not been able to deviate.

The supreme power of the President as Commander-in-Chief is seen in Roosevelt's arrangements with leaders of nations with whom we were allied in World War II. In the conferences outside the country, at Casablanca, Quebec, Cairo, Teheran—and later at Yalta—President Roosevelt entered into agreements affecting not only the conduct of the war but the conditions of peace that have affected every man, woman, and child in the United States. Each conference produced momentous decisions, most of which were not known at the time.

Again a President who had led the nation into war now led the nation toward a peace conditioned by his determination to establish an international organization—this time, a United Nations Organization.

At the time of his death in April, 1945, Roosevelt had in twelve years in office expanded the Executive power and its commitments throughout the world beyond recognition. On the whole, the Senate and House had acquiesced and the public had responded affirmatively. But he was criticized increasingly as the results of his executive role became apparent in the world.[7]

Franklin Roosevelt's accumulated power was to rise to new heights in the presidential careers of his successors, inheriting as they did a legacy of world-wide commitments. As Walter Lippmann has said: "The problem of our foreign policy today will not be fully understood until historians explain how our intervention in the Second World War to defeat the Nazis and the Japanese, became inflated into the so-called Truman Doctrine of the late 1940's, in which the United States said it was committing itself to a global ideological struggle against revolutionary communism."[8]

As the conflicts of nations have come to be contests of leaders, American foreign policies are to be found in presidential pronouncements. Leading from national strength that is geographic, industrial, financial, and military, the President speaks with authority and prestige. His power of persuasion is enhanced by the support of his people as he understands and interprets their outlook to other leaders and their people. While the President has an extraordinary range of powers based on the Constitution, on law, and on precedent, it is increasingly evident that "presidential power is the power to persuade."[9] This power of persuasion, however, is changing, baffling to understand, and often impossible to predict. Yet through his agents—the Secretary of State, his spokesman in the United Nations, and members of his Cabinet—the President has the means, in long-distance negotiation as well as in direct communication, to influence opinion throughout the world.[10] Woodrow Wilson, before he became President, put this in another way. "The President is at liberty, both in law and in conscience," he wrote, "to be as big a man as he can. His capacity will set the limit. . . ."[11]

II.   Harry S. Truman: New Dimensions of Power

Line Engraving from Continuous Tone Negative. Photograph by United Press International

President Truman Calls for National Support to Win the Korean War

★ II ★

Harry S. Truman: NEW DIMENSIONS OF POWER

by RAYMOND G. O'CONNOR

THE PRESIDENT of the United States possesses, one authority asserts, "the highest temporal power on earth."[1] The validity of this claim rests on the accretion of power in foreign affairs during the administration of Harry S. Truman. While exercising the powers of his office as established by precedent, Truman added new dimensions to the role of the Chief Executive in international affairs.

Among significant developments that marked an expansion in presidential power were: (1) production by the United States government of the first nuclear weapons, which meant the predominance henceforth of the military factor in foreign policy; (2) the membership of the United States in the United Nations, accompanied by unilateral responsibility for protection of the free world; (3) peacetime military alliances coupled with programs for the promotion of world prosperity; and (4) the emergence of new machinery for the formulation and execution of foreign policy.

Truman was the first Commander-in-Chief to possess authority *over nuclear weapons.* He employed it to end the war against Japan; to secure legislation placing the control of atomic energy under civilian rather than military jurisdiction; to urge international regulation; to pursue the development of the hydrogen bomb; and to avoid the use of nuclear weapons in the Korean War. He refused at all times to apply the threat of these weapons as an instrument of diplomacy.

17

No preceding President in peacetime had been so dependent on force for the successful implementation of his foreign policy. A drastic change in American military strategy took place during the Truman administration owing to novel methods of warfare, additional precautions on behalf of national security, and increased commitments abroad.

Truman was the first President to serve when the United States became a full-fledged member of an international organization dedicated to the preservation of peace. He supervised the negotiations that led to the Charter and secured its approval by the Senate. He influenced the congressional deliberations that produced the United Nations Participation Act, the enabling legislation which implemented the provisions of the Charter and placed the United Nations representative under presidential direction. Moreover, Truman's concept of presidential responsibilities and national obligation to this organization contributed vastly to its success.

Beginning with his resistance to Soviet expansion during the postwar settlements, President Truman sought to contain Russian ambitions outside the framework of the United Nations. These efforts were most dramatically revealed in the Truman Doctrine and the Berlin airlift during the Soviet blockade of 1948-1949.

Under Truman, the United States concluded its first peacetime military alliance, the North Atlantic Treaty. This treaty set a pattern for subsequent regional pacts in other parts of the world, and Truman resisted congressional efforts to restrict the President's assignment of troops overseas in implementing these agreements.

The Marshall Plan was designed to help European nations restore their economy, which had failed to recover from the effects of the war. The Point Four program promised technical assistance to the under-developed countries throughout the rest of the world. No previous administration had urged or carried out proposals of this type and magnitude.

The National Security Act of 1947 provided for the unification of the Armed Forces, which was aimed at greater co-ordination of effort in military policy. It also created the National Security Council and the Central Intelligence Agency, both designed to provide unity and collaboration among departmental agencies in the development and administration of foreign policy. Truman was instrumental in securing this legislation and was the first President to employ this machinery.

These new dimensions of responsibility and authority have become an accepted part of governmental organization. But at the time of their inception many of these innovations were strenuously resisted by members of Congress and segments of the public. At the same time, however, that the powers of the President were increased, in many respects certain conventional uses of power became more circumscribed. Most of the new American ventures in foreign affairs required Senate or congressional approval, either because they involved treaties or an expenditure of funds. Thus one or both houses of Congress came, in some respects, to have a strengthened voice in the formulation and execution of foreign policy. Also, as the United States became a leader of a coalition or an alliance of nations, it became necessary to consult with friends and allies before carrying new policies into effect. This broadening of the pluralistic nature of the presidency added new areas of authority, but it also placed restrictions on the ways in which this authority could be employed.

No doubt few contemporary observers in the spring of 1945 foresaw the impact that Truman was to have on the office of the presidency. In fact, the new President labored under a host of handicaps that presaged a weak and ineffectual administration.

Truman had been a reluctant compromise substitute for seemingly better qualified but more controversial vice-presidential candidates, which helped deflate his image. Truman had not participated in the great decisions, military and diplomatic, that marked the war years. Not only was he lacking in experience in these matters but he knew little about them, for Roosevelt neither consulted nor informed him about developments. The new Chief Executive also inherited a precedent of summit diplomacy, for the Roosevelt-Churchill-Stalin triumvirate had handled earth-shaking questions on a personal level. In this respect alone Harry Truman was moving into fast company, and he had little preparation for this kind of responsibility.

Not being elected in his own right was a further disadvantage to Truman. Uncertain whether he represented the general consensus, Truman lacked the feeling of confidence and support that a popular mandate provides, and he was deprived of the broad power base that only victory at the polls can produce. This inadequacy was felt by others at all levels, from White House staff to grass roots constituents, in the various communication media, and in all branches of government. The attitude accompanying this feeling was reflected, consciously or unconsciously, in expression and action, which tended to inhibit effective presidential leadership.

Truman was further hindered by inheritance of the policies and commitments of his predecessor. As a loyal New Deal Democrat and a vice-presidential candidate, he had endorsed the practices and proposals of his chief, and upon his accession to the presidency Truman announced that he contemplated no departures therefrom. But even if the new President had wanted to institute changes, in most cases such an effort would have required a modification of party, congressional, and public attitude which generally had supported the late Chief Executive.

As a final handicap, Truman inherited the problems that Roosevelt had not been able to resolve, primarily those dealing with the Russian demands in postwar settlement. Signs of Soviet intransigence and ambition were becoming apparent before Roosevelt's death, and the conclusion of the war in Europe brought a new concern to American and British leaders.

The collapse of the German war machine so soon after Truman entered the White House precipitated an inevitable struggle in the Congress. During the years following the attack on Pearl Harbor Congress had supported the President with little deviation. Now, chafing under restrictions imposed by need for wartime unity and by nearly thirteen years of a strong Chief Executive, the members were anxious to reassert their Constitutional prerogatives. Traditionally, the legislative branch restored the balance of power after deferring to the President during hostilities, but never before had the equilibrium been upset for so long. Truman needed Senate support for the United Nations and the projected peace treaties, as well as congressional authorization for funds to bring relief to areas ravaged by war. These issues, coupled with the enormous problem of converting the nation from war to peace, placed congressional co-operation at a premium and portended a shift in the relationship of the two branches.

Truman was compelled to rely on Roosevelt appointees, many of whom had been selected for reasons known only to the former President. Often the position of such an appointee depended less on professional competence than on ability to function under Roosevelt. Truman quickly learned that changes in personnel, organization, and procedure, were needed before he would possess a satisfactory administrative system. The transition, costly in time and errors, added another burden to an already overwhelming task.

Approval of an order terminating Lend-Lease to Russia immediately offended Stalin and created a good deal of resentment. "That experience," Truman later observed, "brought home to me not only that I had to know exactly where I was going, but also that I had to know that my basic policies were being carried out."[2] Unfortunately, the process of acquiring this knowledge took place during a crucial period for the nation and the world.

Truman's frustration is revealed by an entry in his Diary dated September 20, 1945, where he mournfully confided that it was "almost impossible to get action around here even from the most loyal of the close helpers."[3] Only gradually did he become aware of all that he had fallen heir to.

Perhaps the most damning analysis of the situation was made by Great Britain's wartime leader, Winston Churchill:

> We can now see the deadly hiatus which existed between the fading of President Roosevelt's strength and the growth of President Truman's grip of the vast world problem. In this melancholy void one President could not act and the other could not know. Neither the military chiefs nor the State Department received the guidance they required. The former confined themselves to their professional sphere; the latter did not comprehend the issues involved. The indispensable political direction was lacking at the moment when it was most needed. The United States stood on the scene of victory, master of world fortunes, but without a true and coherent design.[4]

Whether the predicament was as bad as Churchill believed is questionable, and whether Roosevelt could have been more successful under the circumstances is conjectural, but the fact remained that the direction of American foreign policy had passed from the hands of a professional into those of an amateur. No doubt many people throughout the world responded to Truman's plea for prayers in this hour of need.

But all was not on the debit side of the ledger, for the new President had a number of advantages operating in his favor. The many years spent as a public office holder were invaluable, for Truman understood and loved the great game of politics. Experience had provided him with the knowledge and practice of political manipulation, and he was thoroughly familiar with the intricacies of the governmental process. His years in Washington as a Senator gave him invaluable insights into the operations of the Senate and this understanding plus the relationships he had formed were to help him secure advice and consent for major foreign policy measures. As chairman of the Special Committee Investigating the National Defense Program, Truman had come to know "probably more about the over-all war effort, its complexities, its faults, and its failures, than anybody in Washington, with the exception of the President himself."[5]

Perhaps no single experience could have been more valuable in preparing him for the immense role that he had so suddenly assumed.
Truman also found himself, as he later put it, "part of an immense administrative operation. There had been a change of executives but the machinery kept going on in its customary routine manner
and properly so."[6] Thus the normal functions of government continued without making immediate demands on the new President,
and in the majority of cases where decisions were imperative he could
rely on the advice of experienced subordinates. Under the circumstances he had no other choice, and fortunately he could depend on
most of his advisers.

The most pressing problems were the prosecution of the war and
the creation of the United Nations organization. Both of these matters were in capable hands, for Roosevelt had bequeathed a successful
team in the Joint Chiefs of Staff to manage the former, and planning
and personnel were ready for the conference scheduled to convene
in San Francisco. The former President had left much of the strategy
and tactics of the war in the hands of the military experts and Truman was not inclined to interfere. The bipartisan approach to a world
organization with Senate participation also appealed to Truman,
who wanted to avoid a repetition of Wilson's experience.

The new President also benefited from public and congressional
emotional support. A widespread feeling of sympathy for his plight
and a charitable atmosphere strengthened his own resolve and gave
him confidence. Understanding and assistance during the initial
months of trial were accompanied by expressions of pleasant surprise
that Truman was performing so well. His image on acceding to the
office was such that people expected very little of him, and this impression was valuable in sustaining his position.

Much of the support that Truman secured for his major foreign
policies was due to the existence of a bi-partisan, or non-partisan,
approach to external affairs during most of his administration. The
attack on Pearl Harbor had destroyed party division over the conflict, and the Fulbright and Connally resolutions had pledged both
houses of Congress to American participation in an international
organization to preserve peace. Bipartisanship toward war and collective security established a precedent for Democratic-Republican
co-operation in foreign affairs. Truman was able to continue this
joint approach by working closely with members of Congress, who
actually became partners in the formulation and execution of policy.
Though Senator Arthur H. Vandenberg deserves a major share of
the credit for the success of this collaboration, the President usually

was careful to invite congressmen to White House meetings, insure that proposed policies were discussed with members of both parties, and appoint Republican and Democratic Senators as delegates to conferences. Aware that one-third plus one of the Senators present could destroy his program for a postwar world, Truman readily perceived the need for bipartisanship in foreign affairs. The election of a Republican Congress in 1946 intensified the need to remove diplomacy from partisan exploitation if Truman were to carry out his international objectives. The fruits of bipartisanship were revealed by the record. Though much of the administration's key domestic legislation was rejected by Congress, every major foreign policy program was approved. The Congress modified and delayed presidential proposals, but never defeated them.

Truman's concept of the office of the presidency helps explain his role in foreign affairs. "The President," he believed, "must use whatever power the Constitution does not expressly deny him."[7] Thus theoretically, at least, he placed himself in contrast with those who thought they should be limited to powers specifically enumerated in the Constitution. This attitude was to be of vital significance in his role of world leader. Another aspect of his attitude toward the office is vividly revealed by the motto occupying a prominent position on his desk: "The Buck Stops Here." On his first day in office Truman notified the Cabinet that "I would be President in my own right and that I would assume full responsibility for such decisions as had to be made."[8] Advice and disagreement were encouraged in the discussion stage, but the final word was to come from the President, and after he had spoken Truman expected controversy to end.

Truman's concept of the office derived from his own personality, his experience as an elected official, his great admiration for Franklin D. Roosevelt, and his interpretation of history. Though he indulged in periods of self-deprecation, Truman had a streak of stubbornness that overcame what some considered his excessive humility. Often addicted to private and public observations on his shortcomings, he obstinately resisted change once his mind had been made up. So long as he bore the responsibility he intended to exercise commensurate authority. Throughout his career as an elected official Truman had functioned in this manner, and now he was merely extending the same practice to the highest office in the land.

The most impressive example of presidential leadership with whom Truman had been closely associated was Franklin Roosevelt. Truman was greatly impressed by his predecessor's conduct of the office, especially his extensive use of presidential powers. Struck by what he considered to be Roosevelt's success in foreign affairs, particularly the way in which the President had overcome isolationist sentiment in Congress, Truman made himself leader and director in the formulation and execution of foreign policy. In his capacity as President of all the people, and not as Harry Truman of Missouri, he was to do what he thought would be to the best interests of the country. Believing that "Every great president in our history had a policy of his own, which eventually won the people's support,"[9] Truman intended to act as chief educator. Roosevelt, in his opinion, had made his policies prevail by this means and Truman planned to profit by this example.

But Truman was also aware of instances where presidents had not been successful in securing support for their policies. Like Roosevelt, he had been impressed by Wilson's failure to win Senate approval of the Treaty of Versailles on his terms, and he attached considerable importance to the lessons of the past. "I had trained myself to look back into history for precedents," he wrote, "because instinctively I sought perspective in the span of history for the decisions I had to make. That is why I read and re-read history. Most of the problems a president has to face have their roots in the past."[10] Truman often emphasized this theme. "If a man is acquainted with what other people have experienced at this desk," he observed to a biographer, "it will be easier for him to go through a similar experience. It is ignorance that causes most mistakes. The man who sits here ought to know his American history, at least."[11] To John Hersey, preparing a "Profile" for *The New Yorker,* Truman suggested "some biographies of great men; everybody meets up with difficult decisions, and it's good to know how some big men faced things in the past."[12]

On the other hand, Truman tried to profit from the past without becoming its prisoner, for he used the record of human experience to provide him with insights and understanding rather than pat answers to current problems. His broad acquaintance with history of other nations, as well as his own, enabled him to grasp the significance of developments in various parts of the world and see them in a deeper perspective. It also fostered a "long view," by which he could visualize the far-reaching implications of a particular policy. He found this perspective invaluable when confronted with challenges to world order.

Truman was fond of Justice Holmes's observation that "a page of history is worth a volume of logic."[13] His own reading of American history revealed that "a successful administration is one of

strong presidential leadership," for "weak leadership—or no leadership—produces failure, often chaos, and something else."[14] His
heroes, whom he placed in the category of strong presidents, were
George Washington, Theodore Roosevelt, Woodrow Wilson, and
Franklin D. Roosevelt. Each had dominated his administration, established precedents, taken unpopular positions, and usually had his
views prevail. Significantly, each of these presidents faced crises
where leadership determined the outcome. Truman, deeply conscious
of the responsibilities of his office, was ever mindful of the role that
his predecessors had played—or failed to play—when the nation's
future was at stake. Determined to err on the side of action rather
than inaction, he wanted his administration to be remembered for
its accomplishments rather than its derelictions.

His own experience and his reading of history had also convinced
him that "a president has to be a politician in order to get the majority to go along with him on his program."[15] Politics, to Truman,
was man's noblest profession. He rejected the notion that it was an
occupation to be ashamed of, ridiculed, or left in the hands of incom-
petents. The institution of government was one of man's greatest
achievements, and it was designed to provide for the security and
welfare of the people. Since the United States was a republic, not a
democracy, the people placed their trust and authority in the hands
of elected representatives, who by definition were politicians. To
fulfill his obligations, the politician in office exercised an enormous
amount of control over the destinies of the electorate, and the job
had to be placed in a category commensurate with its responsibilities.
The public trust, then, was a sacred trust, and a position of power
was one of prestige and pride. The methods of politics—persuasion
and manipulation—were not to be derided but respected and fostered, and the practice was an art at which the President should be
a master. The Chief Executive had to be the chief politician, for he
was the dominant figure in the governmental apparatus. It was not
enough for him to furnish direction. He also had to obtain support
for the implementation of his policies, a task that placed the greatest
demands on his talents as a politician.

Truman viewed the political process and political power largely
in terms of persuasion. "In the long run," he said, "his [the President's] powers depend a good deal on his success in public relations.
The President must try to get people to do the things that will be
best for the most people in the country. I often say that I sit here at
the President's desk talking to people and kissing them on both cheeks
trying to get them to do what they ought to do without getting

kissed."[16] The symbolism contained in this statement is pertinent, though the method is customarily applied to babies. Perhaps its greatest significance lies in the fact that this commonplace campaign technique has nothing to do with the issues or the professional competence of the candidate. Truman, then, may be inferring that the means by which support for a policy is gained often have little relevance to the merits of the proposal.

In this regard, Richard Neustadt has pointed out that a president's "bargaining advantages in seeking what he wants are heightened or diminished by what others think of him."[17] The image projected by Truman, or at least the way he appeared to others, is somewhat paradoxical. As a presidential figure he lacked the dignity that normally is associated with the office, and in this respect he lacked popular appeal. On the other hand, the public could easily accept him, for he was just "Harry." Moreover, he was a colorful character with his plain talk, flamboyant sport shirts, and ludicrous caps. His folksiness, his eccentricities, and his position made him newsworthy and encouraged reporters to write of his activities in stories that kept him on the front page.

On the other side of the coin, Truman's reputation as a statesman was usually higher in the Washington community than it was with the general public. His abilities as Chief Executive were often more apparent to those closest to the workings of government than they were to the average citizen, who tended to look more at the man than at the office. "Ideally," concludes Douglass Cater, "a president must earn the favor of both these publics if he is not to suffer an erosion of his powers."[18] The very characteristics that made Truman attractive as a *person* tended to detract from his image as a President and weakened his appeal as a national leader. The degree to which this proved a handicap will become clearer in the subsequent portions of this account, especially if Walter Lippmann is correct in concluding that "in matters of war and peace . . . the prevailing public opinion has been destructively wrong at the critical junctures."[19]

At the Democratic Convention in 1956, Adlai Stevenson asked Truman, "What is it I'm doing wrong?" The former President looked out the window and pointed to a man in the street. "The thing you have got to do," he replied, "is to learn how to reach that man."[20] An experienced Washington reporter has concluded that "since power is fragmented in the American system, public opinion is called on more regularly than elsewhere to act as arbiter among the competing policies and politicians."[21] If this be so, then the problem for plain Harry Truman was compounded, for he felt that he knew what had to be done, but his stature made him less effective in this type of leadership. However, he had a key factor acting in his favor. His administration spanned a period of challenges to national security, and appeals for unity at moments of danger have usually been successful. Truman was able to secure congressional and public support for proposed changes in policy by exploiting a crisis. Thus much of his success in directing the course of American foreign relations stemmed from his effective dramatization of the threat to the nation's safety and his grim description of the alternatives facing the country.

When Truman became President he had no idea that a crash project, undertaken by the government to develop an atomic bomb, was nearing completion. Yet, in his role as Commander-in-Chief, he was the first President to direct that the bomb be used. He was faced with the unprecedented problems of dealing with the international regulation of this most destructive weapon; of assimilating it into the national defense structure; of possessing it as an instrument of diplomacy; and of ordering the development of its hydrogen successor. His action in each of these cases was determined by considerations of foreign policy, and control of this weapon added a new dimension to the power of the President in international affairs.

When the Alamagordo blast demonstrated the success of the Manhattan Project, the war in Europe had ended and Truman was engaged in the summit Potsdam Conference. The President's guarded revelation to Stalin that the United States had "a new weapon of unusual destructive force" evidently made little impression on the Soviet leader. Moreover, the use of the bomb as a coercive device for securing concessions from the Russians was considered by the American delegates and rejected. Throughout his administration, Truman refused to employ nuclear weapons as a "big stick" in order to achieve his diplomatic objectives. Even when the Soviet Union violated its agreements in Europe, when the government of Chiang Kai-shek was losing to the Chinese Communists, when the crisis arose over the Berlin blockade, and when imminent defeat faced the United Nations forces in Korea, Truman refrained from brandishing the bomb. In the latter instance an innocuous remark at a press conference to the effect that the government had always "considered" the use of atomic weapons, set off a furor which brought British Prime Minister Clement Attlee to the United States for a hasty conference, though the White House carefully explained that the President's remark was not intended to convey a threat nor an intention. Clearly, Truman could have exploited America's possession of the weapon on these occasions even after the first Russian atomic explosion in 1949, for as late as the Korean War the United States continued to have a virtual monopoly in numbers and means of delivery. It was also well within his power to employ such a tactic, both in his capacity as Commander-in-Chief and as director of foreign relations. He was the only person who could speak authoritatively for the government and the nation on these questions, and the decision was exclusively his.

No doubt there were a number of reasons Truman did not use the threat of what Secretary of War Henry Stimson called "the most terrible weapon ever known in human history." The Russians, he realized, knew that the United States would employ the device in the event of an all-out war, for it had done so against Japan. The Russians were also aware that the state of the American armed forces would not permit the waging of a "conventional" conflict against a major power, so a warning that the bomb might be dropped would be a superfluous provocation. As an admirer of the Republican Roosevelt, Truman was familiar with two of his admonitions: "Speak softly and carry a big stick," and never threaten force unless you are prepared to use it. Truman was not willing to use the bomb to resolve any of the issues that appeared during his administration. His determination to preserve peace, his awareness of the horrors of nuclear war, and probably most important, his conviction that such drastic means would be out of all proportion to the desired end, prevented him from brandishing the atomic arsenal. The Communist strategy of piecemeal aggression, usually by non-military means, furthermore, cast doubt on the usefulness of the atomic bomb as an instrument of diplomacy.

Dropping the bomb on Japan was another matter. A long hard war against a tenacious enemy promised to continue for another year. Believing that Japanese fanaticism ruled out an earlier capitulation, American planners called for invasion of the home islands. Casualties for both sides were estimated in the millions, with an equivalent drain on national resources. The magnitude of the military problem had induced Roosevelt's advisers to press for Russian aid, which he secured only by offering political concessions. At Potsdam Truman adhered to his predecessor's commitments, partly because he wanted to avoid giving the Russians an excuse for violating their agreements.

"The final decision of where and when to use the atomic bomb," Truman has written, "was up to me. Let there be no mistake about it. I regarded the bomb as a military weapon and never had any doubt that it should be used."[22] Nevertheless, following a procedure that became almost a commonplace in his administration, the President sought advice from top civilian and military members of his staff, whose opinions were given orally and in writing, individually and collectively. Conscious of the gravity of his decision, virtually every alternative course of action was explored in depth before the Chief Executive made up his mind. There is no conclusive evidence that he was motivated by a desire to end the war before Soviet forces could occupy strategic positions in the Far East and obstruct the peace in that area. Essentially, his choice was determined by military necessity and the desire to save lives, both American and Japanese.

Impressed by the enormous destructive power of the bomb and its equally great potential for the peaceful application of atomic energy, Truman sought international control of the weapon and governmental jurisdiction over the development of this new force. Congress was willing to provide the necessary legislation but it disagreed with the President on the issue of civilian or military control. The first bill, introduced shortly after the Japanese surrender, provided for military direction of the program. But Truman, in a message to Congress on October 3, 1945, strongly urged that it be placed under civilian authority. Contending that the development of atomic energy was too extensive a task for narrow military administration and that international co-operation would be rendered impossible thereby, Truman wrote public letters, often met with his advisers together with members of Congress, and spoke out vigorously at press conferences. Finally, an amended bill was passed and signed by the President on August 1, 1946. He had succeeded in securing a civilian Atomic Energy Commission. But the new law placed restrictions on the amount of assistance that could be extended to Great Britain in the continued development of this field.

Provision for international control of atomic energy was deemed essential by Truman. American initiative prompted the United Nations to create an Atomic Energy Commission in January, 1946, and in June, Bernard Baruch outlined the American plan before that body. Comprehensive and technically feasible at that stage of nuclear development, the proposal was rejected by the Soviet Union, which demanded the immediate destruction of all atomic weapons as an initial step. Truman was willing to relinquish control of this monopoly to the United Nations, but he believed that neither world peace nor national security would benefit from the elimination of atomic bombs from the American arsenal.

Thus during the crucial period of America's exclusive possession of nuclear weapons and the breaking of the monopoly by the Soviet Union in 1949, Truman secured congressional consent for his approach to the development of atomic energy and general domestic approval of his program for international control. His latter policy was supported by the Western nations and he steadfastly refused to accept the Soviet proposal for unilateral nuclear disarmament. In this added dimension of presidential authority and responsibility Truman had acted vigorously and decisively, exercising restraint or firmness as the occasion warranted. Though one may disagree with his position, he was consistent, he made his views clear, and he did direct the course of the nation in this unprecedented field.

Another crucial area in which the President exercised a major influence was in the effect this new weapon was to have on America's postwar military structure. Roosevelt had envisioned the victorious allies serving as world policemen functioning through the United Nations to preserve peace. America's contribution would be her navy, for he contemplated the withdrawal of troops from overseas and the return to a continental army. As the war progressed Roosevelt began to have serious doubts that China could provide stability for the Far East, and he had begun to suspect Russian ambitions before his death. Truman was immediately plunged into the maelstrom of postwar settlements with the Soviet Union, but no clear-cut military posture had emerged. Ideally, the armed forces, as an instrument of foreign policy, should have been designed to conform with American commitments throughout the world. Yet the extent of these commitments was not clear and an immense confrontation with Russia was not anticipated.

Truman also had to contend with the traditional American attitude toward the armed forces, namely, that when the fight was over they should be demobilized and the temporary warriors be allowed to return to their normal peacetime activities. The United States had enjoyed a large degree of free security due to the huge oceans that separated her from major powers. The navy, as the first line of defense, protected the nation and supported its modest ambitions in foreign affairs. The army existed as a token force that could be rapidly expanded in time of need, and the need was defined as war. What may have been apparent to some, but was accepted by few, was the fact that the second world conflict had drastically altered the defense imperatives of the United States.

As a result of this conflict two new dimensions were added to American vulnerability. First, improvements in weapons systems made possible sudden large-scale attacks on the United States, which ruled out the luxury of leisurely mobilization. Second, the nation was committed to involvement in European and Far Eastern affairs to a much greater extent than ever before. The exact degree to which the United States had become involved was not, at this time, very clear. But it should have been evident that the conventional attitude toward the military establishment had to change in keeping with these drastic innovations. And as the inexperienced helmsman was trying to avoid the shoals of a new and uncharted course, he was confronted with the spectacle of the "ultimate weapon."

There was no consensus as to how the atomic bomb should be incorporated into the American defense structure. If it were placed under international control it could be dismissed as a factor in military planning, and strategic requirements would have to be met with conventional forces. If it were to remain an American monopoly for an indefinite length of time the army and navy, many believed, could be reduced considerably.

The defense dilemma was further compounded by the controversy over the role of aircraft. Strategic bombing had come of age in the war and its exponents bolstered their claims by pointing out that theirs was the only method of delivering nuclear weapons. Truman found himself the focal point of the dispute between the various services over the composition of the armed forces, the portion of the budget that each should receive, and the future role of the atomic bomb. He not only had to determine the merits of the individual service claims in regard to fighting efficiency, but he had to establish American military responsibilities in order to decide what American defense needs should be. These complex decisions had to be made in the midst of a clamor at home for demobilization, a reduction in government expenditures, and a return to normalcy.

Abroad, the President was burdened with the launching of the United Nations, the vagaries of peace settlements, mounting Russian intransigence, and an explosive situation in China. In the midst of this chaos and uncertainty his was the only position of leadership, the only place where people could look for that brave new world promised by Roosevelt, which had fired the imagination of millions everywhere. No one else could do the job, and Truman had no illusions about the role of force in the implementation of foreign policies. What he did not know was how much and what kind of force he needed, and for what purpose. As Truman has observed, "Any schoolboy's afterthought is worth more than the forethought of the greatest statesman."[23] The President made his choice on the basis of what he thought was essential and what he believed could be achieved under the circumstances.

The compromise that emerged placed greater emphasis on strategic bombing with a reliance on nuclear weapons. Congressional support for atomic armament was usually forthcoming, but "on other national defense issues—on demobilization, the draft, universal training, speedy unification—the administration usually stood somewhat ahead of Congress in security-mindedness."[24] Truman insisted on a balanced budget, so when Congress reduced taxes over his veto he pared military appropriations accordingly.

Army planning was dominated by the "citizen army" concept, which envisioned a small professional force that could be expanded rapidly by a mobilization of reserves. Administration attempts to secure legislation for Universal Military Training to implement this program were unsuccessful, though the proposal did reflect the limitations of defense thinking at this time. The planners were preparing for a conflict similar to World War II, with huge armies and swarms of aircraft playing decisive roles. The prospect of limited war was ignored as Air Force proponents emphasized the deterrent value of planes armed with atomic weapons. Thus military policy lagged far behind foreign policy commitments, especially after 1947 when America's determination to contain Communist aggression became clear.

Yet a reappraisal of American military policy in light of foreign policy objectives was accelerated by the adoption of a "containment" policy and the compulsion of two startling events. In August, 1949, the Soviet Union exploded it first atomic bomb, several years ahead of American forecasts. Then, in the latter part of the year, the Communist Chinese drove the last of Chiang Kai-shek's forces from the mainland. These developments prompted the President to order that work on the more powerful hydrogen bomb be continued, and that the State and Defense Departments make a comprehensive study of American foreign and defense policies. A document finally emerged which established "at least some kind of order of priority and magnitude between economy and security, domestic and foreign commitments, economic and military means, American and allied strength, and short and long-run national interests."[25] Labeled "NSC-68" when referred by the President to the National Security Council, this study synthesized ends and means in American strategy. It provided a framework for the rejection of total war concepts in military planning and contained the rationale for the sort of limited conflict that erupted in Korea soon after the study was completed. This shift in strategic thinking was the result of new commitments and new threats, and it was accomplished by a group dominated by State Department officials. The President, in appointing a special committee for the task that minimized Defense Department participation, revealed his awareness of the shortcomings of previous approaches by existing organization.

It seems unlikely that the drastic changes in military policy advocated in NSC-68 would have been accomplished if the Korean aggression had not taken place. As Senator Vandenberg recorded in his diary, "Some of the boys who voted to gut the arms program are pretty sick of what they did in the light of atomic developments twenty-four hours later. But they'll just 'play politics' and blame Truman for not telling us sooner although if he had, they would just as readily accuse him of trying to influence the arms vote with a scare."[26] In order to secure congressional approval of an arms buildup the President had to pose a clear and present military danger to American security. Truman had persuaded Congress to enact legislation to resist Soviet aggression in Europe through economic aid and a military alliance, but even the President contemplated no increase in defense expenditures. The administration budget submitted in January, 1950, for the fiscal year 1951, compiled prior to NSC-68, asked less for the armed forces than was requested the previous year. But before Congress could take final action on the budget the invasion of South Korea had begun.

It may seem strange that the President had not provided for Communist aggression of this type in view of his previous efforts to contain communism by means short of war. As early as October 30, 1947, he had made a note to discuss with the Secretary of State "the military implications of a satellite attack," whether "we need a plan to meet this," and "should we proceed to make one."[27] Apparently, nothing was done to provide for such a contingency, since the Korean incident found the United States woefully unprepared.

The blame for this dereliction can be fixed more easily than it can be explained. "To Truman himself," writes one authority, "belongs the chief responsibility for the poor state of defense preparation in 1950, for he had relaxed his leadership to follow the desires of Congress and the public in restricting military budgets."[28] But there is no indication that the President wanted to spend more for defense at this time. He, too, was dedicated to economy and a balanced budget.

Moreover, the United States had not committed itself to the unilateral military protection of every nation attacked by Communist troops. Secretary of State Dean Acheson, in his speech to the National Press Club on January 12, 1950, had carefully distinguished between those areas that fell within the American defense perimeter and those which were the responsibility of the United Nations. The Rio Pact and the North Atlantic Treaty were regional agreements that envisaged joint resistance to aggression. The former, providing for hemisphere defense, could best be implemented by naval and air power. The latter, in face of the overwhelming superiority of Russian ground troops, relied on strategic air power and the atomic bomb in cooperation with allied forces. Obviously, American capabilities had not caught up with American responsibilities, assumed or implied, and the comprehensive assessment in NSC-68 was still in the planning stage.

During the years immediately preceding the Korean War, the President obtained pretty much what he asked for in military appropriations, and he had established the budget ceilings to which service demands had to conform. Since the requests tended to exceed the ceiling, Truman at times personally reduced the amounts desired. His reliance on nuclear weapons is revealed by the allocation of a steadily increasing share of the defense budget to the air force, and to this extent he, "the armed services, as well as almost all other interested governmental agencies and members of Congress, assumed that if war came it would be total war with the Soviet Union."[29] Truman's shocked reaction to the news of a Soviet nuclear explosion, its contribution to his decision to proceed with the hydrogen bomb, and his order for an overall assessment of military policy, demonstrate the importance he attached to this weapon. But the criteria of economy and preparation for all-out war established a defense policy inadequate to support American foreign policy objectives. The shortcomings of this approach were dramatically revealed when the first act of Communist military aggression took place.

Certainly one of the most vital powers of the President in international affairs is his role as Commander-in-Chief, and Truman "determined the overall level of military effort and the strategy by which it was shaped."[30] The added responsibilities assumed by the United States after World War II markedly increased the peacetime role of force in diplomacy, and the advent of intercontinental aircraft armed with nuclear weapons provided the President with new dimensions of responsibility and power. By failing to co-ordinate American capabilities with American commitments however, Truman endangered national security and world peace. But, after Japan's surrender, he never authorized the bomb's use in war or employed it overtly as a tool of diplomacy. The final decision in these matters was his alone, and his tight control over this ultimate weapon was never relaxed.

America's commitment to the unilateral protection of the Free World developed gradually in response to Russian violation of wartime agreements, Soviet intransigence at postwar conferences, Communist aggression, and the inability of the United Nations to preserve the independence of small nations. The "containment" policy was actually inaugurated by Truman within two weeks after he became President, when he severely rebuked Soviet Foreign Minister Molotov for his government's failure to observe the Yalta accords on Poland. This policy, pursued further in the lengthy negotiations over postwar settlements as the United States sought to prevent the Soviet Union from extending its influence in eastern Europe and the Far East, received its most dramatic exposition in the Truman Doctrine and the Berlin crisis.

"Containment" as a policy achieved its ultimate fulfillment in a series of military alliances beginning with the Rio Pact of 1947 and the formation of the North Atlantic Treaty Organization in 1949. Although the alliances form another dimension of presidential power they constituted an extension of the containment strategy to the ultimate category of resistance. Nor does their collective nature exclude the unilateral factor, for the United States promoted these treaties and provided the military force that made them effective. And every step in the evolution of containment was taken by the President, who adopted or secured the adoption of a strategy designed to check Communist encroachment.

The major American postwar objectives in Europe were to render Germany impotent and restore free governments to those nations that had suffered from Nazi and Fascist tyranny. Assuming that the wartime unity with Great Britain and Russia would continue, peace was to be preserved through the United Nations after the victors had redrawn the boundaries of Europe and provided for domestic stability. Soviet recalcitrance over Poland and Rumania served notice that the Allies were not in agreement on all the political aspects of reconstruction, and the problems were so fundamental that they could be resolved only by heads of state. The wartime summit conferences had established a precedent that seemed to offer a solution to the impasse, and President Truman reluctantly found himself thrust into the role of chief negotiator as he agreed to meet with Churchill and Stalin at the German town of Potsdam.

Truman was not the first President to leave the country in a diplo-

matic capacity but he probably was the least prepared. Wilson and
Roosevelt had the benefit of experience in office and direct participation in the events that led to summit meetings. Truman had been
a somewhat distant observer in spite of his association with the administration, and much of his preparation for the momentous task of
dealing with the British and Soviet leaders was accomplished by a
perusal of background papers on the sea voyage to Europe. Herbert
Feis has noted that the President's method "was not the way of a
patient student of pondering mind, but rather the way of a person
who habitually sought simple versions from which he could arrive at
quick decisions."[31] Not only was Truman lacking in direct knowledge of previous negotiations. He was facing two powerful, seasoned
veterans shortly after assuming office. Few expected Harry Truman
to fill Roosevelt's shoes in dealing with these formidable contestants,
and the prospects for American success must have appeared slim
indeed.

The President had determined beforehand that he would pursue
an independent course. He refused to approach the conference in concert with Great Britain against Russia, primarily to avert Soviet suspicions and preserve freedom of action. Russian trust and friendship
could be maintained, he hoped and believed, if he were firm, fair, and
adhered to the wartime accords. While he was aware of instances of
Soviet duplicity and had been warned repeatedly by certain of his
advisers that Russian aims were expansionist, Truman felt that Stalin
could be trusted so long as the United States made its position clear
and lived up to its own agreements. His attitude and his personality
were to determine the nature of this confrontation with the Soviet
Union, especially after Churchill was replaced by Clement Attlee
following the British election.

The major objectives of the United States at Potsdam were to ar-
range for the completion of the peace treaties, work out details for
the occupation of Germany, clarify the Yalta Declaration concerning
free governments in eastern Europe, and settle the thorny reparations
question. With the exception of Russian policy in eastern Europe, substantial progress was made on every issue—progress which later
proved largely illusory. But the fledgling President gained a good
deal of experience and learned a number of lessons at the conference.

Truman began his personal diplomacy with lack of assurance, then
seemed to gain confidence as the discussions proceeded. Ignorant of
many details, he betrayed impatience when Churchill indulged in long
historical discourses or the conversation drifted from the subject at
hand. The President, in his simplified approach to problems, pleaded

for decisions rather than oratory. Yet his often superficial version of the issues prevented him from perceiving the complex factors which usually ruled out the kind of clear-cut agreement that he wanted, and blinded him to the merits of demands made by the other participants. His effectiveness was further dulled by his espousal of certain pet projects, such as his proposal for the creation of a system of free inland waterways throughout Europe. Bold and foresighted though the proposal might have been, it diverted attention from the more immediate questions and weakened his hold on the conference.

The President's inexperience also led him to rely extensively on the new Secretary of States, James F. Byrnes, for advice. Appointed to succeed Edward Stettinius because Truman thought the person next in line for the presidency should have occupied an elective office, Byrnes had served Roosevelt in the capacity of "assistant president" and had attended the Yalta conference as an adviser. Though Senator Vandenberg deplored Byrnes's appointment on the grounds that he was a partner in the "Yalta betrayal" and would follow a "soft" policy towards Russia, Truman was to rely heavily on the new Secretary until later events produced a break. Wide recognition of Byrnes's influence reduced the President's effectiveness in dealing with leaders of other nations, who were eager to exploit any signs of uncertainty.

One of the greatest limitations on the President's negotiating ability at Potsdam was his lack of bargaining power. At the wartime conferences Roosevelt was in an enviable position, for he possessed the armed might that could determine the outcome of the conflict. Potsdam was the first summit meeting at which the United States was a suppliant, for neither the British nor the Russians needed American military assistance. On the contrary, Truman wanted firm assurances from Stalin that Russia would enter the war against Japan. The erstwhile allies could hope for economic aid from the United States, but Truman was in no mood to hold it out as a *quid pro quo* for acquiescence to American political demands.

Another handicap in discussing territorial settlements and spheres of influence was the overwhelming preponderance of Soviet troops in the areas under dispute. The zones of occupation had been established long before the phenomenal success of the cross-Channel invasion, and Truman had faithfully observed the agreement to withdraw American forces from territory assigned to Russia. The President had also ordered a considerable reduction of troops in Europe to bolster the Far Eastern theater and satisfy the clamor for demobilization at home. A token occupation garrison to maintain order constituted no threat to the mighty Red army. Under the circumstances, the President was compelled to base his demands on Stalin's wartime agreements and the dictator's sense of justice.

For Truman, Potsdam was an invaluable experience. He received his baptism with fire by engaging the foremost world leaders in lengthy, wearisome debate over the most intricate problems. His ability to deal with these men on equal terms, to take issue with them, and at times have his views prevail, gave him an assurance previously lacking in his makeup. Truman also learned a great deal about international relations and the aspirations of other nations, and he gained insight into the nature of the statesmen who conducted the affairs of these countries. The significance of this personal experience is considerable, for by participating in this conference the President had eliminated the middleman, the diplomatic agent on whose reports he had been compelled to rely. The process of education in foreign affairs was accelerated enormously.

In retrospect, Truman's decision to press for Russian entry into the war against Japan may have been a mistake. Of course the agreement had been made by his predecessor, and Truman did not want to furnish the Soviets an excuse for further violation of other accords. Also, as in Roosevelt's case, the President was under heavy pressure from his military advisers to secure Russian intervention. He then, like Roosevelt, in this instance was subordinating political to military considerations, for Stalin secured valuable concessions in exchange for his assistance. Yet Truman, mindful of the wrangling over the joint occupation of Germany, left Potsdam determined that Russia should not share in the administration of defeated Japan. In this effort he was to prove successful.

Potsdam was Truman's first and last summit meeting. Functioning as chief diplomat in addition to his other foreign policy roles had placed an enormous burden on the Executive office, a burden that interfered with the more important task of policy formulation and approval. Moreover, Truman was not temperamentally suited for the interminable haggling over details or the subtleties that characterized diplomatic negotiations. Frustration, not stimulation, was his reaction when talk was substituted for action, and he preferred spending his time making decisions. Always ready to deal with representatives of other nations individually, Truman balked at meeting with them collectively. Perhaps a better informed, more experienced Truman would have responded differently, although he never succumbed to the temptations of a summit conference in the subsequent years of his presidency.

At Potsdam the heads of state had agreed that the European

peace treaties should be drafted by the foreign ministers, and at a Moscow conference Byrnes made concessions to the Russians that caused the President to lose faith in his Secretary of State. Truman for some time had been disturbed by what he considered Byrnes's tendency "to think of himself as an assistant president in full charge of foreign policy."[32] The climax occurred at Moscow, when the Secretary consented to the Russian-controlled governments of eastern European satellite states. This action directly contradicted Truman's position at Potsdam, and the President felt that he could no longer tolerate what he believed to be a usurpation of his Constitutional authority. In a letter dated January 5, 1946, which Truman asserts he read to Byrnes, the President admonished the Secretary of State on his conduct and directed that he refrain from pursuing an independent course in foreign affairs.[33]

Byrnes denies that this letter was ever read to him, or that the President ever indicated disapproval of any position he took on foreign policy.[34] Regardless of whose recollection is more accurate, the President clearly felt that the Secretary of State was exceeding the bounds of his post, and his eventual replacement by General Marshall became a foregone conclusion. Truman's concept of his office permitted no delegation of authority for policy decisions. Responsibility for the conduct of foreign relations had been placed in his hands by the Constitution and he was determined that it should remain there. Challenges by civilian or military appointees were not to be tolerated.

In the summer of 1946, another incident occurred which cast doubt on the President's ability to control the direction of American diplomacy. Secretary of Commerce Henry Wallace felt that Russo-American relations could be improved by making greater concessions to the Soviets, and his ideas were embodied in a speech that he showed the President prior to delivery. Truman, at a press conference, declared that he had approved the speech, though he later explained that he had meant approval of Wallace's right to give the address, not approval of the contents. The startling implications of Wallace's remarks and the indication of presidential endorsement provoked a strong protest from Secretary of State Byrnes, then involved in a foreign ministers conference in Paris, and a threat of resignation if Wallace were not disavowed. Though Truman finally requested Wallace's resignation, the entire episode gave the impression that the President was not master in his own administration and neither understood nor controlled American foreign policy. The impact of this incident on the nation and the rest of the world was startling. Not only did the President's image suffer but the entire direction of American foreign policy was placed in jeopardy. Truman may have been misunderstood, as he insists, or he may have been confused, but whatever the explanation the repercussions of the President's conduct were damaging to American objectives abroad.

Among the many troublesome areas during the postwar years, China provoked one of the major disputes over presidential prerogative in foreign affairs. For nearly two decades the Nationalist government of Chiang Kai-shek had waged a civil war against the Communist forces of Mao Tse-tung, a civil war that had been halted periodically while both sides concentrated on fighting the Japanese. After Japan's surrender, Truman, realizing the need for a strong, unified China to promote stability in the Far East, sent General Marshall as his personal representative to help bring political order to that war-torn country. Neither side appeared to be willing to make the necessary concessions and the civil conflict was resumed. The United States recognized and was sympathetic to the government of Chiang Kai-shek, and Truman did see that considerable military and financial aid was extended to the Nationalists. He believed, however, as did many of his advisers, that drastic reforms were required before the Nationalists could secure popular support, and the President began to withhold aid in an effort to coerce Chiang into making the desired changes. As the war continued members of Congress sought to induce the administration to furnish the Nationalists with aid on the grounds that they were fighting communism, but Truman refused to budge. He believed that Chiang was losing the war not from a lack of supplies, but because the people had lost confidence in his government. Victory would come from political reform, not more weapons nor additional American dollars.

The entire responsibility for America's China policy rested with the President. Even when Congress legislated aid to the Nationalists, Truman withheld much of it because he believed the supplies would be wasted. Convinced that Chiang was responsible for his own destruction, and unwilling to commit American troops to his support, the President refused to advocate or take action to preserve the Nationalist government. Primarily, he felt that Chiang's fate was in his own hands and that the United States should not salvage a corrupt, ineffectual regime.

It is doubtful that Truman ever believed that Mao and his followers were merely "agrarian reformers." But at the time he was not sufficiently dedicated to the containment of communism in the Far East to commit the United States to the defeat of the rebels. Whether the responsibility for the Communist victory in China can be attributed to the President, Chiang Kai-shek, Mao Tse-tung, or other factors is debatable, but the control of American policy toward the conflict remained in the White House. The episode is a revealing example of the way in which a president can thwart Congress in the field of foreign affairs, and pursue a policy of containing communism in Europe through the Truman Doctrine, while rejecting the principle in another part of the world. Not until the Korean war exposed the danger of Communist aggression in the Far East did Truman permit an American military advisory group to cooperate with Chiang's administration on Formosa.

The most dramatic and far-reaching step taken by the President in regard to the unilateral protection of the Free World was his announcement of the Truman Doctrine. Truman himself regards it as "the turning point in American foreign policy, which now declared that wherever aggression, direct or indirect, threatened the peace, the security of the United States was involved."[35] The situation that prompted the doctrine arose out of an agreement between Churchill and Stalin over spheres of influence in southeastern Europe. Britain secured responsibility for Greece and aided the government in its efforts to halt Communist guerrillas who were attemping to take over the nation. In early 1947, England's financial predicament led the British government to notify the United States that it would have to withdraw support to Greece by the end of March.

The implications of this move were appalling, for without aid the Greek government would collapse and the entire eastern Mediterranean, including Turkey, would presumably fall into the Soviet orbit. The President quickly determined to prevent a vacuum by having the United States take over British responsibilities in that area, a view reinforced by the recommendation of the State-War-Navy Coordinating Committee. But the decision to furnish assistance to Greece and Turkey was not so difficult as was the problem of convincing Congress and the American people of the necessity for this action.

To secure support for his proposal, the President called congressional leaders to the White House for a briefing by himself and Secretary of State Marshall. At a second meeting the group was presented with detailed plans for American aid. Senator Vandenberg, aware of the drastic nature of the move, observed that the best method of obtaining the desired legislation would be to go before the nation and "scare hell" out of the people. Following this advice, the President on March 12, 1947, before a joint session of Congress, reviewed the situation, outlined the alternatives, and placed the program in a broad framework of American resistance to a new form of totalitarian aggression.

Over two months elapsed before the bill was sent to the President. Among the congressional modifications was an amendment directing that the aid be withdrawn under certain conditions, including a United Nations resolution asking that it be halted. Nevertheless, the President had obtained authorization for a project that marked a drastic departure in American foreign policy. A Republican dominated Congress had responded to the presidential request because it had been handled adroitly and based on an ultimate threat to national security. Truman's approach, with its emphasis on the crisis proportions of the situation, had won the support of the communications media and the public, both of which made their influence felt in Congress. The latter had responded to Executive initiative largely because of the leadership the United States had gradually assumed in resisting Communist aggression, and this leadership had developed from the direction in which the President had led American diplomacy.

This instance of bipartisan support for presidential policies in foreign affairs was a direct result of the new role accorded the United States in the world, a role fostered by Truman that added significant powers to his office. The precedent established by this congressional action was to endure, for never again was that body to reject a major foreign policy request by the President. From this point onward, it was to serve as a legitimizing and amending vehicle for Executive initiative abroad.

American determination was tested by the Berlin blockade in the summer of 1948, which brought the first confrontation of the United States with the Soviet Union. The city of Berlin, located deep within the Russian zone of occupation in Germany, had been placed under joint control of the allied victors. A dispute over currency provided the excuse for a severance of land and water transportation routes from the Western zones to Berlin, and the United States was faced with a unique dilemma. Since the population of the city could not survive without imports of food, fuel, and other necessities of life, the situation was critical and immediate action was imperative.

Three alternatives were available. The blockade could be recognized and Russia given hegemony over the city. This would amount to a defeat for the Free World, with an attendant loss of prestige and a weakening of resistance to communism elsewhere. Second, an armed convoy could be sent through one of the weaker sections of the blockade. This involved the likelihood of armed resistance and a probable escalation into all-out nuclear war. A third alternative was to go over the blockade by means of a gigantic airlift to provide the beleaguered people with the necessities of life and demonstrate Western firmness.

In making his choice, the President received little help from his advisers. A specific recommendation from the National Security Council arrived too late, and the Joint Chiefs of Staff overcame the President's predisposition for an armed convoy by pointing out the overwhelming numerical superiority of Soviet conventional forces. As one authority puts it, "Both General Clay and President Truman had to take upon themselves the decision to attempt to hold out in Berlin, without the benefit of agreed staff recommendations."[36] And though Clay, the American military governor of Germany, urged resistance, the decision to remain was exclusively that of the President.

Actually, Truman had made his choice soon after the blockade was instituted but he needed help on its implimentation. His military advisers insisted that the proposed solution was impracticable, and they introduced what seemed to them insurmountable obstacles. Thus the President's task was not to convince Congress and the public that the United States should resist the blockade—prior developments and the absence of any need for legislation eliminated those considerations—but to persuade his assistants that the job could be done. That he did so in the face of opposition from within his administration reveals another facet of his exercise of authority, though he did defer to the Joint Chiefs of Staff in regard to the use of armed force.

"Probably no powers granted to the President by Congress," declares one scholar, "were quite as significant to the nation's future in the summer of 1948 as the President's inherent discretionary power over our conduct in the Berlin crisis."[37] The cold war had placed enormous strains on the office, and Truman had called on his Constitutional and accrued authority as the struggle intensified. Hard won congressional approval of one step was interpreted, apparently, as consent for presidential action in subsequent similar situations. The crises occasioned by Communist moves enabled the President to adopt more extreme measures on his own initiative to counter Soviet threats. The Berlin emergency evoked no appeal to the legislative branch or a consultation with congressional leaders. Public opinion and the attitude of other nations evidently played little part in the President's decision. The American response to the Berlin blockade was as nearly complete an exercise of Executive prerogative as the nation had seen since the end of World World II.

It marked the culmination of presidential efforts to commit the nation to the unilateral protection of the Free World, and it revealed that the future of resistance to communism would be determined in the White House.

It must now be evident that President Truman was dissatisfied with the administrative organization bequeathed him by President Roosevelt. The new Chief Executive preferred a more orderly hierarchy, with clear-cut lines of responsibility and authority. He rejected his predecessor's method of establishing agencies and appointing administrators whose duties overlapped, and who could be employed or played off against each other to suit Roosevelt's particular administrative technique. Truman also perceived the need for a reorganization of the nation's security machinery in light of the recent war experience and the enlarged role of the United States in world affairs. He realized the importance of collaboration among the different branches of government whose activities impinged on foreign relations, and he wanted this collaboration to take place outside the White House.

On the other hand, the President had no intention of delegating to subordinates either his responsibility or his authority. Important decisions were his alone to make, and he had no desire to shirk his duties. But, fully aware of the complexities and demands of his job, he wanted to provide himself with the kind of establishment that would enable him to perform his tasks most efficiently and effectively. Executive orders and presidential sponsored legislation helped streamline the system, and a comprehensive study of the organization of the Executive branch of the government was made by the Hoover Commission, whose findings were endorsed by the President and partially implemented by Congress. In the realm of foreign affairs, the primary consideration was the need to provide the President with information and advice on which to base his decisions, and a system through which the action directed would be carried out most expeditiously with a minimum of supervision from the Chief Executive.

Truman, however, did not want others to do his thinking for him. Insisting on a presentation of various points of view, he usually demanded extensive background studies before reaching a conclusion. In seeking the counsel of others he acknowledged the value of experts. But he was aware of their limitations, especially insofar as their overall grasp of affairs was concerned. Truman recognized the need of group effort in attacking momentous international problems, while at the same time he guarded against becoming a virtual prisoner of his staff. Occasionally he found someone who saw things as he did and functioned along similar lines.

George Marshall and Dean Acheson were notable examples of this remarkable affinity, and both men enjoyed an extremely close professional relationship with the President. On no occasion, however, did either attempt to usurp any presidential prerogatives, as Truman felt that Byrnes had done. When Acheson was appointed, the President stressed that the tasks and responsibilities of the two offices were different. He neither intended to perform the functions of the Secretary of State nor allow Acheson to exercise the powers of the Executive. A near perfect harmony prevailed during their long association.

Yet the appointment of Acheson impaired the administration's support in Congress, for he never gained the confidence of that legislative body. Often the Secretary of State is a source of domestic strength for a President's foreign program. The office carries more prestige than any other appointive post, and Truman had considerably enhanced the prospects for acceptance of his foreign policies by the previous appointment of George Marshall. Acheson proved a major liability from the time he served as Under Secretary. Identified with the New Deal and the abortive China policy, British in appearance and giving the impression of haughty condescension, he offered an attractive target for a frustrated and volatile opposition. Though Truman vigorously defended the Secretary at every opportunity, maintaining that critics merely used Acheson as a means of attacking the popular Truman policies, his presence in the Cabinet was a distinct handicap to the President in relations with Congress.

The National Security Act of 1947 created the most significant new machinery to emerge during the Truman years for the planning and conduct of American diplomacy. The impetus for this legislation came largely from the President. It reflected his desire for the consolidation of activities duplicated in the various branches of the government, for duplication required him to consult numerous officials for information and advice on similar matters. Truman sought to unify the armed forces under one cabinet secretary and one chief of staff. He wanted an intelligence agency to gather information and provide a single source for data to be furnished the President and other interested agencies. Finally, he needed a body to provide him with the collective advice of top officials in those branches of government most intimately concerned with foreign policy and defense questions.

The National Security Act of 1947 was intended to satisfy these demands, but Congress was not willing to accept all of the President's recommendations. Though the armed forces were placed in a single Department of Defense, a separate Air Force was created and a civilian head was established for each of the three services under a cabinet secretary. The wartime Joint Chiefs of Staff organization was perpetuated by law, with a regular chairman who possessed no command authority. Thus what had been two departments of the government became, in effect, four, and each branch enjoyed direct access to the President. Interservice rivalries and effective lobbying with members of Congress had thwarted the President's attempt to reduce friction and unite the armed forces in a single direct line of command descending from the White House.

The National Security Act also provided for a Central Intelligence Agency, designed to coordinate and streamline the information-gathering functions of the government under a director responsible to the President. Truman was thus able to secure a single report on what he termed "cloak and dagger'" activities, and the Director became the President's first caller each day to brief him on current intelligence developments. This centralization of the gathering and reporting of data simplified the President's search for knowledge and added significantly to his powers in directing foreign policy. An aura of mystery surrounded this first highly publicized American espionage activity and gave it the unique distinction of virtual infallibility. As a presidential instrument, its status was shared by the Chief Executive, whose monopoly of secret material enhanced the prestige of his office. This exclusive knowledge also gave the President a considerable advantage in disputes over international affairs with members of Congress and others, whose relative ignorance placed them at a disadvantage. In a nation fearful of Communist machinations, the public conceived an inordinate respect for clandestine information. The image of the Central Intelligence Agency, in combination with the other powers of his office, added significantly to the President's stature as the nation's expert on foreign affairs.

Perhaps the most important agency created by the Act of 1947 for the formulation of policy was the National Security Council, which provided a statutory body to coordinate military and diplomatic planning at the highest administrative level. Truman, soon after assuming office, had directed that the State, Army, and Navy Departments consult jointly on political affairs, but he wanted legislative sanction for a permanent arrangement. The National Security Council became a top-level clearing house for suggestions emanating from the various departments. Here the multifarious aspects of American foreign policy were deliberated by the senior appointive officials of the government, whose conclusions were then embodied in a document submitted to the President. The Council, as such, had no authority to determine or execute policy. Its functions were advisory only. But its recommendations represented the combined opinion of the heads of agencies most closely involved with the military and diplomatic affairs of the nation. Theoretically, at least, the President was provided with a co-ordinating body which mobilized the top minds in the Executive Branch of the government for the formulation of American foreign policy.

The new machinery to aid the President in his task of controlling foreign relations did increase his powers in this field. The centralization of effort enabled him to secure rapid, concise, and accurate information on American capabilities and foreign intentions. It furnished him with the combined judgment of senior officials who were compelled to broaden their perspective by exposure to the views of their colleagues. Streamlining the national security apparatus tightened the lines of communication that separated decision from implementation, and thereby expedited the transmission of orders into execution. Moreover, these new agencies constituted power resources on which the President could draw for support. An endorsement of his policies by the Defense Department or the National Security Council weighed heavily with Congress and the public. The National Security Act of 1947 sharpened the weapons at the President's disposal and added a new dimension to his command of American foreign policy.

None of these devices, however, completely removed the problems they were designed to eliminate. The Department of Defense was riddled with interservice rivalry as each branch competed for a greater role in strategic planning and a larger share of the budget. James Forrestal, the first Secretary of Defense, was a tragic casualty of an office that he had prophesied would "be the greatest cemetery for dead cats in history." The reputation of the Central Intelligence Agency was tarnished by its widely publicized failure to diagnose accurately the Korean invasion, when the vital distinction between the gathering of information and its correct interpretation became apparent. Nor did the National Security Council live up to expectations. The long sought-for co-ordination of arms and diplomacy was frustrated by Secretary of Defense Louis Johnson, and co-operation became a reality only when he was succeeded by George Marshall, who usually collaborated with Secretary of State Acheson outside the framework of the Council. The Policy Planning Staff of the State Department continued to initiate many of the proposals later adopted by the President, though these and recommendations of other non-statutory and often ad hoc committees were normally referred by Truman to the Council for deliberation.

In large measure, the operational efficiency of this new machinery depended on the way it was used by the President. Truman, for example, prudently refrained from employing the Central Intelligence Agency as an instrument for executing policy. He did rely heavily on the Joint Chiefs of Staff where military operations were involved, as in the Berlin blockade. The National Security Council was especially valuable for complex, long-term policy questions when circumstances did not demand an immediate solution. The President approved Council recommendations in 1948 and 1949 on the extent of America's military commitment in South Korea. But when the invasion occurred in 1950, he convened an ad hoc advisory group of his own choosing. Significantly, this group was composed largely of Council members, though the choice revealed the President's desire for a speedy and particular type of recommendation. Again, at the time of the Berlin blockade, the National Security Council produced its findings some eight weeks after the incident began. The degree of urgency, then, and the nature of the crisis, determined the type of consultation that took place. In turn, the type of consultation often determined the nature of the action taken. The President, therefore, in selecting the team to which a matter should be referred, usually insured the kind of advice that he wanted.

In any event, the final decision was his own. But independent agreement among his advisers prior to the adoption of a policy strengthened the President's hand. Strong differences of opinion at top governmental levels could delay action, provide fuel for congressional and public opposition, or divide the nation in cases where unity of purpose was essential. Then there was always the danger that interdepartmental committees would, as Dean Acheson puts it, reach agreements by exhaustion. The voices of dissent would become weaker as time dragged on, statements would become more vague and general, until the document that emerged offered little specific guidance for the President.

For Truman, the decision as to *what* should be done was often easy. *How* it should be done troubled him greatly, and in this area of implementation the President relied heavily on his advisers. The new machinery, under his manipulation, augmented the powers of the President in international affairs, and the precedents established by Truman in the utilization of this machinery were not ignored by his successors.

The United States began providing aid to war devastated areas after the first World War by distributing vast quantities of food to the starving populations of Europe. Lend-Lease, enacted in 1941, supplied materiel and financial assistance to nations fighting aggression, and in 1943 America joined the United Nations Relief and Rehabilitation Administration with more than forty other countries to help the liberated peoples. Sparked and financed by the United States, the program ended in 1947, in part owing to objections over allowing other governments to allocate the funds. Thus precedents existed for American alleviation of distress under the circumstances of war or destitution. But the peace created economic problems for the victorious democracies in Europe that appeared insurmountable without help from the United States. Whether it would be forthcoming and in what form was to depend in large measure on the President.

When Japan surrendered in August, 1945, the President, in accordance with the law, ended Lend-Lease to Great Britain. The new Labour government, striving desperately to convert the nation from a war to a peace economy, foresaw a more severe austerity program than had prevailed during the darkest days of the conflict. Truman earlier had told Churchill that he would discuss some kind of postwar economic arrangement with Britain, and he renewed the offer when Clement Attlee became Prime Minister. Negotiations began in September, 1945, with American insistence that any credit arrangement should be predicated on Britain's trading in a world market rather than within the framework of a sterling bloc. The delegations differed on the amount of money to be loaned, and the President finally settled the dispute by fixing the sum at $3,750,000,000. Though less than the minimum desired by the British, the President stood firm on the figure, the interest, and the schedule of payments. Signed December 6, 1945, the Anglo-American Financial Agreement was submitted to Congress for approval.

Securing consent for the British loan demanded an unprecedented amount of effort on the part of the administration. Emphasized in his State of the Union address, the agreement was sent by the President with a special message to Congress, urging approval to implement wartime financial arrangements, stimulate world recovery, and benefit the United States. During the months of debates and hearings, the President wrote personal letters to, and consulted with, members of Congress, obtained endorsements from administration officials and private individuals, and pointed out the dire consequences of failure to grant the loan. But a Congress reacting against years of presidential domination, bent on a sharp curtailment of government spending, balked at aiding a "socialist" government engaged in the nationalization of industry. The antipathy toward traditional British trade practices led to a quasi-filibuster by several Southern Senators, and majority leader Alben Barkley took the unusual step of withholding consideration of other legislation until a vote was taken on the bill.

Administration strategy underlined the fiscal soundness of the loan and its advantages to the United States. Though Congress was eventually persuaded, opinion polls revealed that the public regarded the loan as a virtual gift, for the technical economic ramifications eluded the average citizen. Truman insisted on an agreement that could be justified, and he established restrictions that antagonized Britain. Yet these modifications to the British request did not, in themselves, insure congressional acceptance of the loan. Nor did it simplify the task of explaining the agreement sufficiently to stimulate a groundswell of sympathy from the public.

The experience of securing acceptance of the Anglo-American Financial Agreement alerted President Truman to the difficulties of leading the nation into uncharted areas of international obligation. The war had convinced the nation that it should assume limited responsibility for the preservation of peace through collective security, and the humane feelings of an affluent people condoned temporary relief measures to avoid starvation. But demands for other assistance, whose need was not so obvious and whose significance was not so easily understood, were bound to meet resistance. The presidential art of persuasion would be taxed to its utmost if America were to be led further in the direction of promoting world prosperity through unconventional financial outlays.

The British loan was approved by Congress some seven months after the agreement had been signed. By that time inflation had reduced the actual value of the loan, and the delay, coupled with the harsh words uttered on both sides of the Atlantic, damaged Anglo-American relations. The vivid demonstration of congressional control over foreign affairs requiring appropriations weakened the President's position abroad. A restoration of his image was to await the emergence of a threat to American security unparalleled in the nation's history.

Negotiations with the Soviet Union had deteriorated steadily since the Potsdam Conference, but the President had avoided the temptation to stress the Communist danger. Still hoping that co-operation with Russia was possible, he did not want to risk a break by giving the impression of intractable hostility. Nor could the United States act alone. Other nations, especially France and Great Britain, were partners in the negotiations, and their collaboration was important.

The occasion for a formal American commitment to resist Communist aggression was presented by the British withdrawal from Greece and Turkey, and Truman's decision to support independent nations was revealed in his dramatic address to Congress on March 12, 1947. Elaborating on the Communist threat to world peace, the President stressed American security, contending that it depended on the ability of free governments to defend themselves from subversion and attack. The confrontation of the two great world powers, the United States and Russia, was publicly proclaimed by the President, who combined a warning with an eloquent appeal for support. The fulfillment of Truman's pledge to support independent nations was to compel him to draw on every resource of his office as implications of the pledge appeared to encompass virtually every area of the world.

While the administration followed the painstaking, time-consuming routine of securing congressional approval of the Truman Doctrine, Secretary of State George Marshall returned from abroad with alarming news. Negotiations with the Soviets were at a standstill as they pursued a ruthless campaign to dominate the West. Moreover, the economies of Western Europe were nearing collapse. The expected postwar recovery had not materialized, and widespread poverty furnished rich soil for Communist agitation. Unless something were done to restore prosperity, the western European nations might well succumb to the promises of Moscow-inspired leaders.

Determined that communism should not succeed through American default, Truman pushed studies to assess the economic situation in Europe and suggest methods for its alleviation. The first public indication of administration thinking was contained in an address by Under Secretary of State Dean Acheson at Cleveland, Mississippi, on May 8, 1947. With the President's enthusiastic approval, Acheson reviewed Europe's sad plight, explained America's stake in the prosperity of other countries, and recommended economic assistance. The impact of this trial balloon was not enough to provoke extended comment, either for or against an American commitment. But the lack of concerted or strenuous opposition encouraged the administration to launch the proposal in a more striking fashion.

By late spring, the groundwork had been prepared for a European aid program. Truman's March address had alerted the nation to the dangers of Communist aggression and promised assistance to preserve freedom. But his specific proposal was confined to Greece and Turkey, and it appeared too exclusively military to combat the basic problem. The extension of the President's remarks to more positive lines of activity became a major topic for conjecture among public officials and representatives of the communication media. Acheson's speech had revealed the tentative official line and prepared the way for a major statement of policy by a leading member of the administration.

For this momentous task the President selected Secretary of State George Marshall. Combining the prestige of his office with an exalted reputation, Marshall was an ideal choice to advocate a plan requiring both national and international approval. The veneration accorded a military hero was abetted by diplomatic experience, and he was not vulnerable to accusations of political partisanship. In these respects, Marshall's promulgation of a drastic foreign policy experiment was more influential than if it had been made by the President. No other person could have so impressed the nation and the world with the urgency and merits of the proposal.

This exploitation of one of Truman's most effective sources of power had the desired effect, for Marshall's address at the Havard Commencement on June 5, 1947, set in motion one of the most ambitious projects ever conceived by man. A crash program to revitalize the economy of Europe not only involved a huge financial outlay by the United States but also demanded the enthusiastic co-operation of the governments concerned. Certain European leaders, electrified by the project, threw themselves into its implementation. Others, notably Russian Foreign Minister Molotov, stimulated American support by withdrawing from the preliminary conversations and ordering the satellite governments to refrain from participation. The Communist coup in Czechoslovakia helped induce Congress to provide the required legislation.

Nevertheless, without the total and unremitting efforts of the President, the Marshall Plan, in its projected form, would not have received congressional endorsement. Truman backed his associates fully and consistently from the outset. In speeches, press conferences, informal meetings, and correspondence he fought for the venture. An initial adverse reaction by certain congressional leaders, especially Senator Vandenberg, was overcome by thorough private briefings at the White House and the State Department. Representatives of the news media were handed background information by high officials, and the press made a distinct contribution by presenting a thorough, comprehensive account of the proposal, its objectives, and its progress. Negotiations with representatives of other nations were conducted with the full and obvious support of the President, which facilitated the formulation of detailed plans and expedited final agreement.

What Churchill has termed "the most unsordid act in history" was due to a combination of dedicated individuals and unusual circumstances. The spectre of communism, the prestige of Marshall, the magnificent performance of Senator Vandenberg, the superb staff work of State Department officials, and the enthusiastic co-operation of the press, were among the factors without which there probably would have been no implementation of the Marshall Plan. But the absolutely essential figure in the promotion and adoption of the proposal was the President himself. The least sign of hesitation, the first display of uncertainty, an excess of caution, or an indiscreet move at the wrong time, might have rendered adoption impossible. Facing a Republican dominated Congress in the midst of a major economy move, the President manipulated his power resources masterfully in securing a major departure in American foreign policy. Though he realized that the aid might come too late, Truman knew that it had to be done in a Constitutional manner. That it was provided in accordance with traditional American practices was a tribute to his astute political sense and his understanding of the functions of his office. That it was provided at all is a commentary on the vision and character of the man who occupied that office.

Aware that the Truman Doctrine and the Marshall Plan were temporary measures aimed more at restoring than creating prosperity, the President sought to establish a long-range project for raising the standard of living in the backward non-Western nations of the world. As a fourth point in his Inaugural address of January 20, 1949, President Truman urged the country to "embark on a bold new program for making the benefits of our scientific advances and industrial progress available for the improvement and growth of underdeveloped areas." Again, emphasis was placed on advantages accruing to the United States, among them being an increase in trade and investment and the strengthening of these states to resist the overtures of communism.

Unfortunately for his proposal of this "Point Four" program Truman had not made the careful preparations that marked his previous bold ventures in foreign affairs that required congressional consent.

Perhaps his unpredicted election and the return of a Democratic Congress made him overconfident. In any event, after the address the President directed the Secretary of State to institute planning for the program. Not until June did Truman ask Congress to appropriate money for its implementation, and three months elapsed before the necessary legislation was introduced. Finally, on June 5, 1950, the President signed the bill authorizing the technical assistance program.

Fortunately, the need for the Point Four project was not imperative. In fact, an inability to promote the plan as an emergency device probably accounted for much of the delay. Unlike the circumstances that had made possible the Truman Doctrine and the Marshall Plan, no overriding necessity was evident. Even as late as March, 1950, a phone call from the President to Senator Connally, the Senate Majority leader, attempting to speed up action on the bill, had brought an unenthusiastic response. Truman had not handled the issue properly. His almost impulsive announcement without adequate preliminaries enabled opposition to develop and exploit the obvious shortcomings of what gave the appearance of an act of charity, to be carried out at the expense of the long-suffering American taxpayer. The absence of a crisis and the difficulty of justifying the proposal in terms of national interest, deprived the plan of two vital ingredients: simplicity and appeal. Thorough preparation might have overcome these deficiencies, and in this respect the President had miscalculated. Though it may be true, as one biographer has asserted, that "President Truman considers the Point Four Program the most important peace policy development of his administration,"[38] the President's handling of the undertaking was not commensurate with its importance.

One instance of economic aid was the product of a defeat for the President in his efforts to control foreign policy. Truman had vigorously opposed the Spanish government, which he likened to a police state no different from that of Hitler or Stalin. He had supported the United Nations resolution to withdraw ambassadors from Madrid, and he especially deplored Franco's persecution of Protestants. But two major forces arose to frustrate his position: congressional sympathy for Spain and the desire of military leaders for bases in that country.

Attempts to include Spain in Marshall Plan appropriations were defeated, but the administration reluctantly began to retreat on the exchange of ambassadors. Then, when the Korean War broke out and the administration urged aid to Communist Yugoslavia, the ideological objections to Franco's government were weakened. Subsequently, Congress incorporated a Spanish loan in a General Appropriations bill that included Truman's cherished Point Four funds. In signing the legislation, the President declared that he would indefinitely withhold the sum allocated to Spain, observing that it was not "mandatory" but more in the nature of an "authorization." He further stated that "money will be loaned to Spain whenever mutually advantageous arrangements can be made with respect to security, terms of repayment, purposes for which the money is to be spent, and other appropriate factors, and whenever such loans will serve the interest of the United States in the conduct of foreign relations."

At this stage presidential policy still prevailed. But members of Congress began to press the administration on the advantages that would stem from the loan to Spain. In this effort they received their greatest support from the Pentagon. Eventually the joint pressure of legislators and military experts won over key members of Truman's staff. Finally, with bad grace, the President agreed to extend the loan in exchange for an agreement to permit the United States to establish air bases in Spain. Circumstances and the imperatives of defense had enabled Congress and the military leaders to institute a major change in American aid policy against the wishes of the President. Perhaps his moral and ideological stand had made his position exceedingly vulnerable in a period dominated by considerations of military power. Perhaps, too, his previous reiteration of what constituted the national interest had created a list of priorities headed by security. The device of oversimplification, a technique espoused to secure public support for complex policies, had delivered American economic aid to a government over the objections of the President and altered the direction of his foreign policy.

An opportunity for Executive initiative in the promotion of world prosperity occurred in the field of tariff revision. Legislation had empowered the President to raise or lower duties on numerous commodities under certain conditions, and Truman firmly believed in a lowering of barriers to promote world trade. On at least two notable occasions, the President resisted heavy domestic pressure in order to improve the economies of other countries and promote international goodwill. Urged by numerous groups, including the Tariff Commission, to raise the duties on Swiss watches, he refused in a vigorous message that pointed out the shortsighted attitude of special interests toward American diplomatic objectives. Truman also vetoed a bill to increase the duty on wool imports, and later authorized a United States concession in the wool tariff at a Geneva Conference. "This action of the President," a then Assistant Secretary of State later wrote, "following his veto of a bill which would have resulted in increasing the wool tariff, was the greatest act of political courage that I have ever witnessed."[39]

In sum, Truman provided the leadership for America's sharing of its prosperity with the rest of the world. The major steps were taken under his initiative and his management. He successfully employed the instruments at his disposal in securing the adoption of his proposals, instruments that would have been blunted if wielded in a less expert manner. Only in a Cold War setting could this investment in international well-being have taken place, and only in the hot war atmosphere of Korea could it have been extended to nations such as Japan, Germany, and Spain, the erstwhile enemies of America. But without the determination of a vigorous President, willing and able to exercise his powers in a cause he believed right, the noble experiment might not have occurred at all.

One of the most unique features of the revolution in American foreign policy engineered by President Truman in the years following World War II was the North Atlantic Treaty of 1949, whereby the United States committed itself to the military defense of Western Europe. This departure from the traditional aversion to entanglements was a milestone in American diplomacy, and it established a precedent in regional security pacts to be followed persistently by subsequent administrations.

Like so many diplomatic innovations of the postwar years, the treaty emerged as an evolutionary stage in efforts to halt communism. The United States had been steadily plugging holes in the dike by working through the United Nations, strengthening the economies of nations, and furnishing aid to harassed governments. But it became evident that all these efforts to resist Communist subversion and guerrilla activity would be wasted if the Red army should march into the militarily weak European democracies. Thus an alliance pledging America's armed might to the defense of the remaining outposts of freedom in Europe, seemed a logical and necessary corollary to the containment measures so far instituted. Again, the basic problem was not so much the decision to pursue this objective as was the method by which it could be accomplished in the face of a deeply ingrained American aversion to peacetime military pacts.

An early phase of the process began with the conclusion of the Inter-American Treaty of Reciprocal Assistance, known as the Rio Treaty, signed September 2, 1947. Providing for joint hemisphere defense, this treaty followed a pattern of security commitments by the United States—unilateral, bilateral, and multilateral—extending back to the Monroe Doctrine. The extension of collective security outside the orbit of Pan-Americanism and the United Nations, was to await other developments in the Cold War and the joint initiative of European statesmen.

Opportunity to pursue the plan for collective security appeared with the failure of the Council of Foreign Ministers meeting in December, 1947. Alarmed by Soviet behavior, Great Britain suggested that France and the Benelux countries join her in a defense pact. The Brussels Treaty of 1948 was finally concluded after its strong endorsement in the formative stage by the United States. The Communist overthrow of the Czech government had served as an impetus.

At this time the administration, realizing that the Brussels Pact nations needed more political support and were militarily incapable of resisting the Soviet forces, began careful preparations to bring about American participation. Moving slowly to avoid thrusting the issue into the campaign of 1948, the President made a series of speeches citing examples of Communist aggression and emphasizing the cardinal importance of the Brussels agreement in thwarting Soviet ambitions. Ever bearing in mind Wilson's sad experience, Truman "meant to have legislative co-operation."[40] The step contemplated was so momentous that he wanted the European nations to know *in advance,* that negotiations for a defense pact were supported by the Senate as well as the President.

In pursuit of this goal the President secured the assistance of Senator Vandenberg, and Under Secretary of State Robert A. Lovett was directed to work closely with the Senator to secure a statement of policy from the Senate. On June 11, 1948, Senate Resolution 239, known as the Vandenberg Resolution, was overwhelmingly approved. Containing Senate endorsement of regional security agreements, it laid the foundation for American membership in the North Atlantic Treaty Organization. The President immediately ordered informal military discussions with the Brussels Pact nations and the opening of negotiations to broaden the alliance to include the United States and other European countries.

The entire operation, supervised from the White House, utilized much of the existing governmental machinery entrusted with the formulation and execution of foreign policy. Under Secretary Lovett bore the main burden for conducting negotiations with the Brussels Treaty nations, though he received vital aid from Secretary Dean Acheson and his colleagues in the State Department. The Joint Chiefs of Staff handled the military technicalities, and the National Security

Council provided a forum for comprehensive consideration and synthesis of the final proposal. Truman was regularly informed of every development and he personally reviewed every recommendation.

Final approval of the North Atlantic Treaty by the Senate on July 21, 1949, was the result of a year and a half of patient, painstaking effort on the part of the Executive branch. Encouragement of the Brussels Pact, unflagging co-operation with the Senate, laborious negotiations with representatives of eleven European nations, and the task of securing agreement among the various governmental agencies, marked the adoption of the treaty as one of the more re-markable accomplishments in modern American political history.

Perhaps in no other way could such a drastic departure from national principles have been accomplished. Any other approach would have created such dissension that the administration's containment policy would have been jeopardized or, possibly, destroyed. The presidential strategy anticipated virtually every point of treaty vulnerability. His choice of method, personnel, and procedure insured the adoption of what he considered a principle underlying American foreign policy.

The main purpose of the North Atlantic Treaty was to deter Soviet aggression by serving advance notice that a military assault would be met by the collective strength of the member nations. To put teeth into the organization, the United States became a partner in planning for deterrence as well as defense. Only close co-ordination of military capabilities could erect a shield sufficient to discourage the Kremlin. For this formidable task, Truman appointed General of the Army Dwight D. Eisenhower, whose experience and prestige eminently qualified him to create a peacetime coalition of forces. Choosing the right man for the right job is one of the more demanding responsibilities of a President, and Truman's judgment was sound when he selected the one individual who enjoyed the professional respect and heartfelt admiration of the NATO allies.

During the Senate hearings and debates, two crucial questions had emerged relating to the agreement, one dealing with authority to dispatch troops to Europe in fulfilling the terms of the alliance. Though presidents had often sent forces abroad in the capacity of Commander-in-Chief, no clear-cut precedent was established for doing so in compliance with a military pact. The administration had thwarted Senate efforts to include stipulation on the subject, so it remained an open question. It was, however, complicated by a provision of the treaty which specified that in the event of armed aggression, the type of aid furnished the victim should be determined by each member in accordance with its regular constitutional procedures.

When the Korean War began, it was feared that Russia might take advantage of the conflict to launch an attack on Western Europe, and the President decided to send four American divisions to bolster the NATO defense structure. Truman stoutly denied the need for congressional authority and he carried out the move despite opposition from a small but vocal group of Senators. In so doing, he expanded presidential authority as Commander-in-Chief to encompass the peacetime disposal of forces in meeting the obligations of a military alliance. That he did so without consulting the legislative branch again revealed his concept of the office and his assessment of the strategic demands of the Free World defense perimeter. Still dependent on Congress for the size and composition of the armed forces, Truman, as a result of the Korean crisis, secured legislation for a rapid expansion of the American military establishment. The employment of men and equipment remained at the discretion of the President.

A second question arising during the Senate debate on the North Atlantic Treaty concerned the role of Germany in the proposed European defense organization. Secretary of State Acheson denied categorically that West German rearmament or inclusion in the pact was contemplated. But later, as the truncated nation approached autonomy and its potential value to the alliance became apparent, Truman reluctantly bowed to pressure from Senate critics, the German government, and the Joint Chiefs of Staff. The decision to rearm Germany was especially distasteful to the President, and he made it only under the compulsion of security for the western nations.

The decision to join in a military pact for the defense of Europe marked a return to the balance of power concept earlier rejected by Truman in favor of the United Nations. The Soviet Union had erected a formidable bloc that gave every evidence of hostility to the aims of non-Communist nations. As the former world powers abdicated their previous positions of leadership, the United States, as the only power capable of opposing the Red menace, moved into the vacuum created in Europe by the destruction of Germany and the relegation of Great Britain and France to second class status. The emergence of the Soviet colossus, its aggressive tendencies, and the inadequacy of the United Nations as a device for collective security, created a bipolarization of power between Russia and the United States. Since the latter was manifestly weak in conventional arms and could not hope to halt a Soviet invasion of the continent, the total-war deterrence of atomic weapons had to be supplemented with the land forces of other European states.

In the pursuit of American security the President had led the nation along untrodden paths. An alliance for the preservation of the balance of power in Europe could only have been achieved under the frightening circumstance of a massive totalitarian threat. But the type and degree of the collective response owed a great deal to the nature of the man who occupied the White House. Truman adroitly exercised the powers of his office to secure an unprecedented commitment, and this commitment added unprecedented powers to his office.

American participation in an international organization for the preservation of peace had numerous repercussions on the powers of the President in international affairs. Membership pledged the United States to the concept of collective security, with a commitment to joint action in matters that might only remotely affect the interests of the nation. It demanded full co-operation between the Chief Executive and Congress in order to secure approval of the charter and the enabling legislation, to provide authority and funds to meet the prescribed obligations. Finally, participation in a world organization, both restricted and enlarged the powers of the President in foreign affairs. On the one hand, a unilateral approach to many problems was impracticable, for policies had to be cleared or co-ordinated with representatives of other nations. Conversely, the President could, by effective leadership, secure the assistance of other nations and the machinery of the United Nations for the implementation of American policies. The extent to which American diplomacy was to be advanced or retarded by this new involvement was to depend in large measure on the conduct of the President.

Truman's "first decision" as Chief Executive was to order the San Francisco conference of the United Nations to go ahead as scheduled in spite of agitation for its postponement. His interest in a world organization for collective security was of long standing and stemmed from his reading of history. Speaking before the Senate on November 2, 1943, he declared: "I am just as sure as I can be that this World War is the result of the 1919-1920 isolationist attitude, and I am equally sure that another and a worse war will follow this one, unless the United Nations and their allies, and all the other sovereign nations decide to work together for peace as they are working together for victory." He vigorously supported the Connally and Fulbright Resolutions, by which both houses of Congress pledged American participation in an international organization. But as President he realized that these resolutions did not give him a blank check, and he approved the delegation appointed by Roosevelt, which included two senators and two congressmen representing both parties. Truman's only admonitions were that they "set up an international organization to prevent another world war," and "write a document that would pass the U.S. Senate and that would not arouse such opposition as confronted Woodrow Wilson."[41]

Surprisingly, Truman actually did refrain from interfering with the negotiations, and he provided assistance only when it was requested. In this way he insured that an acceptable charter would emerge, one that met the demands of Congress and the people. The President's major contribution consisted of applying pressure on Stalin to secure certain concessions, such as persuading him to send Foreign Minister Molotov to San Francisco and obtaining a modification of the Soviet position on the veto and voting privileges.

Truman's co-operation with Congress resulted in quick Senate approval of the charter and helped him gain an important concession in the legislation that implemented America's membership in the organization. Known as the United Nations Participation Act, this legislation placed the American representative under presidential rather than congressional control. It did specify, however, that Congress must approve any agreement that promised armed forces would "be made available to the Security Council on its call for the purpose of maintaining international peace and security in accordance with article 43 of said charter." Truman was to interpret this clause in such a way that he, as director of American United Nations policy and Commander-in-Chief, could commit troops without congressional authorization. This interpretation added greatly to his presidential powers.

Throughout his administration, Truman stressed the need for working with the United Nations, which he considered the best guarantor of world peace and a vital instrument of American foreign policy. In following this untrodden path he was dealing with the explosive issue of national versus supranational interests. It became necessary, therefore, for him to show how American objectives would be furthered by co-operation with the United Nations at the same time that he was trying to convince his fellow Americans that they should develop loyalty to the international organization.

In attempting to create two loyalties where only one had existed, Truman risked alienating a large segment of the population, especially when Soviet obstructive tactics threatened to render the United Nations impotent. As the organization developed into a clearinghouse for negotiation and a forum for world opinion, divided allegiance became more of a problem. If the President emphasized American interests in order to satisfy domestic critics he risked antagonizing those nations whose support he sought.

There is some question whether this "multilateral diplomacy is complementary to bilateral diplomacy, not a rival to it."[42] The statement would be true if, in all cases, what was considered good by the United States would be considered good for the United Nations by delegates from other countries. Usually it is easier to satisfy one set of constituents with similar interests than many sets of constituents with diverse interests. One trouble with trying to secure agreement in a group is that a solution often represents the lowest common denominator. Compromises of this kind may well satisfy no one and fail to serve the purpose for which the original proposal was intended. Then, too, the American commitment to accept United Nations decisions demanded strenuous efforts to prevent the adoption of resolutions inimical to the nation's interests. So membership in the organization produced restraints which circumscribed the freedom of action in foreign affairs that previously had prevailed. In this respect American sovereignty was abridged.

But there were advantages which, in Truman's opinion, heavily outweighed the disadvantages. He regarded the organization primarily as a means of preserving the peace, a forum where disputes could be settled and an organ of collective security to prevent aggression. The United States, as the most prosperous and powerful nation, had a duty to furnish leadership in this arena of world affairs. The opportunity was at hand and Truman was determined that it should not be fumbled. Convinced that the League of Nations had failed because none of the major powers had provided direction or lived up to their obligations, the President believed that it was his and America's responsibility to furnish both leadership and an example to insure that the United Nations should not collapse by default.

Truman's most noteworthy action to strengthen the embryonic organization was his commitment of American forces to the defense of South Korea. In the years following World War II the United States had found the United Nations inadequate for the containment of communism. Regional defense pacts such as the Inter-American Treaty of Reciprocal Assistance (Rio Treaty) and the North Atlantic Treaty Organization were created to supplement the security provisions of the United Nations. The Truman Doctrine, the Marshall Plan, and the Point Four program were designed to halt other measures of Soviet aggression. Finding her efforts to expand by non-military means thwarted by the containment policy of the United States, Russia decided to test Western determination by resorting to the only remaining element of competition—war.

Korea appeared ideal for a Communist military challenge. Efforts to unite the divided country, either bilaterally or through the United Nations, had been unavailing. The internal conflict in Korea, therefore, took on all the aspects of a civil war. Communism had prevailed in China through the use of force and the device of a domestic struggle, a struggle in which the only capable Western power— the United States—had failed to intervene. Moreover, Secretary of State Dean Acheson had publicly declared that Korea lay outside the American defense perimenter, and that its protection was a responsibility of the United Nations. These factors, coupled with America's weakness in conventional forces, suggested that the United States would refrain from unilateral intervention.

As for the United Nations, the Soviet Union could well believe that action would be confined to protests and resolutions which, after a rapid conquest of South Korea, would prove ineffectual. Remembering the abortive League activities and the hands-off policy of the United Nations when faced with civil war in China, the Kremlin plotters probably felt reasonably confident that the pattern would be repeated. It has been asserted that the North Korean attack was launched without Russian consent, for the Soviet Union was boycotting the Security Council at this time in protest against the continued seating of the Nationalist Chinese government representative. On the other hand, this may well have been a calculated, deliberate move by the Soviets. For if the United Nations failed to respond to this act of military aggression, it would demonstrate its inadequacy as a device for collective security and go the way of the League, after the conquest of Manchuria and Ethiopia. By absenting themselves from the Security Council, the Soviets avoided having to exercise the veto, and consequently could not be held responsible for what they expected to be the demise of the United Nations. But whatever the motives—and Washington's assessments of Soviet intentions were to influence the reaction—the Communists had posed the ultimate challenge to both the collective security function of the United Nations and the American policy of containment. War, the final arbiter in disputes between nations, had been invoked, and the world's future hung on the nature of the response.

It is important to recall that American military planning had not anticipated this form of aggression. The proposals contained in NSC-68 that advocated preparation for contingencies of this type had not even been approved, much less implemented. Acting on a National Security Council recommendation in the spring of 1948, the President had authorized extension to the South Korean government of economic aid and help in training its security forces. American troops were withdrawn from the area at the suggestion of the Council following a report from General MacArthur. Throughout the spring of 1950, the Central Intelligence Agency warned of a possible North Korean offensive, but, as Truman has noted, "The same reports also told me repeatedly that there were any number of other spots in the world where the Russians 'possessed the capability' to attack."[43] Consequently, when news of the invasion reached the President, no plans were available for guidance in determining American or United Nations action. The element of surprise was complete in every respect.

Though elaborate machinery had been erected to deal with security and foreign policy matters, the urgent and unprecedented nature of the threat left no time for normal deliberations. Only the President, under his constitutional and assumed powers, could deal with the situation. In meeting his responsibility, Truman had to assess the nature of the aggression and its significance in terms of the Communist scheme. If it were merely the first step in a world-wide military offensive, the American response would have to be tempered by demands on defense resources at other vulnerable spots. The limitations imposed on choices by the state of America's armed forces were considerable, for a commitment of troops to Korea would virtually strip other areas. Europe was still considered the most vital Communist target and NATO could not be weakened. In addition to the problem of American *capabilities,* there was question as to the amount of support that Truman might expect from Congress and the public. The bipartisan approach to foreign policy had been seriously impaired by the Communist victory in China, and the administration announcement that military assistance would not be extended to Formosa had brought opposition to the Korean aid bill in early 1950. Domestically, the President was not in a strong position to carry through a policy of heavy involvement on the Asian continent that depended on congressional and public backing.

Probably the overriding consideration in Truman's mind was the future of the United Nations as an instrument of collective security. For years he had pounded home the theme that World War II erupted because the League of Nations had failed to act against aggression, and he had urged American participation in the new organization in order to prevent a third world conflict. Article 43 of the Charter provided that:

> All Members of the UN in order to contribute to the maintenance of international peace and security, undertake to make available to the Security Council, on its call and in accordance with a special agreement or agreements, armed forces, assistance and facilities, including rights of passage, necessary for the purpose of maintaining international peace and security.

While the United Nations Participation Act required that any such "special agreement or agreements" to furnish troops be approved by Congress, Truman, in charge of American relations with the organization, had avoided an agreement of this kind. In the absence of a formal pact he believed that as Commander-in-Chief he could place troops at the disposal of the United Nations. The issue had been raised when American ambassador Austin had indicated that American troops would be supplied as part of a United Nations force to maintain order in Palestine if the Security Council decided to take such a step. The President on this occasion cited historical precedents to back his position, though the examples he mentioned involved a unilateral rather than a multilateral employment of forces.

So the President had the opportunity to preserve what he considered the most vital function of the United Nations, and, at the same time, implement by force his determination to contain communism. By pursuing a multilateral rather than a unilateral course he added legality to his action, gained allies, cultivated world opinion, and helped restore American prestige in the Far East. By operating through the United Nations he could blunt domestic opposition by stressing collective security, the "lessons of history," and international obligations. His policies of the previous years had been, in many ways, a preparation for this moment. Constant repetition of the role of the United Nations in preserving the peace, the rise of the common danger of communism, and the development of the containment policy, all seemed to reach a climax in the challenge of Korea. Under the circumstances it is scarcely conceivable that Truman could have avoided acting as he did, for the circumstances were as much his making as they were factors beyond his control. Almost a prisoner of the past that he had helped shape, both by events and interpretation, he was to encounter his greatest difficulty with execution rather than decision.

The first news of the attack of North Korean forces on South

Korea reached the President on Saturday evening, June 24, 1950, at his home in Independence, Missouri. Secretary of State Dean Acheson phoned the information, and Truman immediately authorized him to "ask the United Nations Security Council to hold a meeting at once and declare that an act of aggression had been committed against the Republic of Korea."[44] The following morning both men agreed that a resolution to this effect would probably be forthcoming, only to be ignored by the North Koreans and their allies. The basic question facing the President was the extent to which the United States should aid the aggrieved party. After directing Acheson to secure recommendations from the service secretaries and the Joint Chiefs of Staff, Truman took off for Washington.

On the three-hour flight the President reviewed the fate of the League and the parallels in the current situation. The issue, as he saw it, was clear cut. If South Korea fell without support from the Free World, other small nations would submit to Communist pressure and eventually a third world war would break out. Moreover, the United Nations would be thoroughly discredited. These sober reflections prompted the President to radio Acheson asking that he, his advisers, and key defense chiefs attend a dinner conference at Blair House that evening.

There is little doubt that the President had already made up his mind to resist the aggression by whatever means necessary. His previous remarks on the role of the United Nations and the failure of the League, his conversation with Acheson, and finally his selection of participants in the Blair House conference, all revealed that he approached the meeting "in decision" rather than "in indecision." By not including all members of the National Security Council, political leaders, or members of Congress, he virtually eliminated anyone who might urge caution. With the knowledge that the Security Council had unanimously denounced the North Korean action, Acheson presented the State and Defense Department recommendations that had the backing of everyone present. After soliciting individual opinions, Truman directed that the recommendations be carried out. These involved the evacuation of Americans from Korea, the dispatch of supplies to South Korea, and the neutralization of Formosa by the Seventh Fleet. The President then asked specific questions of the military chiefs about the location and state of units in the Far East, and directed them "to prepare the necessary orders for the eventual use of American units if the United Nations should call for action against North Korea."[45]

By Monday evening it was obvious that the Security Council resolution was being ignored, and that the South Korean troops could not
successfully resist the attack. The President, therefore, approved
Acheson's recommendation that American forces be committed to
the conflict, and the following day the Security Council appealed to
all member nations to provide assistance for South Korea. The speed
with which these decisions were made and implemented was due to
the existing governmental organization, the co-ordinating efforts of
the Secretary of State, and the administrative abilities of the President. Basically, the efficient manner in which the operation was carried
out reflected the decisive conduct of the President and his unhesitating
acceptance of responsibility and exercise of authority. He had no
doubt about what should be done or whether he possessed the power
to do it.

During the three-day period virtually all of these decisions and
the orders for their implementation were made by word of mouth.
Even the directive to General MacArthur to provide military support was phoned by Acheson at the President's request. The snarls
of red tape that usually impede government activities were cut as the
President infused his subordinates with a sense of the urgency of the
situation. He was determined to leave nothing undone in his efforts
to resist communism, prevent a world holocaust, and preserve the
United Nations. Future historians were not to be given the satisfac-
tion of repeating the old refrain, "too little too late."

The failure to consult any member of Congress before deciding
the extent of the American commitment is surprising in view of Truman's previous efforts at co-operation with that body and the seriousness of the step he was taking. Though he did not doubt his authority
to order forces into combat, he previously had solicited congressional
participation in policy questions relating to the United Nations, and
he certainly would need Senate and House consent for supplementary
defense appropriations. Actually, bipartisanship in foreign affairs
had suffered a decline owing to three developments: the replacement
of a Republican by a Democratic Congress in 1949, the election of
Truman, and the defeat of American policy in China. No doubt these
factors were in the President's mind when he assumed sole responsibility for the American venture.

Actually, on Sunday afternoon, a State Department official did
brief the Far-Eastern Sub-Committee of the Senate Foreign Relations Committee on the Korean crisis. But at that time only the decision to address an appeal to the Security Council for a condemnation

of the aggression had been made. Then on Monday four telephone conversations were held between State Department officers and certain congressional leaders, and Department officials met with the House Committee on Foreign Affairs. The foregoing occurred prior to the second meeting at Blair House. When, that evening, the President did agree to extend miltary assistance to South Korea, he decided to meet with congressional leaders the following morning to acquaint them with the action taken prior to making a public announcement. The leaders received a summary of the situation from Secretary Acheson, and the President "pointed out that it was the United Nations which had acted in this case and had acted with great speed," though he indicated that the neutralization of Formosa was strictly an American move.[46] The eleven Senators and four Congressmen present then registered their approval of the steps taken.

By presenting the Congress and the nation with a *fait accompli* the President had successfully executed a drastic departure in American foreign policy. His choice of consultants, forthright assumption of responsibility, decisive manner, and method of procedure enabled him completely to control the nature of the American response. Opposition and divisive or delaying tactics were eliminated by his not allowing the question to become a matter for private or public debate.

Truman also made and announced his decision to commit American forces prior to the second Security Council resolution requesting such assistance, though it was made with the knowledge that the United Nations call was forthcoming and was clearly consistent with the initial resolution. The American military effort received more official status when the Security Council, on July 7, created the United Nations Command. In practice, however, the command structure was not affected, for the United States was functioning in this regard as the exclusive agent of the organization.

In some respects the Clausewitz dictum that war is merely the continuation of policy by other means was confirmed in Korea. The initial objective of the American and United Nations intervention was to resist aggression and demonstrate the efficacy of collective security. The President was constantly plagued by decisions as to the extent of American bombing operations, the commitment of American ground forces, and, when the United Nations forces finally assumed the offensive, whether the advance should stop at the 38th parallel or proceed with the total destruction of the North Korean army.

Though the United States controlled military operations in Korea, political considerations induced a good deal of restraint. The President, anxious to confine hostilities to a "police action," was especially concerned that Russia not be provoked into war. The need for continued support by the United Nations also placed restrictions on tactical as well as strategic planning, and Truman closely supervised the military operations to insure that they conformed with his political aims.

Each morning he met at the White House with General Omar Bradley, Chairman of the Joint Chiefs of Staff, to review developments. In September, he replaced Louis Johnson as Secretary of Defense with General George C. Marshall. Partly intended to add prestige to the office, the change also reflected the need for greater co-operation between the Defense and State Departments. Johnson had never gotten along with Acheson, and the correlation of the military effort with diplomatic objectives was imperative as never before. In no previous conflict had the Chief Executive exercised such meticulous control over the conduct of the commander in the field, and the uniqueness of this experience was to lead to one of the great debates in American political history.

In another respect the Clausewitz axiom was to prove inaccurate, for military developments prompted a change in the political objectives of the conflict. The routing of North Korean forces after the amphibious landing at Inchon helped convince the President that the war presented an opportunity to end the political division of Korea. On October 7, the General Assembly resolved that United Nations troops might be used to establish a "unified, independent and democratic government" in that ravaged land. Though in accord with Assembly resolutions of much earlier dates, such action had certainly not been contemplated by the Security Council in June. Neither that body nor the United States had originally intended to use the North Korean attack as a means of effecting the unification of the two nations. The United States, under presidential direction, had played a crucial role in promoting United Nations action in Korea. That the President should interpret a General Assembly vote as a mandate or an order to pursue a more drastic course may seem puzzling in retrospect. But in view of the American military contribution it seems unlikely that the Assembly would have passed the October 7 resolution without encouragement from Washington. As President, Truman controlled the behavior of the American representative at the United Nations. As Commander-in-Chief he determined the disposition and activities of the armed forces. Consequently his power was decisive in United Nations action in the Korean crisis. No other national leader had ever occupied a comparable position, and he must be assigned any praise or blame for the subsequent course of events.

In retrospect, Truman was to regret that the advance had not halted at the narrowest part of the Korean peninsula. That it did not was due to many factors, including the nature of his advice, but his meticulous supervision of the venture places even greater responsibilities on his shoulders for any mistakes that were made. The warnings about Communist Chinese intervention were numerous and a more prudent Chief Executive probably would have avoided further provocation. Of course the unusual circumstance of having someone of General MacArthur's stature as field commander placed the President in a difficult position, and his reluctance to interfere with what often appeared to be purely military matters is understandable. But this appearance was an illusion, and it should have been obvious to a President who had been on top of the operation all this time.

The Communist Chinese intervention when the United Nations forces approached the Yalu, placed both objectives of the war in jeopardy and confronted the President with a choice of a vastly greater commitment of resources or a modification of objectives. Though the General Assembly, at American instigation, adopted a resolution on February 1, 1951, branding the People's Republic of China an aggressor nation, neither the President nor the United States was willing to pursue the joint aims of victory and unification. MacArthur's urgent recommendations to bomb Communist China, blockade the mainland, and introduce Nationalist Chinese troops were rejected on various grounds. But primarily, the President and his advisers did not believe that the situation warranted a major war in the Far East. On January 13, 1951, Truman notified MacArthur that American action must be based on what a majority of the United Nations members would tolerate, and that "constant thought" had to be given the preparation for a possible move by the Soviet Union, which constituted the "main threat." Thus military necessity in terms of capabilities and the pressure of "allies" were the imperatives which induced the President to reverse the policy of escalation and return to the initial objective of intervention. This reversal brought Truman into open conflict with General MacArthur and a formidable group in the United States who rejected the concept of a substitute for military victory.

A whole host of grievances combined to spark the reaction against Truman's position. Frustration over the Communist success in China, dissatisfaction with the alleged subordination of the Far East to

Europe in American security efforts, partisan political feeling, resentment toward the United Nations, the desire for final solution to problems, and a reluctance to accept American defeat—all contributed to the criticism. When the controversy between the President and the venerated war hero burst upon the public, the debate was raised to a clear-cut dispute over fundamentals, surrounded by all the dramatic highlights that the communications media could muster. The two eminent protagonists epitomized long developing divergence in many sectors of the nation and cast in high relief an array of accumulating complaints. The American ideal of civilian supremacy was obscured because of a tendency to place the problem in a purely military context, where the judgment of a professional genius was preferred to that of an amateur strategist whose qualifications were suspect.

The President, in effect, was challenging a hero, an institution, and a series of concepts. Perhaps the concepts were his most troublesome problem, for he seemed to be defying basic American traditions. Limited war with limited objectives seemed alien to the American experience and contradicted cherished principles. Compromise with the enemy smacked of treason and forfeited the opportunity to end the threat once and for all. Critics deplored Truman's catering to the wishes of other nations and subordinating American interests to the whims of an international organization. The abrupt and undignified removal of MacArthur added fuel to the opposition. Giving the impression of an attempt to discredit the General and the position he represented, it seemed to reflect the desperation of a frightened, bewildered figure out of his depth in a messy predicament of his own making. Even many who supported the President's point of view were appalled at what appeared to be a spiteful gesture, designed to degrade an illustrious patriot. The martyrdom of MacArthur heightened the animosity toward the President and brought recruits to the General's cause.

Truman finally removed the General because of his alleged disregard of orders, but the two men were fundamentally in opposition over the role of the area commander and the best method of combating communism. MacArthur believed that the Far East was crucial in the world struggle and that a military victory was essential to impress the collective enemy with American determination. Truman, viewing the problem multilaterally, was primarily Europe-oriented, where he thought the Russian threat, as the most dangerous, was directed. The President not only wanted to avoid alienating

United Nations members, but he did not want to create dissent among the North Atlantic Pact nations and imperil the embryonic alliance.

The difference over civil-military responsibilities was more deep-seated and lay at the heart of the controversy. The General felt that once fighting began the statesman should not interfere. As he testified before the special Senate-House Committee on May 3, 1951, "At that stage of the game when politics fails . . . the military takes over." As expressed by the General's former aide,

> MacArthur understood what Truman did not, that the admixture of military strategy with political expediency can produce national disaster . . . . He felt, as experience had long taught, that once the diplomats have failed to preserve the peace it becomes a responsibility of military leadership to devise the strategy which will win the war.[47]

For good or ill, the President perceived the predominance of political aspects of the conflict and conducted affairs accordingly. Though he may have succumbed to the "victory disease" in striving for political unification of Korea, he secured approval for the step from the General Assembly and the major NATO allies. Even after the shattering reverses following Chinese Communist intervention, he stated that there would be no bombing across the Yalu before clearing with the United Nations. The President's efforts to confine the war to Korea and avoid a unilateral approach were successful. As a recent study observes, "The development of the limiting process in the Korean War seems to have been the work, on the whole, of the civilian decision-makers, at least on the American side, in rejecting requests by the military to engage in military operations which would have the effect of expanding the war."[48] On the American side the final decisions were made by the President.

The Korean experience amplified the role of the President in the conduct of foreign affairs. The armed forces had always functioned as an arm of foreign policy, but heretofore the President had not directed their activities in wartime with such a careful regard for political consequences. This detailed control of battlefield operations also enlarged the President's role as Commander-in-Chief, for even Lincoln did not match Truman's interference with military tactics. These factors placed unprecedented strains on relations between the civil and military authorities, and the Truman-MacArthur dispute was an understandable if regrettable consequence. The peculiar nature of the Cold War, the need for multilateral diplomacy, and the horrifying implications of a nuclear conflict placed a greater premium on statecraft than ever before. The further overlapping of military and political activities raised the controversy to the level of a challenge to the civilian supremacy in government and the Constitutional authority of the President. By firing MacArthur the Chief Executive emerged with his image tarnished but with the location of ultimate power clearly established.

The President's task was made doubly difficult by public resistance to his revolutionary course, for the import of his methods was not understood or shared by the nation. As one correspondent wrote at the height of the controversy, "MacArthur promises victory and an eventual end to the crisis; Truman proposes merely that we be patient and endure the crisis."[49] The President had not sold his program to the public, and his prestige declined under the handicaps of an unpopular policy and the humiliation of a hero. Truman later wrote that he "never sought popularity with the press or with the polls," for "if the President is right, he can get through to the people and persuade them, even if he has to risk terrible unpopularity at the beginning."[50] In this instance, however, Truman did not restore his battered image or secure acceptance of his limited approach. MacArthur eventually lost popular support not because he had attempted to usurp authority or because the President eventually won over the people, but because the investigation following the MacArthur removal revealed that the General's program would have resulted in a war of greater magnitude.

Among the innovations made by Truman during the Korean episode was his refusal to ask Congress for a declaration of war. Apparently he believed that it might be necessary if the conflict were extended to the Chinese mainland, but this contingency never arose. Of course Congress still exercised indirect control over what some called "Truman's War" by its jurisdiction over appropriations, though at no time was an administration request for military funds denied. Remarkably enough, while subsequent Presidents have asked Congress for advance authority to employ American troops in a unilateral military action—as in the Formosa Resolution, the Eisenhower Doctrine, and the Vietnam Resolution of 1964—Congress never has given specific approval for the use of troops in a United Nations enterprise. Notwithstanding the implicit intent of the United Nations Participation Act, the Chief Executive has retained this authority as exercised by Truman.

Truman's actions during the Korean incident made a better impression abroad than they did at home. Winston Churchill remarked that Truman's courage during the crisis "made him worthy in my estimation, to be numbered among the greatest of American presidents." The incisive relief of MacArthur also contributed to his international stature, for with his control of nuclear weapons, "nothing adds more to a President's reputation abroad than recognition that he is Commander-in-Chief in fact as well as in name."[51] The significance of this recognition in implementing the President's role as world leader is difficult to exaggerate. Truman had demonstrated America's determination to resist aggression by whatever means necessary and live up to the collective security obligations of the United Nations. His generally prudent conduct of military operations gratified worried allies and reassured skeptical neutrals. His ability to make his policies prevail in the face of formidable domestic opposition established the President as the dependable leader of resistance to communism, a leader who placed the national interest in the broad framework of world responsibilities. This new dimension of Presidential power in foreign affairs emerged in response to the Communist challenge, but its characteristics were determined by the man who held the office at that time.

Truman made more important decisions in the field of foreign affairs than any preceding President. Most of these decisions represented a change in the course of American diplomacy. If they had not, if they had been in the tradition of earlier practice, their import would not have been so great and the decisions would not have been so remarkable. Neither would they have been so difficult, for it is breaking outside the mold of the past that tests a statesman's courage and draws on all his skill as a leader.

One often hears the refrain, "The times make the man." In Truman's case, crisis and opportunity were often present. In their absence his presidency might well have passed with little impact on foreign affairs or on the office he occupied. But it would be a mistake to ascribe his actions to a sort of environmental determinism, wherein he was but a helpless object reacting automatically to external stimuli.

The international responsibilities assumed by the United States during the Truman administration were not "forced" on the nation or the President. Public and congressional opinion in the postwar years was in a state of flux as America attempted to make the transition from the isolationism of the thirties to some form of greater cooperation in world affairs. The extent and form of involvement were uncertain, except for participation in the United Nations. Nor did membership in this organization indicate the *degree* of commitment or the *manner* in which obligations would be fulfilled. Under the circumstances presidential leadership was decisive.

Truman probably would have found it easier to refrain from interference in European affairs, avoid responsibility for the defense of other countries, adopt a passive role in the United Nations, and ignore importunities for aid. In short, confinement to the mainstream of American foreign policy most likely would have encountered less resistance than the departures he advocated. Under another president—a Buchanan or a Harding, for example—the story might well have been different. Truman combined a vision of America's role in the world with a firm notion of the President's role in office. He not only knew where he wanted the nation to go, but he knew what he could do in order to get it there.

President Truman was disdainful of polls, and he perceived the difference between public opinion and published opinion. From the press he asked accuracy and coverage, not caring so much what the editorial page had to say so long as the front page contained the facts. Yet he was not above dramatizing a crisis in order to secure support for a revolutionary proposal, and he knew that the presidential podium was an unequaled source of power. During Truman's presidency the power base of this podium broadened to encompass the world. The Truman Doctrine address of March, 1947, influenced elections in France and Italy two months later, where Communists suffered stinging defeats. Diplomacy by oratory became a potent weapon as America began to extend her influence over the lives of other peoples.

Few presidents have enjoyed thoroughly satisfactory relations with Congress, and Truman was no exception to the rule. Fortunately, on legislative matters a distinction was drawn between domestic and foreign programs. The President's position on foreign affairs was usually shared by the Democratic leaders, and Republicans such as Senator Vandenberg promoted a bipartisan approach that strengthened the President's hand. However, the crisis situations that helped Truman secure legislation were often succeeded by periods of relaxed tension, which jeopardized long-range programs and placed a premium on the constant cultivation of Capitol Hill. Truman, on occasion, dominated or defied Congress, but usually only under the compulsion of extreme urgency. Traditionally, at such times the President's power is virtually irresistible. But if legislative consent was required for any part of his program, the President had to convince Congress that his was the only permissible alternative. Co-operation between the two branches, upon presidential initiative, demanded that the Executive woo congressional leaders of both parties and share with them his information and his policies.

During his administration, President Truman won and pretty well maintained the initiative in foreign policy legislation, and each time he secured unprecedented Cold War legislation through an adroit use of his powers he enlarged the authority of his office. The bipartisanship that lightened his burden could have resulted in a dilution of his programs in order to make them acceptable, a dilution that might have robbed them of their purpose. That it did not is a tribute to the men involved and the skill and perseverance of the President. Willing to compromise on details, Truman persisted on essentials, believing, as he often demonstrated, that in executing the laws he could interpret the letter and the spirit as he saw fit.

The presidency is the focal point for decision in the government of the United States. The extent to which it performs this function depends on the person holding the office, and his behavior sets the tone for the government, for the nation, and, beginning with Truman, for the world. Regardless of the merits of Truman's diplomacy—a subject with which this study is not concerned—the Chief Executive who served from 1945 to 1953 seldom left anyone in doubt as to who controlled American foreign policy or the direction in which it was headed. During this fateful period the scope of action demanded of the President in foreign affairs expanded enormously. Under Truman, presidential power increased in proportion to these demands. In adapting the presidency to the Nuclear Age, Truman added to the Executive new dimensions of power commensurate with America's strength and her pre-eminent position in international affairs. Virtually transformed, the Executive Office was now prepared to provide the leadership and meet the responsibilities assumed by the nation.

III.   Dwight D. Eisenhower: Reluctant Use of Power

Line Engraving from Continuous Tone Negative. Photograph by United Press International

**President Eisenhower Secures Chairman Khrushchev's Agreement
to Negotiate Further on Berlin**

★ III ★

Dwight D. Eisenhower: RELUCTANT USE

OF POWER

by ALEXANDER DE CONDE

Although Harry Truman was the first President of the nuclear age, Dwight D. Eisenhower was first President to be
elected when all knew that the swift changes of the scientific
and technological revolution since 1945 had transformed the executive office. The President's decisions in foreign relations had become a matter of life or death for millions all over the world. The
American presidency was now an institution of world-wide concern,
and the President himself, whether or not he wanted to be, had become a world leader.[1]

Like any modern president, Eisenhower was in a position to take
action in foreign relations at his own discretion that Congress, or the
courts could not, or would find difficult, to reverse. This power in turn
reflected another historical reality. In no part of American political
life did the theoretical, or practical, separation of powers count for
so little as in the President's control of foreign relations.

These factors, among others, have made presidential power in
foreign relations one of the most complex problems in the most complex office in the American governmental system.[2] In view of this
complexity, to understand the use of presidential power under Eisenhower, we must go beyond law and the Constitution. We have to
take into account history, tradition, politics, and even the psychological factors that influenced presidential action. We should be aware
of intangible influences as well as the tangible ones. If possible, we

79

should know something of the literature on the presidency, its strength and weaknesses, and even its contradictions.

One thing this literature shows is that it has internal contradictions, and secondly that scholars who have investigated the nature and extent of presidential power have differed in their interpretations. Despite these differences the idea of studying the presidency through concepts advanced by scholars and statesmen can be a valuable means of evaluating and measuring presidential power in foreign relations, especially when coupled with a study of that power in action. We shall, therefore, use such concepts as those of "weak" and "strong" presidents, as well as historical episodes, to analyze how Eisenhower used presidential power in foreign relations, what he thought of that power, and how his ideas and deeds in situations requiring its use fit the traditions of the presidency.

Before he became President, Dwight D. Eisenhower was a national military hero whose adult life had been spent in the Army, most of it outside the United States. He had had no experience in politics, either local or national. Except for four years as president of Columbia University, he had had no civilian experience of any consequence, and knew little about politics even from theory or casual reading. "I was, of course," he admitted, "a political novice."[3] Yet in 1948 leading members of both political parties wanted him to run for the presidency on their ticket.

The politicians wanted Eisenhower not only because he was that rare commodity, a genuine hero who could probably win elections as such, but also because he was a likeable man who possessed a simple sincerity, an unpretentious manner, and a grin that seemed to light the sky. He seemed, as his nickname "Ike" implied, to inspire friendliness. In him could also be seen some of the most appealing features of the American dream—the small town boy from Kansas who became a world famous conqueror, but who retained his midwestern simplicity among the power-hungry corrupters of Europe.

Even Eisenhower's well-known anti-intellectualism, which appeared out of place in the highest circles of leadership in an age when the intellect had to be nurtured for national survival, belonged to the America of the nineteenth century which many Americans sought, like lost innocence, to recover. When Ike defined an intellectual as "a man who takes more words than is necessary to say more than he knows," millions of those Americans would feel a sense of kinship with him.[4]

Eisenhower's mind, like his personality, was what one writer called standard American. It was strong, simple, pragmatic, impatient with theory, distrustful of fine distinctions, and concerned more with the consequences of ideas than with their abstract roots. He liked concrete concepts and did not give himself to prolonged meditation.[5] His were, in short, characteristics seemingly retrieved from the nineteenth century that Americans knew and admired. Those characteristics in him, it was obvious, had an amazing appeal for the masses, and could be transformed into votes.

Despite these political assets, Eisenhower at first resisted all pressures to seek the presidency, and even gave the impression that he merely wished to enjoy retirement after completing a tour of duty as Supreme Commander of the military forces of the North Atlantic Treaty Organization, usually called NATO. Even later, while striving for the office, he retained this attitude of aloofness. "If they don't want me," he said in reference to the American people, "that doesn't matter very much to *me*. I've got a hell of a lot of fishing I'll be happy to do."[6]

At another time, after completing a term as Chief of Staff, Eisenhower told reporters that he did not desire the presidency because he felt that a man should not try to go beyond his historical peak. "I think I pretty well hit my peak in history when I accepted the German surrender in 1945," he explained.

"Now, why should I want to get into a completely foreign field and try to top that? Why should I go out and deliberately risk that historical peak by trying to push a bit higher?"[7]

The general, we know, changed his mind and did take the risk. What caused him to do so and to seek the Republican nomination for the presidency, he said, was his concern for the principle of collective security and for the President's control of foreign policy. The United States must, he felt, as it did not do in 1919, accept its obligations of world leadership.

"In the overriding question of the United States' commitment to share in the collective defense of the West . . . ," Eisenhower has written, "I was vitally interested." If all quarters of the American government did not support this principle, he believed, NATO's chances for success would be jeopardized.

As the general watched isolationist Republican congressmen attack the commitment to collective security he began to suspect that the principle he cherished might be in danger. To satisfy himself on this point in 1951 he talked confidentially to several Republican senators who had expressed views in keeping with a revived isolationism. From one senator he gained the impression "that he and some of his colleagues were interested, primarily, in cutting the President, or the presidency, down to size." Other Republican visitors left him with the same or similar impressions.

"My disappointment," Eisenhower recalled, "was acute; I was resentful toward those who seemed to be playing politics in matters I thought vital to America and the Free World."[8] His commitment to American leadership in world affairs, he believed, was what divided him from conservative Republicans. With this view in mind, he later fought for the Republican nomination and won.

Even though during the course of the 1952 campaign, candidate Eisenhower made many compromises, some of them with the neo-isolationists he professed to detest, he retained his concern for collective security. "I am not," he is said to have blurted out on one occasion, "going to go around this country making any stupid promises about slashing our defense costs . . . nothing—and I mean *nothing*—is going to come ahead of assuring the safety of the United States."[9]

This attitude reflected another important basis of Eisenhower's appeal. Regardless of its justification in reality, he had a reputation as a wise, moderate, and esteemed figure in international affairs, a man the nation and the world could trust, and to whom all in the Western World could look for leadership. "Let's face it," one of his advisers said, "the only excuse for Ike's candidacy is that he's the man best qualified to deal with Stalin."[10]

Yet, early in the campaign when Eisenhower discussed foreign policy, he seldom rose above fumbling platitudes which left even ardent supporters cold. "Now he's crossing the 38th platitude again," a reporter remarked on one of these occasions, but even critics such as this would probably concede that Ike had the gift for speaking platitudes sincerely.[11] Later, as his speeches began to take fire, he appeared to borrow some of the exaggerated rhetoric on foreign policy heard at the Republican National Convention, such as the charge that the Democrats under Harry S. Truman had abandoned China, and hence had betrayed American interests to the Communists.

One aspect of Truman's Far Eastern policy, the war in Korea, became the most sensitive question of the campaign. Republican strategists considered it their foremost issue, placing it first among three basic issues: Korea, Communism, and Corruption in government, known by the formula $K_1 C_2$.

In September, 1952, criticisms of Truman's policy in Korea ran through many of Eisenhower's speeches, but it was not until late October that he and his advisers decided to exploit the issue fully.

On October 24, in Detroit, Eisenhower pledged that if elected he would himself go to Korea. Three days later he announced that "if a journey to Korea and a close study of our military and political problems there, can save the life of a single American soldier and bring peace of mind to a single American family, I must make that journey."[12]

Some political analysts have maintained that this pledge marked the turning point in the campaign, that it clinched the election. This is an inflated claim, for Eisenhower's personal popularity was so great that he probably could have won the election without any declaration on Korea.[13] Nonetheless, the declaration gave life to Republicans, dismayed Democrats, and recognized not only the importance of foreign policy, but also the depth of public feeling toward it in the world of 1952.

Eisenhower had suggested that he would end the stalemate in Korea and replace a blundering leadership in foreign policy with initiative and dynamic leadership.[14] The sweep of his victory, which made him a landslide winner, certainly indicated that the voters believed him. They seemed to have more confidence in him than in his party, for other Republican candidates did not do nearly so well as their standard bearer. Ike's magic was not strong enough to carry many of them into office. His was the personal victory of a hero, not of a party.

Between the day of election and inauguration Eisenhower, as he had promised, visited the Korean battlefields. On the way back, in the second week of December, 1952, he spent three days in conferences with his advisers and future cabinet officers aboard the cruiser U.S.S. *Helena*. Foreign policy, particularly the Korean War, received considerable attention. "There was," Eisenhower wrote later, "general agreement with my conclusion that we could not tolerate the indefinite continuance of the Korean conflict; the United States would have to prepare to break the stalemate."[15] Beyond that the President-elect, according to the available record, made no important foreign policy decision on the *Helena*.

Yet, as Eisenhower himself pointed out, the most complex and urgent problems confronting him as he prepared to enter the White House as the first Republican President in twenty years were in international affairs. The pressure from foreign problems would never cease; it would continue throughout his Presidency and be with him to the day he drove away from 1600 Pennsylvania Avenue.

The President-elect's preparations for a transition that would allow him to grasp at least the essentials of foreign problems from men who had worked with them, or understood them through study, was inadequate. During the campaign, for example, he had turned down invitations from President Truman to go to the White House to discuss the more pressing problems of foreign policy with cabinet members and others, and had also refused to receive weekly reports from the Central Intelligence Agency.[16]

Later, as Eisenhower gathered about him a group of advisers, called "the team," which he planned to bring into the White House with him, there seemed to be considerable concern for the handling of foreign relations in a time of crisis. But this concern, too, masked inadequacy. With the exception of John Foster Dulles, chosen to be Secretary of State, the team was noteworthy for its lack of experience in, and knowledge of, foreign affairs.

After the election, it is true, Eisenhower visited Truman at the White House where the discussion centered on problems of foreign policy. Secretary of State Dean Acheson reviewed problems in Korea, NATO, Iran, Indochina, and elsewhere. The exchange between the President and the President-elect lasted only twenty minutes and was so cold it might have frozen alcohol.[17] Truman was disturbed by Ike's lack of responsiveness and by the "frozen grimness" he displayed.

Eisenhower's liaison officer for foreign policy, Henry Cabot Lodge, conferred for fifty minutes with the head of the State Department's Policy Planning Board, a body that analyzed current policies and projected others into the future. Except for housekeeping matters or procedural details, this was the extent of the Eisenhower team's effort to meet the problems it would immediately confront when it took power. "The door was wide open," one of Truman's assistants remarked later, "but nobody came in."[18]

Ironically, eight years later, Eisenhower and his staff complained about the shallowness of John F. Kennedy's preparation for the transition. Eisenhower himself expressed concern over inexperienced newcomers taking over control of crucial problems in foreign relations with inadequate instruction.[19]

Despite the weaknesses in the transition from Truman to Eisenhower, it was an improvement in co-operation over previous transitions. Outwardly, at least, it suggested national solidarity in foreign policy, despite some of the bitterness and extreme charges of the campaign.

Eisenhower's inaugural address, directed to the rest of the world as well as to the nation, appeared to support this expectation. This message, couched in terms of general ideals, pledged his administration to support the principle of collective security. "In the light of this principle," he announced, "we stand ready to engage with any and all others in joint effort to remove the causes of mutual fear and distrust among nations. . . ." He also stressed what most Americans wanted to hear, that he would dedicate himself to a quest for peace. "The peace we seek," he said, is "more than the stilling of guns, it is easing the sorrow of war . . . , it is a way of life."[20]

This immediate concern for foreign policy was in keeping with what most Americans expected. Eisenhower had been elected in part because the people considered him capable of handling foreign relations well, and his orientation was, in fact, clearest on matters of foreign policy. Most people apparently looked upon him as a new George Washington—a not entirely inadequate image—who was patriotic, able, experienced in the large issues of world affairs, and concerned about the national welfare in a manner that transcended narrow partisanship.

Eisenhower apparently accepted this image of himself, believing that he was fit for the Presidency because of his wartime experiences and his natural endowments. This feeling of fitness and self-confidence did not, however, encompass the role of politician and initiator of policy. For this he was unequipped by experience, by knowledge, by temperament, and even by taste. He brought to the White House a view of the Presidency not far removed from the nineteenth-century Whig concept of the office as one of three equal branches of government. This was the concept of a relatively weak executive.

Ike embraced the Whig view of relations between the President and Congress because of personal preference, and also because in the preceding twenty years Republican power had survived mainly in Congress. There resentment against the man in the White House burned deeply, and the Whig idea of presidential power had become almost a matter of Republican faith. Since Eisenhower had no clear idea of the President's responsibilities and tended himself to view presidential power in terms of his personal relationship with others rather than in terms of institutional relationships, it was logical for him to go along with the Whig concept.

Eisenhower soon showed that, as expressed in the Whig doctrine, he distrusted and discounted power in the presidency, approaching issues which required the use of the broader powers of his office with hesitation, respect, and even timidity. Almost always, it seemed, he used power himself in the big issues with reluctance, as a last resort. He had not sought power; it was thrust upon him. He could, therefore, and did, take an aloof attitude toward power, whereas his

Democratic predecessors were impressed, even fascinated, by it. Apparently he looked upon himself not as one who should wield power to lead and create, but as one who should bind the wounds of the past, act as a father to the people, and bring unity to the nation. Scholars have pointed out that he wished to arbitrate, not to master; to serve, not to enhance the power of his office; to crown a reputation, not to make one.[21]

At times it seemed as though Eisenhower did not trust his own judgment enough to use power and make decisions on his own. Early in his presidency he revealed a willingness to disperse and delegate the powers of his office. One critic even maintained that during his first six years in office, Eisenhower delegated so much of his power "as hardly to be President at all." Eisenhower himself denied that he delegated basic responsibilities. "I would make one thing clear," he told a press conference in May, 1956, "no President can delegate his constitutional duties."[22]

Since the tasks of the modern President are so demanding that one of his essential functions is to delegate authority, the important question is not delegation itself, but to what extent did Eisenhower delegate power, to whom, and to what degree?

Scholars have pointed out repeatedly that the personality of the President, his training, and his thinking as an individual, often more than theory, party philosophies, or even historic forces, have governed his concept of the office and his use of power. What he thought of the presidency has, not infrequently, been a measure of his achievement, and of how he used power.

This was true of Eisenhower. His approach to power and to leadership in the presidency reflected his military experience, which was in large part that of a staff officer, not that of a combat commander, probably even more than he himself realized. He thought the presidency should be, and he tried to make it, an efficient machine, combining the features of a military staff and a corporate board of directors. He immediately made this concept a practical working one, and relied on it with confidence. "One of my first responsibilities," he wrote, "was to organize the White House for efficiency."[23]

Faith in efficiency and the staff system never left Eisenhower. "I believed, and still do," he wrote after leaving office, "that the careful development by the President of a personal staff, able to assure the effective and unobtrusive performance of . . . several duties on his behalf, is one of the most important things he can do in the interests of efficient government."[24]

As a military man, moreover, Eisenhower appeared to assume

that when he gave a command it would be carried out, but the presidency was not the army and politicians would not function as efficiently and smoothly as well-trained members of a military staff. "The President still feels," an aide to Eisenhower remarked in 1958, "that when he's decided something, that *ought* to be the end of it . . . and when it bounces back undone or done wrong, he tends to react with shocked surprise."[25]

Regardless of such shock, Eisenhower did bring order and efficiency to the Cabinet and to the National Security Council. For each body he created the post of secretary. In the case of the Cabinet, the secretary would prepare an agenda for each meeting, which usually took place on Friday morning and lasted about three hours. Each item on the agenda would be supported with a memorandum, giving background details and outlining the points at issue, and with a financial statement indicating probable cost if the proposal were adopted. In most instances the papers were circulated to the Cabinet members and the problems defined earlier in the week.

The Cabinet secretary kept a record of each meeting, and after the meeting representatives of the department heads would come together in the White House where they would record the decisions taken so that they could follow up whatever action had been promised.[26] Unlike the British cabinet, the American Cabinet had no power of decision, that power rested with the President. Under Eisenhower, however, the Cabinet's recommendations helped to shape decisions in a way unknown in the past.

More than most presidents, Eisenhower consulted the Cabinet and other advisory bodies before arriving at a decision. "The Cabinet, as well as the Security Council," Eisenhower's chief assistant wrote, "became under Eisenhower a force in the determination of government policy that it never had been in previous administrations." One reason for this was that Eisenhower required a consensus of the Cabinet, or of his staff, or even of Congress to arrive at judgments.[27]

This system made innovations difficult and led to some strange decisions, even to contradictions within the administration on matters of policy. By the standards of the day, and by the admissions of his advisers, Eisenhower headed a conservative administration. By the same standards those within the administration who dealt with domestic affairs were the most conservative of his advisers. Those who might be called "liberal" or "modern" Republicans, such as Henry Cabot Lodge, John Foster Dulles, and Harold Stassen, handled foreign relations. This meant that at times Eisenhower's policies in foreign relations were fairly liberal, but at other times, when domestic considerations came first, those policies could be quite conservative.

Under the Eisenhower system problems of foreign policy usually went to the National Security Council, but new issues in foreign affairs also went to the Cabinet for review. In the first Cabinet meeting, an unofficial one at the Commodore Hotel in New York a week before the first inauguration, Eisenhower told his department heads that each one would be responsible "for making government policy. No major decision will be made by the National Security Council but what will be reviewed by the Cabinet and brought back to the NSC."[28]

It has been said that Eisenhower institutionalized the presidency, meaning that he practically suffocated it in a cluster of institutions designed to produce foreign policy out of conferences or consensus. This is an exaggeration, for other presidents, too, contributed to this institutionalization. None, however, went as far as he did. Firm organization, as we have seen, suited his temperament and training. He was, some critics argued, a prisoner in his over-organized house. Yet he designed a system long recommended by experts on problems of the presidency, and along lines urged by the Commissions on Organization of the Executive Branch of the Government, headed by Herbert Hoover.[29]

Eisenhower's emphasis on staff procedure did tend to rigidify the presidency, because under the American system only the President could co-ordinate the Cabinet, the National Security Council, and the federal bureaucracy. Eisenhower usually preferred to let administrators, or staff members, proceed on the lowest common denominator of agreement rather than have their debates and arguments, at least on issues and details, pushed up to him.[30] Disliking quarrels, he felt that wrangling between the President and Congress, as under Truman, had weakened respect for the presidency. Yet, even he could not entirely avoid arguments or hard decisions. "There are no easy matters that will come to you as President," he told John F. Kennedy, his successor. "If they are easy, they will be settled at a lower level.[31]

Since most problems of national security, and hence of foreign policy, went to the National Security Council, that council became a powerful agency, and one of the most important arms of the presidency. Eisenhower used it regularly as his machinery for reaching decisions in foreign relations.

The purpose of this agency, created under Truman in 1947, was to advise the President on the integration of domestic, foreign, and military policies relating to national security; to "assess and appraise the objectives, commitments, and risks of the United States in relation to our actual and potential military power." It was designed to keep the various agencies which dealt with security matters from acting on their own without over-all direction. For example, Eisenhower was concerned with economy. He immediately had George Humphrey, the Secretary of the Treasury, attend the Council's meetings. "Thus," Eisenhower wrote, "the responsibilities of the NSC as an advisory body were broadened to recognize the relationship between military and economic strength." Later, he required "that every National Security Council policy paper include the estimated cost of the program it proposed."[32]

Some analysts have maintained that the basic difference between the Cabinet and the National Security Council under Eisenhower was that the Cabinet dealt mostly with domestic affairs and the Council with security and foreign affairs, though in fact the President encouraged Cabinet officers to express themselves on foreign relations. Another difference was that procedure in the Council was more formal. It functioned almost entirely through carefully prepared staff work, and usually dealt with questions that required a specific recommendation to the President for action.

If, for instance, Eisenhower had some problem he wanted studied, he would refer it to his special assistant for security affairs, a position held for several years by Dillon Anderson, a conservative lawyer from Houston. Anderson would then pass the question to the department concerned, or to several departments, for comment. After that the material would go to the permanent staff of the National Security Council. That staff would then prepare the material relating to the problem for the consideration of the Council's Planning Board.

That Planning Board, which did the basic research and analysis, and much of the Council's thinking, was the principal interdepartmental committee concerned with issues of war and peace. Its members, anonymous and usually invisible, were high-ranking civil servants, or non-political experts. Although they denied this, they wielded considerable power, for many of their policy papers, after approval by the President, became official statements of government policy.[33]

The Operations Co-ordinating Board, established in 1954 with a membership composed of officials at the level of Under Secretary, had the task of following-up and seeing to it that policies laid down by the National Security Council, and approved by the President, were carried out in a coordinated manner. These three bodies, the Planning Board, the National Security Council, and the Operations

Coordinating Board constituted a staff system for policy formulation, decision, and execution, and theoretically of strengthening presidential leadership in policymaking, that Eisenhower viewed with pride.

Another element in this staff system, about which little is known, was the Central Intelligence Agency, created in 1947 as a servant of the National Security Council. It was entrusted with the mission of gathering, analyzing, and disseminating information concerning national security and foreign relations. Although the Central Intelligence Agency was not itself a policymaking body, its head, Allen Dulles, the brother of the Secretary of State, served as a principal adviser to the National Security Council, had direct access to the President, and hence was in a position to influence foreign policy, and at times did so.[34]

The members of the National Security Council, like the Cabinet officials, based their discussions on the carefully prepared papers of the Planning Board, and were often, despite Ike's dislike of argument, unrestrained in their debate, discussion, and criticism. The men who prepared the papers, for the National Security Council, and for the Cabinet, were key figures, regardless of how much they denied their power. They provided the President with solid staff services, but they could not substitute for him in the use of power. In short, these interdepartmental committees sometimes suffered because they lacked a clearly defined mission, and often because they did not have the authoritative direction that only Eisenhower himself could give.

This was true, to a certain extent, of the National Security Council itself. The Council and its Planning Board could recommend, but the Constitution imposed on the President the duty to decide. Although he could and should seek help, he could not, if he were to decide intelligently, avoid immersing himself in the hard and often frustrating task of choosing between dangerous alternatives. Too often, critics said, Eisenhower, whose schedule left no time for intense study of world affairs, left these tough decisions to his subordinates.

Eisenhower used the meetings of his Cabinet and of the National Security Council to shape government policy in every important field. More than any other president before him he relied on the collective judgment of his advisers to resolve the tough questions headed for his desk.

This staff concept, more than any other, stamped the Eisenhower administration as one devoted to teamwork and co-ordination of policy. That concept also made possible a pattern of collective judgment that the President accepted. His decisions were not usually the result of his own thinking, influenced by the advice of one or two Cabinet officers, but of the collective thought of the team or staff.

It would be wrong to give the impression that the staff system was unique with Eisenhower. He did not originate the concept. The Executive Office of the President was created in 1939, and after that the staff grew. In a few years it became a central feature of the presidency.

All recent presidents have had to rely, to some extent, on a staff system in dealing with foreign relations. Foreign affairs have become so complex that a president can grasp only a small part of them. He must, therefore, rely on a variety of staff members, often on nonpolitical permanent experts in the lower ranks, for help in arriving at decisions.[35] This does not in itself vitiate presidential power in foreign relations, for the ultimate decision always belongs to the man who is President. Also, he himself can handle only a few of the functions imposed on him for the conduct of foreign policy, and hence he must, as a simple matter of administrative principle, delegate "responsibility." Most students of government agree, nonetheless, that Eisenhower, through his staff system, carried the principle farther than had any other president.[36]

Despite the efficiency of the staff system, there were occasional blunders, and even lack of co-ordination. In February, 1953, for example, Eisenhower made public his decision not to pardon Ethel and Julius Rosenberg, two American Communists who had been condemned to death as Soviet spies. World opinion against the penalty, fanned by Communist propaganda and heated by moral indignation, was intense and could influence American policy in many parts of the globe. Logically, the Department of State was concerned not only with the President's decision itself but also with its proper handling by diplomats and American propagandists, especially those employed by the Voice of America radio. Yet the President and his staff did not consult the State Department on the decision. Its officials read about it in the morning papers.[37]

Personal inclination, as well as addiction to the staff system, led Eisenhower to take a detached view of the conduct of his subordinates. According to his own theory of government, free of any link to legal or historical reality, Cabinet officers were independent office holders, each with his own views of appropriate policy. Once broad policy was made, therefore, he allowed Cabinet members a wide range of autonomy in carrying it out. The President, he believed, had no warrant to interfere with his department heads in their implementation of policy.

"You have full authority. I expect you to stand on your own feet," Eisenhower is reported to have told his Cabinet officers. "Whatever you decide goes. The White House will stay out of your hair."

This detachment, this attitude of reigning rather than ruling, led to contradictions within the executive branch on matters of policy. Despite the emphasis on consensus within the staff system, department heads might, and sometimes did, publicly challenge presidential policy. This theory of department heads as independent sources of policy, when coupled with the concept of the staff system, left considerable power in their hands, and fragmented or weakened Eisenhower's own use of power.[38]

When Eisenhower suffered a heart attack in Denver, in September, 1955, he became unable to control foreign policy, but his staff system worked so well that the policymaking machinery continued to function without him. The President had set up the business of government in such a way, Vice-President Richard M. Nixon told reporters, "that it can go ahead despite the temporary absence of anyone."[39]

Policymaking did not, however, go on as well as Eisenhower's partisans claimed. This was so because the making of many decisions involved political issues which were beyond the influence of subordinates. Even though Eisenhower had already delegated a large measure of responsibility to his subordinates, was willing to have them confer together, and to go right ahead with their tasks while he was gone, only he, as President, could truly coordinate foreign policy.

Without personal direction from the top, foreign policy on the big issues could not be left in the hands of bureau chiefs and other staff members in the Department of State and the National Security Council. For six months, while Eisenhower was stricken or recuperating, he could offer no such direction. Not even the Secretary of State could act as effectively in foreign policy as when Eisenhower was in active command. Fortunately, at this time, the government faced no new big emergency problems, hence neither the Cabinet nor the National Security Council was forced to exercise extraordinary authority. As Vice-President Nixon, who umpired interdepartmental disputes, pointed out, the regents "realized that our team government would be inadequate to handle an international crisis, such as a brushfire war or an internal uprising in a friendly nation or a financial crisis of any ally."[40]

In 1956, when Eisenhower ran for his second term, the performance of his presidential duties became a campaign issue. Democrats charged, that because of his heart attack he would be only a "part-time President." Some even argued that he had never been more than that. Eisenhower himself brought up the issue, when he told the American people that if re-elected he would continue to handle personally "all the important duties" of the presidency, but would delegate other tasks that he had himself discharged before his heart attack.

John Sparkman of Alabama, who had been the Democratic vice-presidential nominee in 1952, accused Republicans of trying to shrink presidential power, and thus weaken this "central pillar" of the American system of government. Other Democrats complained that Eisenhower, even before his illness, and increasingly since, had been delegating vital functions to a "regency," most members of which were the President's personal appointees, not men elected by the people. He was not, one critic wrote, "boss of the works."[41]

Eisenhower hotly denied that any of his proper constitutional duties were being discharged by others. Yet he insisted that his subordinates would perform other less important chores. He worked on the principle that a subordinate had "within his own area of delegated authority and within the limits of established policy, to solve his own problems." If Eisenhower had to make a decision "that properly belonged to a subordinate," he explained, he would tolerate such procedure only once. After that he would replace the subordinate.[42]

Some critics argued that the efficiency of Eisenhower's staff screened, but not effectively, a lack of decisiveness in the use of presidential power, or what they called "massive indecision." During the first administration, Robert Frost, the poet, visited the White House and later commented on the various commendable qualities in President Eisenhower. "But I sense," the poet explained, "from around the country, something troubling. It comes from the young people especially. It is one fear and one want. It is *a lack of decisiveness.*"[43]

There was some truth in this observation, and also in another voiced frequently by friends and detractors alike, that Eisenhower's reliance on collective judgment and on his personal theory of Cabinet responsibility increased the power of his Secretary of State, John Foster Dulles. Too often, critics said, Eisenhower left tough decisions to Dulles, who enjoyed his respect and confidence. Few Secretaries of State, if any, have received as much confidence from any president. Eisenhower admitted that he gave Dulles responsibility for initiating foreign policy. Since Eisenhower was reluctant to use power in foreign relations himself in a direct and forceful manner, and willing to disperse or delegate his power, Dulles was ready, willing, and even eager to assume this authority.[44]

Before becoming Secretary of State, Dulles reportedly told the

President, "With my understanding of the intricate relationships between the peoples of the world and your sensitiveness to the political
considerations involved, we will make the most successful team in
history."[45] Eisenhower accepted this rather arrogant assumption because of his own reluctance to use power and because he came to
have confidence in Dulles's use of it in foreign relations.

This was not always the case. Initially, leaders of the Republican
party had insisted that Dulles was the most competent and experienced member of the party in foreign affairs, and had urged his appointment as Secretary of State. Although Eisenhower followed this
advice, at first he showed little enthusiasm for Dulles and seemed
bored by him. Very quickly, however, the President developed the
habit of deferring to his judgment in matters relating to foreign relations, and came to see the world through Dulles's glasses. Eisenhower invariably defended his Secretary of State against critics, calling him at various times "indispensable," and "the most brilliant man
I have ever known in foreign affairs."[46]

After the death of the Secretary of State in 1959, Eisenhower explained that Dulles had been his closest friend and confidant who had,
for six years, supplied the brains and heart in the formation of foreign
policy. "The fact remains," Eisenhower said on another occasion, of
Dulles, "that he just knows more about foreign affairs than anybody
I know. In fact, I'll be immodest and say that there's only one man
who has seen *more* of the world and talked with more people and
knows more than he does—and that's *me*. And I can't take his job
and move over there. . . ."[47]

There was some truth in this comment. Foreign relations, as we
have seen, was Eisenhower's area of prime concern, and the one in
which he was prepared to proceed with most confidence based on his
own experience. Those close to the President pointed out that he
"was more confident and incisive in discussions of global strategy at
meetings of the National Security Council, than he was in many of
the detailed debates on domestic issues with the Cabinet."[48]

Eisenhower did not, as some critics have maintained, abdicate control of foreign policy to Dulles; he just delegated big pieces of that
power while retaining the power of final decision. "Behind closed
doors," Eisenhower said of Dulles, "we worked as partners," but
we both recognized that "the final decision had to be mine." Eisenhower had simple convictions in foreign policy: peace, the rule of law
in the world, faith in the United Nations, in America's national interest pursued with some generosity, and in the American way of life
as a criteria of a good society everywhere. These principles served

as guides for the Secretary of State. Beyond them, Dulles was on his own.[49]

One of Dulles's earliest announcements, for example, reflected Eisenhower's own approach to world affairs. The administration's foreign policy, Dulles said, would operate on three principles which "were in accord with what used to be the great American traditional foreign policy . . . openness, simplicity, and righteousness."[50] The Secretary of State's manner of expression implied that these vague virtues held the secret of the sound American way of conducting foreign policy, that the Democrats had somehow lost the secret, or had deliberately strayed from the path of virtue, and that the Eisenhower administration had rediscovered the virtues.

Furthermore, the basic orientation in foreign policy reflected Eisenhower's belief that the United States must assume a role of leadership in world affairs. "Within that framework," Sherman Adams explained, "Eisenhower delegated to Dulles the responsibility of developing the specific policy, including the decision where the administration would stand and what course of action would be followed in each international crisis."[51]

Eisenhower admitted that Dulles originated much of the planning in foreign policy, meaning that the Secretary of State provided the rhetoric and ideas for that policy. At his press conferences it seemed, at times, that Eisenhower merely repeated what Dulles had said the previous day. Quite often he would refer the questions to Dulles.

If Eisenhower had desired to do so, there was nothing that could have stopped him from taking over direct control of foreign affairs. What prevented him from doing so was his own personality, his image of himself as President, his concept of the Secretaryship, and his method of using power. He accepted Dulles's advice because of these things, and because it was congenial to his own thinking.

Knowing of Dulles's control of power in foreign relations, newspapermen called him "the giant of the Cabinet" and "the most powerful Secretary of State of this century." Aware that such power came from the President personally, Dulles would allow nothing or no one to come between himself and Eisenhower. On occasion he confessed privately that he feared Eisenhower's possible "naïveté." He watched closely, therefore, all officials having or seeking direct access to the President.

Unlike other department heads, Dulles had instant access to the President. "You don't ever need to announce him," Eisenhower told his appointments assistant. "I'm here whenever he is."[52] This relationship of Dulles to Eisenhower illustrates the truism that presidential power in general, and specifically in foreign relations, had been personal.

Unlike a British Prime Minister, who has to make sure he has the support of his cabinet before acting, the President can make decisions entirely on his own. Eisenhower, for example, did not have to rely on his Cabinet, or even on the National Security Council for independent advice. He did not have to consult these bodies if he did not wish to do so. If a president so desires he can manipulate foreign policy to create situations from which escape, except by war, may be impossible.[53] He has this power merely by his control of day-to-day events in foreign relations.

Entirely on his own, using his powers as Commander-in-Chief, President Eisenhower could have started a nuclear war. If it had been physically possible and if necessary, he could have sent troops to the moon. In the use of such vast military power the President may, in some situations, be as prudent or capricious, as clumsy or skillful as his temperament or mood permit. In this age of nuclear warheads and hurtling missiles the American people have entrusted the President with the survival of their homes, their own lives, and those of their children.

This power of life and death in the hands of the President has tended to increase with the advances in weapon technology. In Eisenower's time and since, during crisis, particularly when tension over the possibility of war is high, national leaders, even democratic ones such as the American President, tend consciously or unconsciously to confine deliberations to a handful of men. In the midst of crisis, when time is short, "concentration of power can most readily be placed in the chief executive."[54]

Eisenhower knew that in a world policed mainly by American armed forces his decisions and actions affected the lives of millions of allied and neutral peoples, as well as those of his own. As President, he also knew that he had the power to influence world order and social stability.

In addition, Eisenhower entered the presidency with a public support that may have been greater than that given to any man since Washington. Few, if any, presidents had an equivalent opportunity for vigorous leadership. This immense personal prestige, combined with his control, as President and Commander-in-Chief, over the world's largest nuclear arsenal, placed in his hands a power that few, if any other, mortals have had.

In foreign affairs, especially, Eisenhower's position was unique. Because of deep divisions in foreign policy among the people, linked to a domestic hysteria over communism, no Democratic president had or could enjoy the political freedom to act decisively in world affairs that Eisenhower could. Under attack by the Republicans for allegedly being too soft in dealing with the Soviets, the Democrats could make no diplomatic concessions to the Russians which might help to ease world tensions. They would have been attacked as being "soft" on communism. Eisenhower's prestige was such that he could make such concessions and survive politically.

Almost as soon as Eisenhower took office, he was confronted with the need to use his personal and presidential power in foreign relations. The Korean War was in its thirty-first month, had entered a stalemate punctuated by brutal small encounters, and had become more frustrating than ever because of long, drawn-out truce negotiations which appeared to try the nerves of Americans more than those of their Asian foes.

Soon after his inauguration, Eisenhower took the first step in what he had promised would be a dynamic new foreign policy, by "unleashing" Chiang Kai-shek, the head of the Chinese Nationalist government based on Formosa, whom Truman had barred from attacking the Chinese mainland from his island sanctuary. The Seventh Fleet, the President told Congress, would no longer "be employed to shield Communist China." Some Americans now feared that Chiang would raid the mainland and drag the United States into war with Red China, but the Generalissimo was too weak to act effectively, and nothing happened.

Despite this striking announcement, the stalemate in Korea continued, and on the surface the Eisenhower policy seemed as cautious as Truman's. Since Eisenhower was more or less committed to the aims of the foreign policy he had inherited, the comparison was valid enough.

An example of the new President's caution can be seen in his reaction to a request from General Mark Clark, the American commander of the United Nations forces in Korea. Clark suspected that the Communists were building up forces in an area of sanctuary, and asked permission to attack first if he became convinced that the Communists were themselves preparing to attack. "This authority," Eisenhower wrote, "I thought unwise to delegate at that time."[55]

Everyone, it seemed, wanted to find some way to end the war. Even a conservative businessman who had become Secretary of Defense, Charles E. Wilson, could blurt out a drastic proposal for terminating the war. "Is there any possibility for a package deal?"

he asked. "Maybe we could recognize Red China and get the Far East issues settled."[56] This suggestion was ignored.

The President and Dulles formulated what they claimed was a bold policy. Eisenhower decided to try once more for a truce and if he failed, to fight for victory with tactical atomic bombs if necessary. He let the Communists know, through various sources, including India's Prime Minister, that "without satisfactory progress" in the truce talks, "we intended to move decisively, without inhibition in our use of weapons, and would no longer be responsible for confining hostilities to the Korean Peninsula."[57] Eisenhower claimed that this decision, involving the "danger of an atomic war," broke the deadlock in the truce negotiations and brought the Communists into line. Whether or not the atomic threat was decisive, the truce talks were resumed in April 1953 and on July 27 the negotiators signed an armistice.

Regardless of the decisiveness of the threat, Eisenhower and Dulles had used presidential power in foreign relations to threaten war, but with the objective of peace. The threat was not a public one. Only those immediately involved knew of it at the time.[58] To the public it seemed that Eisenhower had played the role of peacemaker as he had promised, and thus he became more firmly established in public favor than before. Yet, his use of presidential power in this instance could have been a decision for war, a nuclear conflict with millions of casualties.

There were Republican conservatives who distrusted the use of such presidential power, even when in hands of a president of their own party. In particular, they challenged the President's prerogatives in the making of treaties and other international agreements. Resenting executive agreements, such as those made at Yalta in 1945 by Franklin D. Roosevelt, Senator John W. Bricker, a Republican from Ohio, sponsored an amendment to the Constitution that would have given Congress, in addition to its authority over treaties, the power to regulate all executive agreements with foreign countries. This Bricker Amendment cut across party lines and gained vociferous support from isolationists, states righters, the American Medical Association, Daughters of the American Revolution, and other conservative groups, and aroused considerable emotion in Congress.

At one time Eisenhower had shown sympathy for the amendment but when he recognized the impact it would have on the presidency, he turned against it. This reversal in attitude was in keeping with the traditions of the office, and with his own feeling that he could delegate power but would resent any direct effort to curb it. Even weak presidents have reacted to challenges to their constitutional authority, and Eisenhower was no exception to this rule.

The President was under considerable pressure to go along with the amendment. Even his brother Edgar, "a constitutional conservative," urged its approval. "Both of us felt so strongly about the amendment," Ike wrote, "that by common consent it was finally dropped as a subject of correspondence between us." He also reacted against the pressure in other ways. "I'm so sick of this I could scream," he said at one time about Bricker's efforts. "The whole damn thing is senseless and plain damaging to the prestige of the United States."[59]

As the showdown approached, Eisenhower, advised by Dulles, took the position that duty compelled him to oppose the amendment. "As President," he said, "I have taken an oath to defend the Constitution. I therefore oppose any change which will impair the President's traditional authority to conduct foreign affairs." At another time he explained that "the President must not be deprived of his historic position as spokesman for the nation in its relations with other countries."[60]

Eisenhower had precedent and practicality on his side. In the government of the United States there is no machinery, not even in Congress, which could replace the President in the conduct of foreign relations. Yet through this amendment, neo-isolationists sought to shackle presidential power at a time when international crises were crowding each other with frightening speed, and the President needed more, not less, flexibility in his conduct of foreign relations. Despite Eisenhower's stand, when the Senate voted on a modified version of the Bricker Amendment on February 26, 1954, it was defeated by only one vote. Even William F. Knowland, the Republican leader in the Senate, voted for it.

If Eisenhower had not used his personal influence and that of his office to defeat the proposal, it undoubtedly would have passed. He fought, he said later, "with every tool I could get. I talked, I made speeches, I wrote letters, and I certainly—I got my own group working on people in the Congress. It was, to my mind, it would have been an unjustifiable invasion into the Presidential powers...."[61]

Some have viewed the struggle over the Bricker Amendment as merely a squabble between internationalists and isolationists. For the presidency it had a deeper meaning than that. It reflected a modern dilemma, the continuing need for constitutional control over presidential power in foreign relations, contradicted by the requirement of the nuclear age, that the President be able to act quickly and decisively in a foreign crisis to defend the nation.

An example of the need for presidential flexibility and decisiveness in foreign relations occurred a short time later, in the spring of 1954, when events in Southeast Asia threatened to pull the United States into a war there. That war had been going on for a long time, but when Eisenhower took office the French were deeply involved in Vietnam, part of their former colony of Indochina, fighting a nationalist political organization called Viet Minh.

On the theory that if the Communists triumphed in Vietnam, all the states of Southeast Asia, like a row of dominoes, would fall to them, Eisenhower greatly increased American aid to the French. Within a year the United States was contributing almost eighty per cent to the total of all French military expenditures. If necessary, Eisenhower was willing to intervene with troops, but only after France asked for them, after Britain and other allies indicated they would go along, and after Congress had expressed support for his contemplated action. These conditions were never met.

In the spring of 1954, the war took a disastrous turn for the French, and touched off a crisis in American foreign policy. The Viet Minh trapped some twenty thousand French and supporting Vietnamese troops in a remote fortress, called Dien Bien Phu, in Northern Vietnam. In desperation, on April 23, the French finally appealed for American intervention, primarily for a massive air strike from carriers to relieve besieged Dien Bien Phu. This plea became known to the public, leading many Americans to fear that if heeded, Vietnam would become another Korea, or worse, the starting point of another world war.

Earlier, in a widely publicized speech, Vice-President Nixon had suggested that the United States might have to send troops into Indochina to stem Communist expansion. "I think the Executive has to take the politically unpopular decision," he said, "and do it."[62] This caused a furor and revived talk of restricting the President's power to use the armed forces as he saw fit.

At a news conference on April 29, 1954, a reporter asked the President about a rider attached to an appropriations bill on the previous day, which would limit the President's authority to send troops anywhere in the world without the consent of Congress. Eisenhower replied that "such an artificial restriction would damage the flexibility of the President in moving to sustain the interests of the United States wherever necessary."[63] To kill the rider, he said, he would veto the bill. The rider did not pass.

This, however, did not meet the French plea for the air strike. To this question Eisenhower replied, for the information of his advisers, that "there would be no intervention without allies." Through Dulles he also approached the British once more, telling them that intervention would require the consent of Congress, and that such consent would be more likely if Britain agreed to joint action. Preferring negotiation, the British, for the last time, refused.

Secretary of State Dulles, Chairman of the Joint Chiefs of Staff Admiral Arthur W. Radford, Senator Knowland, and others, nonetheless persisted in urging the air strike against Dien Bien Phu for its psychological effect. The President listened but would not act. Since the crisis required action, the President could not wait too long before making a firm decision, and he did not. Against the views of most of his close advisers in foreign affairs, he ruled out the air strike, or other unilateral action in Vietnam. Conditions in Indochina, he wrote later, "were such as to make unilateral American intervention nothing less than sheer folly."[64]

Here Eisenhower showed a decisiveness that detractors said he lacked, and a strength of will that would not allow pressure to force him to act hastily against his own convictions and better judgment. In this crisis, Eisenhower also revealed his attitude of dependence on Congress, and that when pushed he could and would use presidential power meaningfully to decide a foreign policy issue on his own.

Similarly, in a lesser crisis in Guatemala, Eisenhower allowed detailed conflicting advice to reach him. Then, on the basis of immediate military and strategic considerations, rather than on those of long range foreign policy, he made his decision.

Through Colonel Jacobo Arbenz Guzmán, who had become president in 1951, local Communists had gained control of key posts in Guatemala's government. Policymakers in Washington, occupied with crises in Asia and Europe, had paid little attention to the growth of communism in the small Central American republic. In August, 1953, the Department of State quarreled with Arbenz over his expropriation of lands belonging to the United Fruit Company, a North American corporation. A month later the Assistant Secretary of State for Inter-American Affairs, John Moors Cabot, publicly charged Guatemala with "openly playing the Communist game."

The American government never questioned Guatemala's right to expropriate the disputed property; it merely sought adequate payment, which Arbenz would not offer. After Arbenz, in February, 1954, refused to bring the dispute before the Court of Arbitration at The Hague, as provided for in the fruit company's contract, American officials became convinced that Communists, in part at least, had inspired the attack on the fruit company. Guatemalans, who had some legitimate grievances against the company, believed that the charges were camouflage for Yankee economic imperialism.

Unwilling to endure a Communist regime in the Western Hemisphere, especially near the Panama Canal, Eisenhower and his advisers decided to bring the issue of communism in Guatemala before the Organization of American States for multilateral action to get rid of the Communists. If the United States acted alone, the Department of State realized, the Latins could accuse it of violating pledges against intervention in the internal affairs of a sister republic.

At the Tenth Inter-American Conference of the Organization of American States, which met in Caracas in March, 1954, the United States offered a general anti-Communist resolution. Although it did not mention Guatemala, the resolution could serve as a means of measuring Guatemala's conduct. "What we need to do," Secretary of State Dulles said, "is to identify the peril; to develop the will to meet it unitedly if ever united action should be required. . . ."[65]

The Latin Americans were not truly behind the resolution. Many of them had gone to Caracas to discuss their economic problems, but supported the resolution because they knew that only those who opposed communism would receive the aid that all desired. The resolution passed, therefore, by a vote of 17 to 1. Only Guatemala voted against it. Costa Rica, which had refused to attend the conference, cast no ballot, and two larger states, Argentina and Mexico, abstained. Even though the vote was a questionable triumph for the United States, and the delegates showed considerable sympathy for Guatemala, Dulles, who represented the United States, was satisfied.

In its final form the resolution, entitled the "Declaration of Solidarity . . . against International Communist Intervention," condemned international communism as a threat to the peace and security of the Americas. It called for consultation, according to existing treaties, to consider appropriate action in case any American state fell under Communist control, and for the exchange of information on Communists and their activities.

Two months later relations with Guatemala reached a more critical stage. On May 17, 1954, the Department of State announced that a shipment of 1900 tons of Communist arms, manufactured in Czechoslovakia, had arrived at Puerto Barrios, Guatemala. "By this arms shipment," Dulles announced several days later, "a government in which Communist influence is very strong has come into a position to dominate militarily the Central American area." And, he added, "the extension of Communist colonialism to this hemisphere would, in the words of the Caracas resolution, endanger the peace of this hemisphere."[66]

The United States sought, but failed to obtain, permission from its North Atlantic allies to search their merchant ships suspected of carrying arms to Guatemala. It also promptly began airlifting arms to Nicaragua and Honduras, with whom it had hastily signed mutual security treaties. Under the Caracas resolution it made arrangements for an emergency conference in July of foreign ministers from the Americas, but events in Guatemala came to a head before the ministers could meet.

In the early morning hours of June 18, Colonel Carlos Castillo Armas, an exiled Guatemalan army officer, led a makeshift army of about two hundred men from Honduras into Guatemala to overthrow Arbenz. In support of the "invasion," three obsolete military planes of United States manufacture buzzed Guatemala City, and bombed the ordnance depot. On June 22, Allen Dulles, of the Central Intelligence Agency, reported to President Eisenhower that two of the three bombers were lost.

This development produced a crisis, and drew the President directly into the situation. That afternoon Eisenhower met with Secretary of State Dulles, his brother Allen, and Henry F. Holland, the new Assistant Secretary of State for Inter-American Affairs. They discussed, and the President had to decide, whether or not to replace the bombers for Castillo Armas, and hence step-up the involvement of the United States in the conflict.

Eisenhower's advisers disagreed. Holland insisted that the American government should keep hands off, pointing out that other Latin-American republics would, if the action of the United States became known, interpret the shipment of planes as intervention in Guatemala's internal affairs. The other advisers felt, however, that Castillo Armas and the anti-Communist *Putsch* could succeed only if the United States supplied additional planes.

"What do you think Castillo's chances would be," the President asked Allen Dulles, "without the aircraft?"

"About zero," Dulles replied.

"Suppose we supply the aircraft," Eisenhower went on. "What would the chances be then?"

"About 20 per cent," the head of Central Intelligence answered.

On the basis of this exchange, and his own evaluation of the situation, Eisenhower decided to act. "On the actual value of a shipment of planes," he explained later, "I knew from experience the important psychological impact of even a small amount of air support. In any event," he continued, "our proper course of action—indeed my duty—was clear to me. We would replace the airplanes."[67]

In less than two weeks the Arbenz govement collapsed, and Castillo Armas assumed power. The President believed that his decision to support Castillo Armas was critical.

Eisenhower also thought that "the rest of Latin America was not in the least displeased" with the manner in which Arbenz was overthrown, an assumption not supported by reports from various parts of Latin America. In many cities demonstrators denounced what they called a revival of "big stick" diplomacy, some publicly burned the stars and stripes, and others hanged Eisenhower in effigy.

Even though Eisenhower may have been mistaken in some of his assumptions, this episode reveals that despite his reluctance to do so, he would weigh conflicting advice, would reach a decision, and would use presidential power in foreign relations, even with a heavy hand if necessary. In particular, he took seriously his obligation as Commander-in-Chief of the armed forces, to defend national honor and security.

This role of Commander-in-Chief, enhanced by the changed nature of war, underwent change in the Eisenhower years. It practically permitted the President to exercise the warmaking power without prior consultation with Congress. The President, Eisenhower insisted, "is in a very definite sense responsible for all measures that are taken to defend the United States and provide for securing its rights everywhere in the world."[68]

Understandably, Eisenhower felt a special competence in military matters and was sensitive to any criticism of his discharge of defense responsibilities. In October, 1957, when Democrats were attacking his foreign and defense policies, he exploded. "The idea of *them* charging *me* with not being interested in *defense!*" he sputtered. "Damn it, I've spent my whole life being concerned with defense of our country."[69]

Another episode wherein Eisenhower concerned himself with a problem of defense, but slighted the political realities of foreign policy, affected relations with France and Western Europe. When he became President he supported, as had his predecessor, Western European unity as a foremost objective of foreign policy. His administration also launched what came to be called the "new look" in military policy. Under the slogan of "substituting machines for men," this program emphasized the use of nuclear weapons to fill gaps in manpower.

Since the new look appeared to commit the United States to the idea of nuclear warfare as basic defense policy, it alarmed Europeans. They realized that in any atomic war with Russia, Western Europe would be the most likely target. This fear, plus the death of the Soviet dictator Josef Stalin in March, 1953, led many Europeans to talk about "peaceful coexistence" with the Soviets. In France it encouraged resistance from those who opposed a plan for merging German units into an integrated European army controlled by a European Defense Community of six nations, France, West Germany, Italy, Belgium, the Netherlands, and Luxembourg. This community would be linked to the United States through diplomatic agreements.

Although the idea had been proposed originally by a Frenchman, the French now began having second thoughts about the European Defense Community. They feared that a rearmed Germany might once again threaten their security. Taking into account Eisenhower's new look, the French began asking if nuclear weapons were to be substituted for manpower, why rearm the Germans?

This attitude upset Americans. They wanted prompt approval of the European Defense Community Treaty. This impatience became evident in July, 1953, when Congress began to consider an amendment to an appropriation for mutual security funds, which would prevent the President from obligating any of those funds until the various European governments ratified the treaty. Looking upon this action as much too drastic and as a challenge to his control of foreign relations, Eisenhower protested to Representative Walter Judd of Minnesota. Among other things, Ike said, "it was an insult . . . for a Republican President to face such a restrictive policy when the Congress had not forced it on his Democratic predecessor."[70] As was the case with the Bricker Amendment, Eisenhower again had to fight legislators of his own party to preserve presidential flexibility in foreign relations, and to shield that power against congressional encroachment.

Nonetheless, Eisenhower and his advisers shared Congress' impatience, particularly over France's delay in approving the treaty. In December, 1953 Secretary of State Dulles announced that without the European Defense Community he doubted that continental Europe could be made a place of safety. If France did not approve, he warned, "that would compel an agonizing reappraisal of basic United States policy."[71] This statement suggested that the United States might rearm West Germany on its own, or pull out of Europe and rely on its own nuclear power for defense. Either was a distasteful alternative to its allies, who also resented Dulles's pressure.

Several months later, in April, 1954, Eisenhower himself tried to overcome French fears of a revived Germany. He "indicated that the United States would keep armed forces in Europe, including Germany, as long as the need existed, and would do everything possible to bring about the closest integration between EDC forces on the one hand, and United States and other forces (meaning principally British) on the other."[72]

Despite Dulles's tough policy and Eisenhower's assurances. American diplomacy could not save the European Defense Community. In August the French National Assembly defeated the treaty. Eisenhower called it a "major setback" to American foreign policy, which it was. It was also a setback to Eisenhower, and to Dulles who had unsuccessfully used delegated power to pressure the French, and had failed to achieve his objective. In this instance, too, the depth of French feeling, expressed politically, against Germany was strong enough even to resist pressure from Eisenhower himself.

One of Eisenhower's most effective, dangerous, and controversial uses of presidential power in foreign relations occurred not in Europe, but in Asia. Early in August, 1954 Chou En-lai, Red China's Premier, announced his government's determination to "liberate" Formosa, also called Taiwan, from the control of Chiang Kai-shek's Nationalist government. "Any invasion of Formosa," Eisenhower replied, "would have to run over the Seventh Fleet."[73]

The Chinese Communists did not attempt to invade Formosa but threatened a number of small islands, including the Tachen, Matsu, and Quemoy groups, strung out for some 350 miles along the China coast and held tenaciously by Nationalist troops. On September 3, the Reds began a heavy bombardment of the two Quemoys, located about five miles outside the port of Amoy. This "marked the commencement," Eisenhower wrote, "of a sequence of events which was to extend through nine months, threaten a split between the United States and nearly all its allies, and seemingly carry the country to the edge of war, thus constituting one of the most serious problems of the first eighteen months of my administration."[74]

Eisenhower had to decide quickly what policy he would adopt toward Red China's attack. Before making a decision he turned to advisers. The Joint Chiefs of Staff agreed that the offshore islands were not essential to America's defense of Formosa, and that the Chinese Nationalists could not hold them without American help. Since the loss of the islands would have bad psychological effects on the Nationalists, the chiefs, with one exception, advised the use of forces to defend them. Admiral Radford and General Nathan F.

Twining of the Air Force urged American bombing of the mainland to aid Chiang.

The President disagreed with this reasoning. Such a conflict, he said, could not be confined to Quemoy. "We're not talking now about a limited brush-fire war," he pointed out. "We're talking about going to the threshold of World War III. If we attack China, we're not going to impose limits on our military actions, as in Korea."

"Moreover," Eisenhower explained, "if we get into a general war, the logical enemy will be Russia, not China, and we'll have to strike there."

Privately and publicly Senator Knowland demanded, especially after the Reds imprisoned thirteen American airmen for "espionage," a naval blockade of China. The President again dissented. He admitted that he, too, suffered from a feeling of frustration, and a desire "to lash out" against the Reds. "But I knew," he wrote later, "such a response would be self-defeating."

"The hard way," Eisenhower said, "is to have the courage to be patient."

Eisenhower thus "rejected a hot-headed plunge into atomic war as a solution to the Chinese problem." He also showed that he would not use his power recklessly.[75]

To bolster Nationalist morale at this time Secretary Dulles stopped at Taipei, the capital of Formosa, on his way home from a conference in Manila. After talks with Chiang, he agreed to an alliance with the Nationalist regime. In Washington, on December 2, the United States and the Republic of China, Chiang's government, signed a mutual defense treaty, or alliance. Each country, the treaty stated, would recognize an attack on the other's territories in the Western Pacific as dangerous to its own peace and safety. To meet the danger, each would act according to its constitutional process.

The treaty did not define the extent of Chiang's domain, but declared that the word "territories," in respect to Nationalist China meant "Taiwan and the Pescadores." In supplementary notes dated December 10, the signatories said the United States could act in the offshore islands but was not bound to do so. No one knew, therefore, whether or not Eisenhower would defend the islands. Many Americans, and their allies, feared that a thermonuclear war would follow if the Communists invaded the islands, for the Soviet Union, by treaty, was pledged to aid Red China in case of war.

Fear of war also stemmed from Chiang's avowed objective of reconquering the Chinese mainland. Eisenhower did not want to commit himself to a war in which the United States would have to do most of the fighting, solely to serve Chiang's interests. Yet he did not wish to deny Chiang's claim to the mainland. To have done so would have been an admission that the Communists were China's true masters, and, hence, the logical incumbents of China's seat in the United Nations.

The supplementary notes got around this difficulty by pledging Chiang not to use force, except in self-defense, without American consent. That agreement, by precluding a unilateral attack on the mainland, once again placed Chiang on a leash.

The Communists denounced the Formosa alliance, continued the heavy shelling, and on January 18, 1955, invaded the island of Yikiang, eight miles north of the Tachens. Eisenhower and Dulles immediately indicated that they did not consider that island and the exposed Tachens essential to the defense of Formosa, some two hundred miles away.

Five days later Eisenhower asked Congress for clear authority to deal with any emergency that might arise in Formosa Strait. Although as President he already had this power, and knew that he did, he and Dulles wanted the Communists to know that retaliation would be supported by Congress if they attempted to invade Quemoy and Matsu. "I resolved that this time," Eisenhower wrote, "no uncertainty about our commitment to defend Formosa should invite a major Chinese Communist attack." He also wanted to give a lift to Nationalist morale, and "to dispel doubts in foreign capitals that the United States was acting on constitutional grounds."[76]

This request revealed a great deal about Eisenhower's use of presidential power in foreign relations. It showed that he was much more sensitive to the wishes of Congress than most people realized, and that he would himself admit openly. He considered the President to be under a moral obligation to seek Congress' approval, when time permitted, for the use of power in what has been called the constitutional twilight zone of warmaking. This approach was in keeping with Whig doctrine, but it was not an innovation, for other presidents had acted in a similar manner. At this time, moreover, it was good politics.

A friendly biographer maintained that Eisenhower believed Congress should have the last word in national policymaking. Sherman Adams, who ran the White House staff at this time, implied this, saying that Eisenhower "was also determined not to become involved militarily in any foreign conflict without the approval of Congress."[77]

In this instance Congress responded immediately with a joint resolution authorizing the President to use the armed forces to protect

Formosa and the Pescadores, and "such related positions and territories of that area now in friendly hands. . . ." The House approved the Formosa Resolution on January 25 by a vote of 409 to 3, and the Senate three days later by a margin of 85 to 3. Eisenhower signed it on the following day. To allay fear that Chiang or some excited American military officer in the area might trigger a war, the President announced that he alone would decide on when and how to use the authority Congress had granted him.

In addition to revealing Eisenhower's attitude toward power and Congress, this episode illustrated several important aspects of modern presidential power in foreign relations. From the beginning, as we have seen, the President has had all the powers necessary to carry on foreign relations. Although he shared some powers with Congress, he, and not Congress, almost always has exercised the power of initiative in foreign policy. This was particularly true in negotiation. Only the President or those who represent him can negotiate, a point that Eisenhower himself made with some exaggeration, saying that "the power to negotiate, the responsibility for negotiating with others, rests absolutely and completely in the Executive."[78] Most presidents have recognized nonetheless that in the long run their initiative, even in negotiation, and their foreign policies can be meaningful only with the support of Congress. This is another reason why Eisenhower turned to Congress.

Contemporary students of government, ironically, offered conflicting interpretations as to the significance of Eisenhower's action. Some critics argued that he had taken Congress into partnership in the making of foreign policy, and hence had weakened presidential power. In the future, they said, his action would haunt and restrict presidential action. Any president who neglected to ask permission of Congress under similar circumstances would be accused of ignoring Eisenhower's principle of 1955.

On the other hand, other critics maintained that Eisenhower's action illustrated how presidential power in foreign relations had grown and how that of Congress had been diminished. Once a president had staked American prestige on a sensitive issue, as in Formosa Strait, Congress had to go along with him or repudiate his policy before the world, or at the least, weaken his hand in a crisis. One senator put it this way, "Eisenhower is passing the buck."

Congress, in effect, was placed in the position of either helping the President, or indirectly, of aiding the nation's enemies. This was, critics maintained, no choice at all. Congress' freedom of action, in this instance, was more theoretical than real. Congress practically surrendered, beforehand under given conditions, its power of declaring war to the President.[79]

Leaders in Congress were aware of this problem but they had faith in Eisenhower. Senator Walter F. George, the Democratic chairman of the Senate Committee on Foreign Relations, accepted all of Eisenhower's assurances. "I believe that President Eisenhower is a prudent man," George announced. "I believe he is dedicated to a peaceful world. I believe what he says, and I am willing to act upon it."[80]

George was right about Eisenhower being prudent, for the crisis in Formosa Strait passed without the use of American force. In August, 1958, however, a new crisis burst in the headlines when the Chinese Reds resumed their massive shelling of Quemoy, practically cutting the island off from the outside world. American warships, with orders to shoot back against any attack, convoyed Nationalist supply ships to within three miles of the guns trained on Quemoy and Matsu.

This time the President said he would repel any Communist attack, and announced that the protection of Quemoy and Matsu, primarily because Chiang had committed about one-third of his troops to those islands, had become "increasingly related to the defense of Taiwan." Soviet Premier Nikita S. Khrushchev, in several letters to Eisenhower in September, then warned that he would support his Chinese ally if the United States became involved in any attack on the Chinese mainland.

Again many Americans feared war, but this crisis, too, passed without the President using force. He did not shrink from the possibility of having to use force—even small atomic weapons—but he was determined to use every means for keeping peace. He felt that the Red Chinese did not want war.[81] When Eisenhower left the presidency he, in effect, turned over his Formosa policy to his successor, for the Formosa Resolution was construed not as a grant of power to him personally, but to the President of the United States. In June, 1962 President John F. Kennedy explained that he accepted Eisenhower's Formosa policy and would, if necessary, use the power that went with it.

These episodes in Formosa Strait were called performances in brinkmanship by critics and other observers because Secretary of State Dulles claimed that he and President Eisenhower, especially in the crisis of 1955, "had walked to the brink" of war in Asia in a deliberately calculated risk to advance foreign policy and preserve peace. He claimed that this policy, also called deterrence, had "not only prevented the 'big' hydrogen war but the little wars as well."

Dulles elaborated on these views in an article written about him in *Life* magazine in January, 1956. "Of course, we were brought to the verge of war," he said. "The ability to get to the verge without getting into war is the necessary art. If you cannot master it, you inevitably get into war."

Then the Secretary of State added, "We've had to look it square in the face—on the question of enlarging the Korean War, on the question of getting into the Indo-China war, on the question of Formosa. We walked to the brink and we looked it in the face. We took strong action." Although Dulles appeared to claim this policy as his own, he did admit that "it took a lot more courage for the President than for me," and that the ultimate decision was Eisenhower's. In each crisis, the Secretary said, "the President never flinched for a minute . . . he came up taut."[82]

Dulles's claim to the success of these policies, even with his deference to Eisenhower's leadership, was questioned by critics, and by those close to the President. "I doubt," Sherman Adams wrote, "that Eisenhower was as close to the brink of war in any of those three crises as Dulles made him out to be."[83]

As he had in Asia, Eisenhower encountered perplexing foreign policy problems in the Middle East. As in the case of Formosa, he ultimately turned to Congress for advance assurance of support in case he should have to use force to meet some of those problems head on.

Under Eisenhower the United States and its Western Allies attempted to strengthen their military position throughout the Arab world. To do so they worked out a plan for a Middle Eastern collective security defense organization. It would, they hoped, protect the region against Soviet attack. Egypt, a leader of the Arab bloc, refused to join the security organization.

In 1954 both the United States and Britain thought that perhaps a young colonel, Gamal Abdel Nasser, who had emerged as Egypt's strong man, would reverse the policy of his predecessors and join a new alliance system that Dulles was shaping along the "northern tier," that is among those states of the Middle East closest to the Soviet Union. Nasser would have nothing to do with the alliance, called the Middle East Treaty Organization, or the Baghdad Pact because it was signed in that city, but he did accept American economic aid. He also turned to the Communist bloc for arms, announcing in September, 1955, that he would pay for the arms by mortgaging his country's cotton crop, its major source of revenue.

As part of his reform program Nasser wished to build a huge

dam and hydro-electric power station on the Nile River at Aswan, some 800 miles south of Cairo. Since Egypt lacked the resources to pay for the project, he sought outside assistance. In December, the United States said it would help finance the dam, offering an initial grant of $56 million. Britain also offered help, $14 million.

Since the United States attached a distasteful condition to its proposed grant and loan, that Egypt could make no side deal with the Communists, Nasser delayed his acceptance and dickered with the Soviets, apparently seeking better terms. In May, 1956, as if contemptuous of American good will, he withdrew recognition from Chiang Kai-shek and established diplomatic relations with Communist China. Egypt, it seemed clear, would not be able to hold up her end in financing the Aswan Dam, and was determined to follow an anti-Western policy.

In July, under pressure from members of Congress and others who opposed the Aswan project, Secretary of State Dulles, after consulting with the President who approved the contemplated action, suddenly reversed himself by withdrawing his initial offer of economic aid for the dam. Britain also cancelled her offer.

A few months later Eisenhower had some second thoughts. He asked Dulles if the withdrawal from the Aswan Dam project had been perhaps too abrupt or "undiplomatic." The Secretary of State denied that he had in any way shocked the Egyptians.[84]

Regardless of Dulles's view, Nasser reacted as if he were shocked and deeply humiliated. He took America's "great refusal" as an effort to topple him. A week after Dulles's action, Nasser struck back by nationalizing the Universal Suez Canal Company, owned mainly by British and French stockholders, and announced that Egyptians henceforth would run the canal.

On Britain and France, Nasser's act had a shattering impact, not so much the nationalization itself, as the fact that an international waterway vital to their economies was now at the mercy of a man they distrusted. Britain's Prime Minister, Anthony Eden, said his country would fight if necessary to protect her access to Middle Eastern oil, and labeled Nasser's deed "an act of plunder." The French National Assembly adopted a resolution calling Nasser "a permanent menace to peace."

Eisenhower and his advisers opposed the use of force or even stringent economic measures against Nasser, though the American government did freeze Egyptian assets under its control. Seeking a solution by negotiation, Dulles suggested a Suez Canal User's Association, a vague international body that would manage the canal and its shipping. As proposed by Dulles, the association was unacceptable to all parties immediately concerned. Disgusted by what seemed indefinite talk and no results, the British and French concluded that they would have to impose a solution on Egypt.

Israel, which was technically at war with Nasser and suffered from persistent raids across its borders by Egyptian suicide squadrons, had also decided, in concert with the British and French, to attack. On October 29, 1956, Israel's army knifed into Egypt with the objective of wiping out the raiders' bases and overthrowing Nasser.

On the following day Britain and France, without informing the United States, sent ultimatums to Israel and Egypt ordering them to keep their armies ten miles from the Suez Canal. Their own troops, the British and French said, would occupy the canal zone and would use force if resisted.

In a lightning campaign, the Israelis overran the Sinai Peninsula and routed the Egyptians. As expected, Nasser rejected the Anglo-French ultimatums. British and French planes bombed Egyptian airfields and other targets for four days, and then British and French troops invaded and occupied Port Said and the western end of the Suez Canal.

Eisenhower was surprised and stunned by the action of the British, French, and Israelis. The American people, then involved in the last days of a presidential campaign and frustrated by their inability to aid Hungarians who were in rebellion against their Communist masters, were shocked by the attack on Egypt. The United States, on October 30, immediately placed a resolution before the Security Council of the United Nations calling on Israel and Egypt to stop fighting, and on Israel to withdraw her forces from Egypt. Britain and France vetoed that resolution, and a similar one offered by Russia. The Suez case then went to the General Assembly under a "Uniting for Peace" resolution of 1950, designed originally to circumvent Soviet use of the veto in the Security Council.

On the following morning, at Dulles's suggestion, Eisenhower telephoned Eden in London, objected to the ultimatum sent to Egypt, and gave the Prime Minister a tongue-lashing in barracks-room language. Sick and emotionally upset, Eden burst into tears.

All of Eisenhower's advisers agreed that if the Soviets went openly to Nasser's assistance, a war involving the United States was inevitable. Although not aware of the gravity of the inside developments, many Americans feared war. That evening, President Eisenhower spoke over radio and television about the crisis, explaining that he had not been consulted by his allies about their actions, or even informed in advance, and assured the people that he would keep the peace. "There can be no peace without law," he said. "And there can be no law if we were to invoke one code of international conduct for those who oppose us and another for our friends."[85] The United States thus joined Russia in condemning the British, French and Israeli attack. So unpleasant did Eisenhower find his position, that he considered this, aside from his periods of sickness, the worst week in the presidency.

On November 2, 1956, the General Assembly passed a resolution, introduced by Dulles, calling for an immediate cease-fire and the withdrawal of foreign troops from Egypt. Within the next few days a number of other resolutions favoring Egypt were also passed.

At the same time the Soviet Union threatened to use arms, even guided missiles, against the British, French, and Israelis, and announced it would send "volunteers" to assist Nasser. On November 5, Russia suggested joint action with the United States to end the "aggression" in Egypt, a proposal Eisenhower promptly rejected as "unthinkable." The United States, he said, would use force to prevent Soviet interference.

Faced with hostile world opinion, with Soviet threats, and with the opposition of their major ally, the British and French gulped their pride, stifled their resentment, and agreed to withdraw from Egypt. Israel was left with no choice. She, too, after being threatened with economic sanctions, ultimately had to agree to pull out her troops.

In this crisis Eisenhower delegated considerable authority to Dulles but he himself took part in all the major deliberations. The Suez crisis showed how closely Eisenhower and Dulles could work together under pressure. "The President," Under Secretary of State Robert Murphy remarked, "behaved like the chairman of the board, leaving it to his Secretary [Dulles] to handle details. . . ."[86] Regardless of the precise nature of his role, Eisenhower assumed a more active role in this crisis than in other diplomatic conflicts, mainly because he felt deeply about the principles involved, especially those relating to peace and aggression. These principles seemed to the President more self-evident and simple in this case than in most others. He did not, therefore, hesitate to use presidential power swiftly, and on his own.

During and after the Suez crisis, Russia exploited her newly acquired prestige as an opponent of aggression, moving into the Middle East with enhanced influence. She replaced the guns, tanks, and planes Egypt had lost, mostly to Israel, and sent arms to Syria. To counter the stepped-up Soviet penetration, to salvage what remained of Western influence in the Arab world, and to fill the power vacuum created by the British and French retreat, the United States pondered emergency measures. American policymakers took a first step in November, 1956, when they assured the northern tier members of the Baghdad Pact that a threat to their territorial integrity and political independence "would be viewed by the United States with the utmost gravity."

Those states were not satisfied. They wanted a stronger commitment to the defense of the Middle East. In response, Eisenhower decided to issue a unilateral warning to the world that the United States would defend the whole Middle East against Soviet attack. In a special message of January 5, 1957, he personally presented the declaration of policy, which became known as the "Eisenhower Doctrine," to Congress, and asked the legislators, as he had during the first Formosa crisis, to support it with a joint resolution.

The President and his advisers realized that the plan had weaknesses, particularly in its inability to cope with internal Communist subversion. "I just do not believe," he told congressmen nevertheless, "that we can leave a vacuum in the Middle East and prayerfully hope that Russia will stay out."[87]

The President's request passed the House without difficulty but ran into opposition in the Senate. As had been the case with the Formosa Resolution, some senators felt that the desire for legislative support in the possible use of military force during an indefinite future emergency, was merely another attempt to force Congress to share the responsibility for a decision that belonged to the President, and that he was reluctant to make on his own. Others argued that Eisenhower was asking for authority which the Constitution had entrusted to Congress.

After two months of debate Congress slightly modified and finally approved the Eisenhower Doctrine. The President signed the joint resolution on March 9, 1957. The United States, the doctrine read, "regards as vital to the national interest and world peace the preservation of the independence and integrity of the nations of the Middle East." When the President decided the need for it, the resolution authorized him to use the armed forces to assist any Middle Eastern nation which requested help in resisting "armed attack from any country controlled by international communism." The doctrine also offered those countries economic and military assistance, and authorized the President to spend initially, without restriction, $200 million already appropriated for such aid.

The United States thus assumed almost entire responsibility for

Western defense for the Middle East. No one could now assume that President Eisenhower would avoid a fight for the Middle East. In this sense the Eisenhower Doctrine was a dramatic turn in foreign policy, and a bold use of presidential power. Yet, in a broader context, it could be seen as a weak link in a world-wide chain of regional treaties and alliances that Secretary of State Dulles was constructing in an effort to contain Communist expansion, and that the President accepted without too much questioning.

A year later events in Lebanon exposed the difficulty of applying the Eisenhower Doctrine to a specific development. In May, 1958, civil war, mainly between Moslems and Maronite Christians, broke out in Lebanon. Camille Chamoun, that country's president and a Maronite Christian, accused the United Arab Republic, Nasser's name for an enlarged Egypt, of instigating and aiding the rebellion, and formally complained to the Security Council of the United Nations, that Nasser was interfering in Lebanon's internal affairs and endangering the peace of the Middle East. The United Nations failed to find evidence to substantiate these charges.

Suddenly, on July 14, a group of army officers in Baghdad overthrew the government, murdering the king, the crown prince, and the prime minister, and announced the founding of the Republic of Iraq. The new regime, headed by Brigadier General Abdel Karim Kassim, quickly dissolved a union made with Jordan earlier in the year, and concluded a defensive alliance with the United Arab Republic.

The swift success of the Iraqi revolution upset the Eisenhower team, which had looked upon Iraq as a main bulwark in the Baghdad Pact. Iraq's new rulers made it clear that they considered the alliance undesirable and would withdraw from it, and hence Dulles's northern tier was left with a gaping hole.

Frightened by the developments in neighboring Iraq, and fearing that he too was marked for destruction, Lebanon's Chamoun meantime had sent an urgent plea for help to Eisenhower, saying his country could not survive both domestic rebellion and "indirect aggression."

Earlier Eisenhower had warned congressional leaders that he might have to risk war by intervening with military force in Lebanon, and that he might not have time for prior discussion with Congress. With this idea still in mind, the President reacted quickly to Chamoun's plea.

At 9:45 a.m. on July 14 Eisenhower met with the National Security Council and obtained its support for his plan of intervention. That afternoon at 2:30 p.m., he and Dulles spoke to congressional leaders from both parties, telling them what the administration intended to do to prevent further deterioration of the American position in the Middle East.

The legislators had difficulty differentiating between the application of the Eisenhower Doctrine and interference in what appeared to many to be purely an internal civil war. Some of them believed it was as logical for the President to send troops into Iraq as into Lebanon. None of the leaders attemped, however, to dissuade Eisenhower from intervening as he had planned. Instead, they let him know "they had little enthusiasm for his decision and no desire whatever to share in the responsibility for it."[88] Although Eisenhower wanted congressional approval beforehand, he was left, for the second time, to act alone without such support.[89]

Although fearing that the Soviets might retaliate and set fire to the Middle East, and perhaps to the world, Eisenhower did act on his own, swiftly. In this instance he made up his mind to use presidential power decisively because he knew his area of authority was clear and because he himself thought the issue was clear-cut.[90].

On the following day, July 15, he rushed 5000 marines to Beirut, Lebanon's chief port, to defend that country's independence. "I have concluded that, given the developments in Iraq," he told Congress, "the measures thus far taken by the United Nations Security Council are not sufficient to preserve the independence and integrity of Lebanon." He also announced that in his view the Lebanon case fitted the Eisenhower Doctrine. Ultimately, 14,000 American soldiers and Marines occupied strategic areas in Lebanon, but with orders not to shoot unless shot at.

To the United Arab Republic, Eisenhower's intervention was "another Suez," and to the Soviets it was an "open act of aggression." When the United States, on the day of the initial landings, asked the Security Council to establish an international military force to preserve Lebanon's independence, the Soviet delegate vetoed the American resolution. Ominously, the Russian press announced that on July 18, military maneuvers would begin near the Turkish and Iranian frontiers.

In October, after some involved international political maneuvering by all concerned, American troops evacuated Lebanon; alien infiltration ceased; and the crisis ended. The general worldwide reaction to America's first military intervention in the Middle East was unfavorable. But by showing that he was willing to use force in the Middle East, Eisenhower may have given pause to aggressive plans in Cairo and Moscow.

For Eisenhower himself this use of presidential power, without backstopping by Congress, was an agonizing experience. His closest advisers knew, and he himself later admitted, that he had acted reluctantly. The irony of it all is that his speedy action may not have been necessary, for he and Dulles probably overestimated the external danger to Lebanon, involved the United States in a domestic Lebanese quarrel, and gained few positive results from the intervention.[91]

At the time of the Suez crisis another came to a head in Eastern Europe. In Budapest on October 23, 1956, students began a national anti-Communist revolution. As the revolt spread, the Hungarians demanded not only freedom within the Communist bloc, but freedom from communism as well. In November they denounced their alliance with the Soviet Union, known as the Warsaw Pact, and appealed to the United Nations to help them defend their neutrality.

That effort to escape from the Communist bloc brought a massive invasion of Soviet tanks and artillery. In one of the most heart-rending and unequal struggles in the twentieth century, young Hungarians, almost with bare hands, futilely fought the Soviet tanks block by block in battered Budapest. The Russians brutally crushed the rebellion and clamped a regime composed of loyal Communists on Hungary.

Shocked and frustrated, Americans could do nothing to help the Hungarian "freedom fighters." "In the name of humanity and in the cause of peace," Eisenhower pleaded with Nicolai A. Bulganin, at that time Soviet Premier, to withdraw Russian troops and accept Hungary's right to self-government. Bulganin replied that Hungary's affairs were none of America's business.[92] Americans thought otherwise, but Eisenhower, cautious as usual about actions that might endanger peace, would not intervene at the risk of touching off a third world war.

Hungarians were bitterly disappointed. Aware that as part of a dynamic Republican foreign policy, Dulles had announced that the United States would move beyond the policy of containment to one of "liberation" of those peoples who lived under despotism behind the Iron Curtain, the Hungarians had hoped for aid from the West in their fight. Critics, at home and abroad, accused Dulles and Eisenhower of recklessly inciting captive peoples with slogans to revolt, only to face helpless slaughter.

Eisenhower replied that with the policy of "liberation" he had never urged "any kind of armed revolt that could bring about disaster to our friends."[93] Yet American prestige and perhaps foreign policy suffered. Few could distinguish the difference between encouraging "peaceful liberation" and inciting rebellion. In this instance by not acting, Eisenhower showed that he understood the limitations of presidential power even when needed for a commendable cause, and that despite considerable pressure he could be counted upon not to move recklessly and endanger the welfare of the nation.

Two years later, on November 10, 1958, Premier Khrushchev set off another diplomatic crisis by suddenly announcing that the Soviet Union had decided "to renounce the remnants of the occupation regime in Berlin." In subsequent notes to the United States, Britain, and France on November 27, he demanded that they withdraw their occupation forces of some 10,000 men that had been in West Berlin since the end of the Second World War, declare Berlin a demilitarized "free city," and negotiate directly with the East German government on terms of access to the city. He was willing to discuss the status of Berlin, but in any event, he said, if the Western powers did not make an agreement with the East Germans within six months, the Soviet Union would give the Communist "German Democratic Republic," which the Western Allies refused to recognize, control of the Western supply routes to the city.

In January, 1959, Khrushchev suggested separate peace treaties for West and East Germany. If the Allies did not agree, he said, later, Russia would make a separate peace treaty of her own with East Germany.

Taken together, the Soviet demands sought to force the Western powers to leave West Berlin, to recognize the East German government, to abandon their announced goal of a re-unified Germany, and to accept a *status quo* in Eastern Europe favorable to the Soviet Union.

"We are most solemnly committed to hold West Berlin," Secretary Dulles said in his initial reaction to Khrushchev's demands, "if need be by military force."[94] Khrushchev responded that if the United States attacked the East Germans, Russia would retaliate. Both sides subsequently made it clear that the use of force would mean war.

Since the United States and its Allies did not recognize the East German regime, they had no agreement with it on their right of access to West Berlin, about 110 miles within East Germany. That right rested on four-power agreements concluded at the end of the Second World War that Khrushchev had denounced. Thus the Soviet moves endangered the Western supply routes to West Berlin and threatened to blockade the city as Josef Stalin had done in 1948.

Efforts to settle the Berlin question through negotiation failed, but the Soviets extended the time limit on their demand without removing the menace. This was the situation when Dulles became gravely ill with cancer and had to give up his command of American foreign policy. He died on May 24, 1959, and was succeeded as Secretary of State by Christian A. Herter, who was never entrusted with the extensive powers Eisenhower had given Dulles.

In the last stages of Dulles's sickness the President himself took command of foreign policy. After Dulles's death Eisenhower not only retained direct command, but also abruptly changed the tone, if not the direction, of that policy. This change was understandable, for even those close to the President maintained that "the hard and uncompromising line" the United States had followed toward Russia and Red China "was more a Dulles line than an Eisenhower one."[95]

Earlier, Sherman Adams, considered the most powerful of Eisenhower's assistants, one who was said to have acted as an assistant president, had been forced to resign. With Dulles and Adams gone, the critics quipped, this was "the year Eisenhower enjoyed being President."[96] Reporters and columnists talked of a "new" Eisenhower, all of which helped dampen criticism of his ineffectiveness in the previous year. But, as one analyst has pointed out, in 1959 Eisenhower received extravagant praise for sporadic spurts of leadership such as Woodrow Wilson and the two Roosevelts had shown all during their presidencies.[97]

As Eisenhower sought to come to grips with the Berlin situation, he came to feel that it was so pressing that a discussion on the highest level with the Soviets might break the stalemate. In July, 1959, therefore, on his own initiative, he decided to offer Khrushchev a qualified invitation to visit the United States and he expressed willingness to travel to the Soviet Union in return. To avoid the appearance of a retreat before Soviet pressure, the President insisted that Khrushchev's visit would not be a trip to the summit, that he did not intend to negotiate with the Soviet leader, and that the only purpose of the invitation was "to melt a little of the ice" of the cold war. Through a misunderstanding of the President's motive, State Department officials issued a much less restrictive invitation than Eisenhower had intended. If Dulles had still been around, the President felt such a slip-up, which angered him, would not have occured.[98]

Khrushchev accepted the invitation and arrived in Washington on September 15, less than forty-eight hours after Russia's second planetary rocket, Lunik II, had scored a direct hit on the moon. Basking in the glow of this scientific triumph, he insisted that capitalism and communism could coexist. After that he made a spectacular pilgrimage across the continent and then returned for final talks with the President at Camp David, a presidential retreat in the mountains of western Maryland. There the Soviet Premier waived a time limit for negotiations on Berlin.

This concession cleared the way for a summit meeting of the leaders of the Big Four powers, the United States, Russia, Britain, and France, that Khrushchev desired. In explaining the agreement, Eisenhower said that "we now can negotiate . . . without an axe hanging over our heads."[99] Since the Eisenhower-Khrushchev agreement pushed the idea of war over Berlin into the background of cold war issues, the Russians spoke of the "Spirit of Camp David," but Eisenhower never used the term. He knew that neither side had retreated on fundamental issues.

Before the summit meeting, scheduled for May 16, 1960, in Paris, could take place, the "Spirit of Camp David" was shattered by a new crisis. On May 1, over Sverdlovsk, an industrial city in the Ural Mountains some 1300 miles within Russia, a Soviet missile brought down a high-flying American reconnaissance plane, more a glider with a motor than a conventional military aircraft, called the U-2. The administration reacted to this news, announced by Khrushchev on May 5, by saying that a weather plane was missing and may have strayed into Russia. The Department of State denied any deliberate attempt to violate Soviet borders. Yet the President himself had authorized the use of U-2's in spying missions over the Soviet Union four years earlier because he was convinced that the photographic intelligence they could gather was important to national security.

Then, after the American denial, Khrushchev sprang his trap. He called the American version of the flight a lie, said the pilot, Francis G. Powers, was alive and had confessed to espionage, and that photographic equipment on the plane had been recovered with exposed shots of Soviet military installations. Secretary of State Christian A. Herter then compounded the blunders by admitting that American planes had been making high altitude flights into the Soviet Union for several years and implied that they would continue to do so.

Khrushchev countered with a warning that foreign bases used by the United States for spying missions would be showered with rockets, a threat he later supported by giving military orders to Soviet missile installations to do just that, if the flights continued. In an action unprecedented in espionage cases, President Eisenhower assumed personal responsibility for the spy flights, terming them "a distasteful but vital necessity" in efforts to penetrate Soviet military secrecy.[100] He also refused to cancel his trip to the summit meeting in

Paris. "For me," he wrote later, "the attendance had become a duty." With this attitude he left for Paris. As he did so, Press Secretary James C. Hagerty denied published reports that the U-2 flights had been suspended. Yet Eisenhower himself had given orders to stop the U-2 flights over Soviet territory.

At Paris, in the elaborate surroundings of the Elysée Palace, Khrushchev destroyed the summit meeting in three hours. In a storm of invective he demanded that the United States call off all flights over Russia, apologize for past "aggressions," and punish those responsible for them. Furious over Khrushchev's harsh language, Eisenhower denied his Press Secretary's denial. "These flights were suspended after the recent incident and are not to be resumed," he told the Russian. "Accordingly, this cannot be the issue." The flights, obviously, were no longer a vital necessity. Eisenhower rejected the other terms, for they would, in effect, have caused him to punish himself.

Khrushchev then suggested that the summit meeting be postponed for six to eight months, and culminated his attack on the President by withdrawing his invitation to Eisenhower for the visit to Russia, scheduled in June. "The Russian people would say I was mad," Khrushchev had commented earlier, "to welcome a man who sends spy planes over here."[101]

Few could deny that the Soviet Union had won a great propaganda victory, for the United States had illegally violated the borders of a sovereign state. Any government, certainly the American one, would have been furious under similar circumstances.

As for the President's role in this affair, it was a humiliating one. Despite the vaunted efficiency of Eisenhower's staff system there was chaos, contradiction, and just plain lying among his advisers. All could see that the staff procedure had either broken down, or had suffered from lack of communication and co-ordination. Some critics charged that the difficulties stemmed from Eisenhower's procedure of delegating too much power. Yet this was, as critics themselves have pointed out, the period when Eisenhower was himself in command of foreign policy. The sad fact seemed to be, as Eisenhower later admitted, he suffered from a lack of sound judgment. He had not taken into account the consequences of the flights at this time if one of the planes should be shot down, and hence had allowed the flights to continue while preparing for the summit conference.

Originally Eisenhower had planned to follow his visit to the Soviet Union with a trip to Asia, with Japan, where three U-2's were based, a major stopping point. With the fiasco in Paris fresh in mind and with newspaper headlines shouting that Tokyo was wracked with anti-American violence, some members of the team advised against risking further humiliation, and even the President's safety, in Tokyo. Others urged him to take the risk, so he went ahead with the established plans.

The source of much of the anti-Americanism in Japan was a Mutual Security Treaty signed by President Eisenhower and Premier Nobusuke Kishi of Japan in a White House ceremony on January 19, 1960, to replace a similar treaty concluded in 1951. Unlike the old pact, which merely called for consultation in case of an attack, and which many Japanese felt did not commit the United States strongly enough to the defense of Japan, the new one pledged each signatory to treat an armed attack against the other as dangerous to its own peace, and to act to meet the common danger. This alliance allowed the United States to base military forces in Japan for ten years, but also committed it to consult with the Japanese on deployment of the troops.

Details were spelled out in an exchange of notes, and in a communiqué issued after the signing in which Eisenhower declared that "the United States government has no intention of acting . . . contrary to the wishes of the Japanese government."[102] It was at this time that the White House announced that the President would visit Japan in June 1960 and that he had invited Crown Prince Akihito to come to the United States.

Kishi considered the treaty a distinct gain for Japan, but many of his countrymen did not. Neutralists, Socialists, Communists, and others viewed the alliance as leading Japan to entrapment in the cold war. Some denounced the treaty because it failed to return the Ryukyus, Okinawa, and the Bonins—islands occupied by American forces—to Japan, and others because it gave Japan no right of veto over the deployment of guided missiles and nuclear weapons within her borders. After the U-2 crisis, some warned that the pact might invite Soviet and Red Chinese retaliation against Japan for actions within her borders by Americans over which she had no control. Still other Japanese were upset by privileges for Americans embodied in the lengthy status of armed forces agreement linked to the treaty.[103]

The chief opposition party, the Socialist, tried to kill the treaty with violent student demonstrations. This turmoil did not prevent Japanese government's ratification, which came in May, so left-wing demonstrators demanded that Kishi cancel Eisenhower's visit. Leftists feared that the visit would strengthen the position of the unpopular Kishi and assure approval of the treaty. A few days before Eisenhower was scheduled to arrive, some 12,000 students in Tokyo stormed the Diet in the most violent riot of that spring, some of them carrying signs that read, "We Dislike Ike." Secretary of State Herter said that Eisenhower would not cancel the trip because of the mob actions, especially since a postponement would deal a serious blow to Kishi's prestige and encourage the opponents of the security treaty.

Nevertheless, on June 17, 1960, two days before Eisenhower's scheduled arrival, Kishi asked him to postpone the visit, admitting that his government could not guarantee the President's safety. Eisenhower, who had already started on a nine-day good will trip to other parts of Asia, received the humiliating news in Manila with the cheers of thousands ringing in his ears.[104]

The cancellation damaged American prestige throughout Asia, and stimulated Asian neutralism. Almost everywhere it was accepted as a setback for the United States and as another cold war victory for communism. Many observers pointed out that Eisenhower should never have allowed his subordinates to have maneuvered him into this position which brought a loss of prestige to him and to his office. Yet the subordinates were not entirely to blame. The President was aware that the invitation might be canceled at the last minute, but he stubbornly refused to change his plans. He contributed to his own embarrassment. Again Eisenhower's staff system, and his own judgment, had failed to save him from a humiliation that could have been avoided.

To most students of the presidency, to most intellectuals, and even to some of those who worked closely with Eisenhower while in office, the sum of the foregoing episodes, and others, indicates that he lacked skill in the use of power in foreign relations. One reason for this, as we have seen, was that his definition of the office, and hence of its power, was narrow. He did not, moreover, attempt to judge the acts of his presidency by any theoretical standard of the extent or limitations of presidential power.

This does not mean that Eisenhower ignored power. As his memoirs indicate, he did think about the power of the presidency in foreign relations, and probably more than he did any other aspect of the presidential office. Yet, as available evidence suggests, he did not have a sound philosophical understanding of presidential power and how it should be used most effectively, for he had little interest in theories of power, of leadership, or of history. At times he seemed uncertain as to what his powers were or as to how he should exercise them.

To obtain full use of power in foreign relations a president must know what it is, know how to use it effectively, and have a desire to use it. He can delegate its use, but not the responsibility for its use. In using his influence, the President, in the final analysis, as Eisenhower came to realize, must rely on himself. Power in foreign relations more than any other area of executive responsibility, belongs to the President by law, tradition, and by the fact that the people have entrusted that power to him, and to no other individual.

In the middle of the twentieth century, it has been said, the people expected the President to do something about everything. This is an exaggeration, but it does reflect a social acceptance of the idea that government should act, initiate, and reform, rather than simply protect the established order. Certainly the people expected him, as Eisenhower knew, to do something about foreign policy. That was a main reason for electing him. In this area the President must be a leader, and frequently Eisenhower was not.

Eisenhower deliberately set out to be a president in the Whig, or caretaker, tradition. The orientation of the modern Republican party suggested it, and Senator Robert A. Taft and other leaders of his party virtually demanded it. Eisenhower's personality and methods of operation, which leaned more toward conciliation, negotiation, and compromise than toward personal creativity and dominant leadership, complemented the historical situation. He deferred to Congress to the point of permitting congressional intrusion into executive affairs. When he desired support for action that involved risk, or skirted the twilight zone of presidential power, as in the cases of the Formosa Resolution, the Eisenhower Doctrine, and the Lebanon intervention, he tried to clear the way by advance consultation with congressional leaders, and was usually open to reasonable compromise.

Nonetheless, under Eisenhower presidential powers in foreign relations grew, but not because he consciously sought to expand them. They grew because of the demands of the cold war, and the complexities of America's worldwide responsibilities.

Eisenhower's views on the presidency were not in the main stream of historical tradition. Those, like him, who embraced the Whig concept of the weak executive, headed the least distinguished administrations in the history of the presidency. In the past, even under weak presidents, such as James Madison and James Buchanan, in periods of crisis, the nation had always come through safely, but in the Eisenhower era foreign relations were much more vital to survival than in the past, and the nation suffered some harsh blows because of weakness in presidential leadership.

The diplomatic history of the United States tends to justify the insistence of the strong presidents that they themselves must be in control of the conduct and determination of foreign policy.[105] In historical perspective it can be seen that the interests of the nation have been served best by those presidents who saw their power in foreign relations rooted in a broad concept of their office. The strong presidency evolved out of a history that cannot be changed, or ignored, for that history made the office one of the most venerable and powerful among executive offices of the great nations of the world.[106]

Those presidents who have distinguished themselves in the conduct of foreign relations have usually insisted that the presidency was not the servant of Congress but a virtually independent government agency, and the only one capable of wielding power effectively in foreign relations. Eisenhower was not such a president. Although he believed Congress could not itself limit the power of the President in foreign relations, he did not, as strong presidents usually did, believe that the presidency was superior to Congress. In his view Congress was an equal to the President, and he had to influence it with logic and persuasion.

Eisenhower's policy in dealing with Congress, therefore, was consistent, and based on conscious intent. "Now, look, I happen to *know* a little about leadership," he would say when his handling of Congress was criticized. "I've had to work with a lot of nations, for that matter, at odds with each other. And I tell you this: you do not *lead* by hitting people over the head. Any damn fool can do that, but it's usually called 'assault'—not 'leadership.' . . . I'll tell you what leadership is. It's *persuasion*—and *conciliation*—and *education*—and *patience*. It's long, slow, tough work. That's the only kind of leadership I know—or believe in—or will practice."[107]

According to some recent analysts of presidential power who have concerned themselves with the limitations of that power rather than with its expansion, this aspect of Eisenhower's formula for leadership could be considered sound. To them the power to persuade, and hence to bargain, was basic in presidential leadership. In this matter of persuasion, they point out, the President has many advantages over others in government. Especially in foreign relations he has a status and authority that no one else can approach.

Since George Washington's time, as we have seen, no president had more of this authority, status, and prestige than Eisenhower.

The problem was, critics maintained, that he failed to use his power to persuade in bargaining situations so that he could achieve positive results. When he did attempt to persuade, he did so reluctantly. In the view of one prominent student of the presidency, "no President in history was ever more powerfully armed to persuade the minds of men to face up to the inevitable—and then failed more poignantly to use his power.[108]

Ironically, the very source of Eisenhower's personal power contributed to his reluctance to use it. Like George Washington, he accepted the popular image of himself as national hero, a leader above the turmoil and stress of party. He thought the presidency was, or at least should be, a moderating influence, a unifying force for the whole nation. In no area did he believe this concept to be more important than in foreign relations. This concept, as we have seen, had in fact drawn him to the presidency, where the role of Chief of State appealed to him more than did the roles that required active, tough leadership. Yet the pressure of events compelled him to act more often in a forceful manner in the handling of foreign relations than in domestic affairs.

Despite Eisenhower's reluctance to be a leader, and the alleged public preference for strong presidents, he remained immensely popular to the day he stepped out of the White House. "The public loves Ike," one critic observed in February, 1957 after his overwhelming election to a second term. "The less he does the more they love him. That, probably, is the secret. Here is a man who doesn't rock the boat."[109]

What Eisenhower lacked in leadership, one historian maintained, he covered up with that amazing personality of his that seemingly never failed him. His personality became a substitute for presidential leadership, dominating, for most people, national and international politics. As though he were a king, the people overlooked faults of omission or commission, or attributed them to his assistants, not to Eisenhower himself.

During the eight years Eisenhower held the presidency he seemingly never lost his appealing sense of humility. He seemed to be a living rebuke to those who argued that the military leader, the man on horseback, by historical definition, constituted a danger to democratic government. When he decided to leave the nation a farewell address, somewhat as had that first soldier-president, George Washington, Eisenhower chose to warn his countrymen to stand guard against the dangers inherent in an increasingly powerful "military-industrial complex." "This was," he believed, ". . . the most challenging message I could leave with the people of this country."[110]

No one could accuse Eisenhower of being power hungry, nor of fitting Lord Acton's maxim that power corrupts. He saw the democratic process which he headed as essentially a diffusion of power. In him there were no compelling ambitions in politics at home or on the world scene. His highest ambition, it seemed, was to be liked, and he was a man who could be liked. Who could quarrel with this?

In a world torn by struggles for power, constant conflict, and undying hatreds, Eisenhower was a man to be trusted, one whose devotion to peace was as understandable and as simple and sincere as his personality. "You know, it is *so* difficult," he once said. "You come up to face these terrible issues, and you know that what is in almost everyone's heart is a wish for peace, and you want so much to do *something*. And then you wonder . . . if there really *is* anything you can do . . . by words and promises . . . You wonder and you wonder. . . ."[111]

Early in his administration, in a speech called "The Chance for Peace," Eisenhower made clear to everyone his own desire for peace and disarmament by proposing a "peace plan." He denounced war and armaments, saying "we are only for sincerity of peaceful purpose attested by deeds." Stressing that he sought "a peace that is true and total," he announced that his government was "ready to ask its people to join with all nations in devoting a substantial percentage of the savings achieved by disarmament to a fund for world aid and reconstruction. . . ."[112]

Years later Eisenhower admitted that as President he could never put aside the questions of peace and war. He was involved incessantly in decisions pertaining to the dispersal of atomic weapons all over the world. "My every footstep," he explained, "was followed by a courier carrying a satchel filled with draft war orders to be issued by code number in case of emergency."[113]

Even in his commitment to peace, which mattered to him more than almost anything else, critics maintained, Eisenhower showed no compelling leadership. So general were his purposes, it has been said, he could provide no substantial guidance on specific undertakings in the name of peace. Yet few of his predecessors provided any sounder or more specific leadership in this area, for peace, like love and motherhood, is a universal ideal that defies those who wish to box it in, hold it, or lead it.

While in the White House Eisenhower repeatedly indicated that he would eagerly go anywhere in quest of peace. "I have said time and again," he told newsmen in March, 1955, for example, "there is no place on this earth to which I would not travel, there is no chore I would not undertake, if I had the faintest hope that, by so doing, I would promote the general cause of world peace." Two years later a public opinion survey suggested that what the people liked most about the Eisenhower administration "was 'peace' but what they liked least was, paradoxically, the administration's foreign policy."[114]

Observers could and did point out, however, that Eisenhower would contradict his sentiment of traveling in search of peace with comments that revealed a naïve approach to diplomacy, or just plain ignorance of history. "This idea of the President of the United States going personally abroad to negotiate—it's just damn stupid," he said. "Every time a President has gone abroad to get into the details of these things, he's lost his *shirt.*"[115] In its essentials, this was a view held by Dulles, and also by Dean Rusk, a later Democratic Secretary of State.

Despite this view and Dulles's strictures on summit diplomacy, in Eisenhower's last year in office, as we have seen, advisers persuaded him to play the role of "the Man of Peace" on the widest possible stage, that of the world itself. In this role Ike traveled to Asia, Europe, and Latin America, and did help to get across the idea he was committed to a policy of peace. But he also encountered frustration, disappointment, and failure. After the failure of the Paris summit meeting in 1960, he apparently regarded Dulles's opposition to such meetings as wise indeed.

Even in pursuing peace, as in his travels, Eisenhower seemed reluctant to wear the mantle of personal authority. Despite this reluctance, we must remember that his use of power in foreign relations had some positive aspects. He never abused that power, and never took advantage of his role as hero. In reaching decisions, especially when he was personally involved, he moved slowly and cautiously because he wanted desparately to have them come out right, and he always measured them with the yardstick of national interest as he understood it. Unlike some of his more conservative supporters and more impatient advisers, he realized that the possession of tremendous power in foreign relations imposed responsibility for its prudent use.

For example, Eisenhower resisted those advisers who wanted to use the nation's nuclear power to solve world problems, as if that were possible. "Any notion that 'the bomb' is a cheap way to solve things," he told his official family early in his administration, "is awfully wrong. It ignores all facts of world politics—and the basic realities for our allies. It is cold comfort for any citizen of Western Europe to be assured that—after his country is overrun and he is pushing up daisies—someone still alive will drop a bomb on the Kremlin."[116]

This attitude, and others revealed in his memoirs, suggests that Eisenhower, a cautious man, was at times a more decisive, courageous, and thoughtful President in the use of power in foreign relations than many critics have been willing to concede. On his own terms, which were of course limited, he was a successful President in the conduct of foreign relations. He "kept the shop" faithfully, if unimaginatively, and often in the vital issues he was himself in command of foreign policy. What critics rightfully lamented, over and over again, was that he was equipped to do much more than he did. The American people had a right to expect more from him than from a Harding or a Coolidge.

Eisenhower's strength as President, following a period of bitterness, division, and frustration in foreign affairs, lay in his role of national unifier, in his image of a father-like man who could accommodate different points of view rather than provoke controversy. He exhibited enough strength to ward off assaults on the presidency but not enough to mark it with his own imprint.

Eisenhower knew that students of government and history considered him a weak President. At the last meeting of his Cabinet in January, 1961, the chairman of the Council of Economic Advisers, Raymond J. Saulnier, remarked that newspapers said, as though his group had been dead, that in the new Democratic administration "the council will be reactivated."

"Don't worry," Eisenhower replied. "According to the papers, so will the presidency."[117]

Eisenhower was also aware that he had been criticized for not keeping fully informed, and for frequently avoiding controveries within his administration. Such comments, he felt, showed a lack of understanding of his staff system. As President, he believed, he had refined that system so that it worked well. He was convinced that the results obtained from it over the years had proved its worth beyond that of any method of executive procedure he knew.

Like others who had held the office in modern times, Eisenhower believed that the various constitutional duties assigned to the President made the presidency too much for one man to handle. Because of this, and especially because of demands in foreign relations, he felt that "the President must have authority to delegate more work and responsibilities to others."[118] This might be done, he thought, by raising the stature and authority of the President's immediate assistants. Then the President could free himself from routine government management and find time to concentrate on the bigger problems of world peace, disarmament, national security, and domestic welfare.

A noteworthy feature of this attitude is its emphasis on foreign affairs which were of major concern to Eisenhower while in the White House. He once told Sherman Adams "that he had become completely convinced that every important decision of the government, no matter what field it was in, had a direct effect upon our relations with other nations."[119]

Even Eisenhower's harshest critics could not deny that he took seriously his constitutional duty to lead the nation in foreign policy. What crippled him in this leadership, among other factors, was his narrow view of constitutional authority. He looked upon the Constitution, and the concept of the separation of powers, as did many patriotic Americans, with a simple, innocent, and perhaps naïve reverence. For example, he sometimes spoke of the Constitution and the Declaration of Independence as the "founding documents," as if they were animate and capable of creating the nation. He was, a friendly biographer wrote, "the most Constitution-conscious President the country has known in a generation." "Our government is a government of checks and balances," he once told the National War College. "The President cannot do certain things without checking with the Congress." His concern and respect for the limitations of presidential power in constitutional government was striking to all, and especially to those who worked closely with him.[120]

In view of this attitude, it is understandable that critics, and friends too, wrote appraisals of Eisenhower's presidency which say that under him the powers of the office suffered serious erosion, that he had been unable, unwilling, or reluctant to use many of his powers. His presidency, such accounts suggest, was a reversion to the nineteenth-century practice when isolation was the guide in foreign policy and ceremony the President's main concern. He himself, moreover, suffered a loss in historical stature.

Some presidents, as men, have increased in stature when they used power, but not Eisenhower. His towering reputation, logically, had led many to expect too much of him, hence his failures appeared greater than they were. He did, nonetheless, seem smaller as President than he did as the military hero.

It is true that in modern dress Eisenhower refurbished the Whig concept of the presidency that many had assumed had become obsolete as a result of events since 1933. Yet we must not forget that this tagging of presidents as weak or strong is merely a convenient device used by scholars and accepted in popular political literature. It does not take into account steadily accumulating evidence to the effect that in a time of recurring crises, mainly in foreign relations, demands are made on the President that he finds difficult or impossible to meet. Eisenhower faced such demands, and tried to meet them, but not as weak President. In other words, in the use of presidential power in foreign relations he may not have been the dynamic strong President some would have liked, but neither was he the ineffective weak President his detractors have said he was.

This analysis suggests that the concepts of weak and strong presidents, as a means of evaluating the presidency, are too simple and may give a distorted view of history. Certainly Eisenhower, with his tremendous popularity, weakened, if he did not destroy, the theory that the people demand constantly active, strong presidents. His years in the White House showed, more than anything else it seems, that in the use of power in foreign relations events beyond his control, as much as his own concept of power, may force a president to be weak or strong, and that in the twentieth century there was still room for a president who distrusted power and used it reluctantly.

IV. John F. Kennedy: Experiments with Power

Line Engraving from Continuous Tone Negative. Photograph by United Press International

President Kennedy Reports to the Nation that Cuban Missile
Bases are Being Dismantled But U.S. Will Insist on
International Inspection

★ IV ★

John F. Kennedy: EXPERIMENTS WITH POWER

by MARTIN B. TRAVIS, JR.

WHEN IT CAME to foreign policy issues in the 1960 presidential campaign, the Republican Party presented a formidable threat to the Democratic ticket of John F. Kennedy and Lyndon B. Johnson. Indeed, the Republican candidate, Richard M. Nixon, could chart the developments which led to his almost uncontested acceptance by the Republican National Convention in Chicago in terms of his personal involvement as Vice-President in dramatic foreign crises. Mr. Nixon's trip to South America in the spring, 1958, resulted in front page headlines across the United States when he was stoned and spat upon by mobs in Lima, Peru, and in Caracas, Venezuela.

The Caracas crisis, followed that year by popularly received Republican decisions to defend the small islands of Quemoy and Matsu against Chinese Communist attacks, and to send Marines to support the threatened Lebanonese regime, carried Mr. Nixon's popularity to an all-time high. But the decisive break for Mr. Nixon came in July, 1959, when he traveled to the U.S.S.R. for a meeting with Mr. Khrushchev, which involved a dramatic and widely reported exchange of opinion over the relative merits of the two systems of government.

The pace of world events during 1960 favored those candidates who could most successfully present the image of experienced and mature statesmen. Soviet aggression, anarchy in the Congo, Castro's

135

Cuba, Khrushchev's shoe-pounding demonstration at the United Nations, were front page issues right up to the election.

With ranks closed in both parties after their respective conventions, the final and most intensive thirteen weeks of the campaign got under way. Each presidential candidate had long since determined his strategy.[1] Nixon's was that of world leadership—as he had said at the Chicago convention, "If you ever let them (the Democrats) campaign only on domestic issues, they'll beat us—our only hope is to keep it on foreign policy."[2]

Senator Kennedy's own record in foreign affairs fell short of that of his opponent. His recent book, *Strategy of Peace,* suggested that Kennedy had not entirely neglected the field, but any experience gained by his participation on the Senate Committee on Foreign Relations was limited by a poor attendance record. Once a candidate, Mr. Kennedy was briefed on world affairs by Allen Dulles, Director of the Central Intelligence Agency. Kennedy's "Brain Trust" could be relied upon to think, winnow, analyze, and prepare data on the substance of foreign as well as domestic policy, thence channel their material through Theodore C. Sorensen, whom Kennedy called his "intellectual blood bank." But by the last month of the campaign, Kennedy subsequently told Nixon, this team was less used, while Sorensen and Richard N. Goodwin (who was then assisting him with campaign speeches) were relied upon more and more because they could react to and reflect up-to-the-minute tactical shifts in basic strategy. It was also true that specific issues regarding defense, China, or Latin America in the last month had ceased to matter. Intangible issues like style and personality by then weighed most heavily in the balance.

One of the first direct confrontations of the candidates on any foreign policy issue[3]—that relating to Quemoy and Matsu—best illustrates the advantage enjoyed by Nixon. During the course of the second TV debate on October 7, 1960, Senator Kennedy declared that these small offshore islands were strategically indefensible, they were not essential to the defense of Formosa, and that the U.S. should undertake negotiations in regard to the future status of the islands. Kennedy's position seemed to imply that the islands had little value and might be traded to the Communist Chinese in return for a cease fire in the Formosa Straits. Kennedy quoted a two-year-old statement of Secretary of State Herter to support the strategic vulnerability of the islands, and in the third TV debate quoted President Eisenhower as declaring in 1958, "No American need feel the U.S. will be involved in military hostilities *merely* (sic) in defense of Quemoy and Matsu." Nixon warned that a policy of withdrawal from the islands represented a kind of appeasement.

The Cuban question was one in which the Democratic candidate could freely exploit a popular mood of frustration, unrestrained by the actual formulation and implementation of any proposed policy. Kennedy drew his first blood on the Cuban issue the day before the first TV debate, when he held the administration responsible for policies which he said encouraged the Batista dictatorship and gave rise to conditions that paved the way for Fidel Castro to impose his Communist regime in Havana. It did not matter that Kennedy had described Castro as "part of the legacy of Bolivar" in his book published the previous January, and was still supporting the Cuban policy of the Eisenhower administration in May. Then, a day before the fourth and last TV debate (October 20), Kennedy demanded that the non-Batista, anti-Castro forces be strengthened. Thus far, he noted, these fighters for freedom had virtually no support from the United States government.

Nixon fully appreciated that a tougher line against Castro was overwhelmingly favored by public sentiment. Indeed, Nixon, as early as April, 1959, shared with J. Edgar Hoover and Kennedy's personal friend, former U.S. Ambassador to Cuba, Earl E. T. Smith (though not with the Department of State), the view that Castro was either incredibly naïve or under the discipline of communism. Nixon's tougher line finally prevailed over that recommended by the Department of State in early 1960. The CIA was accordingly given instructions to provide secret arms and training to Cuban exiles. The Kennedy proposal paralleled the precise secret action which had been taken but it also stole the fire from Nixon's proposal (two days earlier) for an all-out quarantine of the Castro regime—if possible in full association with the rest of Latin America.

Under the circumstances Nixon could not disclose the secret operation and thereby destroy its effectiveness—if for no other reason than that he was strongly advocating it be implemented *before* the election. An administration which had ousted Castro would be counted on to receive the continuing support of the people in an election year. Thus Nixon reluctantly chose a deceptive approach, piously arguing that if we were to follow the Kennedy recommendation, we would not only violate five treaties, but lose all our friends in Latin America, be condemned by the United Nations, and invite Mr. Khrushchev to come into Latin America and engage us in civil war. But Nixon reminded his TV audience of 60 million, that the U.S. policy of "quarantining" the Arbenz regime in Guatemala had been successful in ousting that Communist government. The attentive public in the U.S. and Latin America well knew that this had been a successful CIA maneuver, and Nixon, in his fashion, may have hoped to communicate to them that Castro was likewise doomed.

Scolded by the attentive public and the communications and intellectual elite he most appreciated, Kennedy was to deny that he ever had advocated intervention in Cuba in violation of U.S. treaty obligations two days after he had intimated as much on TV before 60 million Americans. The denial, as Nixon was correct in pointing out, satisfied Kennedy's critical attentive public, while it did not reach the minds of the action-oriented, Castro-hating mass public.

In the broader issues of foreign policy, Kennedy agreed that the greatest issue of the campaign was that of war or peace, and while both candidates agreed on their broad generalizations of doing more to win the cold war, Kennedy warned that his opponent was a risk-taker abroad and a conservative at home. The question of whether U.S. prestige had fallen during the course of the last seven and one half years had been an area staked out by Kennedy even before the campaign started. As treated by the campaigners, and particularly Kennedy, the prestige question little deserves the dignity of contemporary analysis, but Nixon clearly worried about its impact on the voters. He deplored the "poor mouth" image of America—just barely limping along in second place behind the dynamic Soviets with the gap widening day by day.

Both candidates promised to increase defense spending even if taxes had to be increased.

Kennedy would make the United Nations the central instrument of U.S. energies and policies in Africa, and would call for a conference of Israel and the Arab states to consider their common problems. He would institute a Peace Corps of talented young men, willing to serve the country abroad as an alternative to the Selective Service, in assisting underdeveloped nations in agriculture, road-building, and other skills. Both candidates would encourage the continuing development of the North Atlantic Alliance.

Perhaps more important in the outcome of the election than their diagnoses of world ills and prescriptions for remedies, were the candidates' views of the office of the presidency. Both favored a political president and an active leader. Kennedy, however, placed more emphasis on presidential initiative while Nixon dwelt on restraints. The office will demand, Kennedy declared, that the President place himself in the very thick of the fight, that he care passionately about the people he leads, that he be willing to serve them at the risk of incurring their momentary displeasure. Nixon talked about a new reorganization—giving the Vice-President new powers, while Kennedy talked about new men. Kennedy was clearly more interested in ideas and style; his model of the presidency was that of the ebullient, disorderly, highly personal executive, Franklin Roosevelt, and not the orderly, self-effacing Eisenhower.

In final analysis, did the foreign policy issue affect the outcome of the campaign? Both the *New York Times* (November 6) and the *Christian Science Monitor* (November 7) agreed that the intangible issues (image and religion) outweighed the tangible issues (substantive policies). Scholarly analyses have subsequently confirmed these latter statements: the issue of religion exceeded any other, and was not helpful for Kennedy; the TV debates strengthened existing partisan support for the candidates, while the issues debated therein were not important.[4] One final conclusion should be noted—had Kennedy accomplished his purpose of alerting voters to the importance of foreign affairs, there is every reason to believe that he would have lost support, since voters, in line with their previous inclinations, would have decided that the perilous times called for an experienced Republican in the White House.

That Kennedy's spirit and style should have weighed more in the balance, that he was held accountable for his energy, grace, looks, speech, and manner, and not necessarily for his campaign statements on foreign policy was, however, welcomed by those most experienced in international affairs.

The Kennedy administration learned at least as early as February 9, that the missile gap to which it had called attention during the campaign did not exist. More time would elapse before its view of the world situation would parallel that of the professionals in the field.

In view of the narrow margin between the Democratic victor and the Republican vanquished (roughly 100,000 popular votes), was the impact of the campaign notable upon the candidate himself—if not upon the voting public—insofar as it concerned foreign policy?[5] President-elect Kennedy did give some indication to Nixon when they met in Florida, November 14, that his campaign speeches had moved him toward a new policy for the Far East. At that time Kennedy raised with Nixon the possibility of admitting Communist China to a seat in the UN General Assembly, and thereby adopting a "two-China" policy. Nixon advised against such a policy because Communist China would not meet the UN requirement of "peace loving," and its membership would increase its respectability in Asia.

The Kennedy brain trust, which had been increasingly neglected toward the end of the campaign, was once again mobilized after the election for the preparation of task force studies. Adlai E. Stevenson, with the assistance of two Washington, D.C. lawyers, George Ball and John Sharon, had prepared a 200-page report for President-elect Kennedy, which dealt with decisions to be made between election day and inauguration, and with the probable foreign policy issues which would preoccupy the new administration after January 20. Sharon suggested going beyond the report with the establishment of task forces; a dozen were thereupon established, involving more than 100 consultants working on foreign policy recommendations. Those dealing with foreign economic policy (balance of payments, foreign aid, commerce) reported to Ball while the rest (including USIA, disarmament, geographic areas) worked under Sharon. The consultants included David K. E. Bruce, Paul H. Nitze, Chester Bowles, Harvard professors, and foundation employees. Most of them were asked to come to Washington. As secretarial positions were filled, the new officers became ex officio chairmen of task forces that concerned them.

It is doubtful that the task force recommendations readied by December 31, directly influenced President-elect Kennedy's thinking on foreign policy. Together with his immediate staff he was preoccupied with the preparation of his inauguration address and the appointment of key administrative officials during January. For the participants in the task forces, however, who were to hold high appointive office—like George Ball—the exercise was meaningful. For them, indeed, it was an intensive and high level seminar which prepared them in some depth for the substantive issues with which they were to be concerned.

The rhetoric of the new administration was never better than in the Inaugural Address. President Kennedy called upon the country and the world to co-operate in dynamically new policies. "Let us never negotiate out of fear. But let us never fear to negotiate." The Soviet Union was called upon for a new beginning and was warned that "civility should not be mistaken for weakness." The President would "push back the jungles of suspicion" in a new endeavor, not simply for a new balance of power, but rather a new world of law where the strong are just and the weak secure and the peace preserved. A stronger NATO, unqualified support for the United Nations, assistance to undeveloped nations in breaking the bonds of mass misery, and in particular, an alliance with the free men and free governments in Latin America to cast off the chains of poverty, were all invoked.

It was the first awesome task of the President to organize a government which would implement these millenial objectives. As the youngest elected president in history, Kennedy at 44 brought to the office tireless working habits and an exceptional self confidence which reflected his wealthy upbringing and his successful political career. Intolerant of incompetence, Kennedy cherished those decisions which he or others had based on abundant information and careful analysis. He had yet to learn that in foreign affairs all relevant information would never be available, and more importantly, forecasts of the consequences of alternative policies were often based upon insightful judgments drawn from experience. Withal, Kennedy was an activist, and did not "agonize over decisions."

For the success of his administration, the new President counted heavily upon the quality of his appointments to key foreign policy posts. It would be difficult to generalize on the overall nature of these appointments, for they were an odd mixture of idealism and cynicism, of liberals and conservatives, and of professors and politicians. If the average age (47) of the cabinet was ten years younger than that of the two previous administrations, both the Secretaries of State and Treasury exceeded this average by five years. Kennedy's narrow margin of victory also made it desirable to have Republicans appointed to the Defense and Treasury posts, thereby reassuring the public of the administration's intent of pursuing fiscal responsibility. Following a recommendation of Senator Jackson's Subcommittee on Government Operations, more high-level officials from private life and career service with experience in more than one agency were appointed to the principal departments dealing with national security.

A soft-spoken Georgian, Dean Rusk, who for nine years had been president of the Rockefeller Foundation, was named Secretary of State. Previously unknown to the President, Rusk's qualifications reflected the personality and qualifications which Mr. Kennedy would have in his first Secretary. An article Rusk had written the previous April for *Foreign Affairs* clearly indicated his conviction that the President himself should provide the leadership in the formulation and the execution of foreign policy. Kennedy has phrased it somewhat differently—the Secretary of State, he had said, should be intelligent and self-confident enough to solve minor problems satisfactorily on his own responsibility, yet wise enough to identify the major problems and take them to the President for a joint solution. Rusk's own five-year experience (1947-1952) at the Assistant Secretarial level in the Department and his distinguished intellectual attainments (he was one of 20 former Rhodes scholars appointed to the new administration) qualified him as a candidate for the post. Personally self-effacing and quiet, Rusk was also free from controversial positions. As a highly qualified technician, the new Secretary could be expected to give his entire energy to the execution of a Kennedy policy in much the same manner as his colleagues in the Foreign Ministries of Moscow, Bonn, Paris, and Berlin (all of them unspectacular efficiency experts).

Rusk's role as Secretary was further inhibited by the appointment of internationally known specialists in foreign policy, including Adlai E. Stevenson as U.S. Permanent Representative to the United Nations and Chester A. Bowles as Under Secretary of State for Political Affairs. In return for his willingness to accept a lesser position in the administration, Stevenson was promised an enlarged role for the UN position. He was to add to the U.S. Mission a distinguished galaxy of new personnel, and to be accorded cabinet rank (as was his predecessor, Henry Cabot Lodge). Stevenson's direct superior in the Department, the 43-year-old J. Harlan Cleveland, Assistant Secretary of International Organizational Affairs, looked to him for policy guidance, as did the White House special assistant Arthur M. Schlesinger, Jr. Within the administration, Bowles and Stevenson represented the more forward-looking approach to foreign affairs (critics claimed they were soft on communism); their restless minds were less content to accept a simplified image of a world divided between good and evil. Within this more complex and diversified world, as they saw it, they stressed the importance of such long-run problems as developmental assistance, an expanded role for the United Nations, and more flexible political approaches towards the many-hued Communist nations.

Among others on his staff, Secretary Rusk had George W. Ball as Under Secretary for Economic Affairs. Ball had had government experience in foreign economic assistance, and had headed Kennedy's brain trust during and after the election. Other political appointments within the Department included the defeated candidate for governor in Michigan, G. Mennen Williams, who became Assistant Secretary for African Affairs, and a Harvard law professor, Abram Chayes, as Legal Advisor. At his first staff conference, Chayes was candid in confessing that he was virtually innocent of international law, and much the same could be said of the seven appointees he made in the legal office (more "political" appointees than had been made in any previous post-war administration).

The Republican appointees to the commanding foreign policy posts outside the State Department included Robert S. McNamara as Secretary of Defense, C. Douglas Dillon as Secretary of Treasury, and the reappointment of Allen Dulles as Director of the Central Intelligence Agency. Dillon, as Under Secretary of State in the Eisenhower administration, was an investment banker (his father had founded Dillon, Read & Co.) who would provide continuity for the Inter-American assistance program which he had negotiated in Bogota, Colombia, the previous August. His background and training also suggested that he would search for international (rather than restrictively national) solutions for such problems as the continuing depletion of U.S. gold reserves.

Robert S. McNamara, as an intelligent and prodigious worker, had at 44 just become president of the Ford Motor Company. A former Harvard Business School professor, he was a specialist in cost control and represented modern business management. He, more than others, would have to cope with the problem of which Eisenhower had warned in his farewell message: the conjunction of an immense military establishment and a large arms industry provided the potential for the disastrous rise of misplaced power. The second most important civilian in the Pentagon was Paul H. Nitze—Assistant Secretary of Defense for International Affairs. A former member of the State Department Policy Planning staff, he was to develop new disarmament proposals.

Crisp, tough, able men were selected for the White House staff. There were the brilliantly able political technicians—the so-called "Irish Mafia" or "Boston Originals" who had started out with Kennedy's political career. There was Theodore Sorensen, who believed his assignment as principal speech writer was in fact a policy-making assignment. The 32-year-old Sorensen had joined Kennedy's Senatorial staff in 1953 and has been as influential as any single person in "liberalizing" the Senator.[6] He was a shy, abstemious puritan whose relationship with the President had developed into his whole life—anything that threatened that relationship was a threat to life itself. Almost alone among the White House staff, Sorensen treasured anonymity.

Of the three remaining "intellectuals" the 42-year-old McGeorge Bundy soon emerged as the most influential. Assigned as the principal staff aide on foreign policy and security matters, he had been a candidate for the position of Secretary of State, and had been vetoed by Dean Rusk as Under Secretary. Bundy's, perhaps, was the most conservative mind of the group.

Walt Whitman Rostow (44 years old) resigned his professorship of Economics at MIT, to share some of the White House foreign policy assignments. Until he became director of State Department's Policy Planning Staff in November, 1961, Rostow served on the White House staff. He had supplied Kennedy with basic position paper on defense during the campaign, and on the White House staff was assigned South Vietnam, Germany, guerrilla force (Bundy was given Cuba, Laos, disarmament).

The 43-year-old Arthur M. Schlesinger, Jr. was at the same time the most liberal and the most partisan.[7] He was the former speech writer for Adlai Stevenson, and resigned his Harvard professorship to accept the White House assignment. He came to be viewed first as an expert on Latin America, and subsequently on the United Nations. Professor Jerome Wiesner, 46, an MIT scientist, was the disarmament specialist. Convinced that it was better to accept some risk that the Soviets might cheat than to follow the path towards nuclear holocaust, Wiesner was neither popular nor influential with the Pentagon and other powerful circles.

There were others—David E. Bell as budget director, John J. McCloy as disarmament chief, and Robert F. Kennedy, the President's 36-year-old brother who was appointed Attorney General. In the free-wheeling Kennedy government, Robert Kennedy had more continuing influence in foreign as well as domestic policy making than any other official—certainly more than any previous Attorney General. When the President was absent from Washington at a time of some international crisis, Robert Kennedy would move to a command post in the State Department. The President's dependence upon his brother necessarily was reflected in the White House staff's ready reference to him.

If the Kennedy administration considered that its toughest job was to get the right people to take the top positions, as Robert Kennedy declared in January, 1962, the problem of effective executive organization may have been even more important simply because it was often purposefully neglected. John Kennedy's view of leadership had been changing even before he reached the White House and was to change again within his first year of the presidency.[8]

In his first book, *Why England Slept*, (1940) he developed the thesis (largely influenced by his father) that the chief villains of Britain's failure to keep pace with German rearmament were the unthinking British public, not the politicians. Fifteen years later, in his *Profiles in Courage,* Kennedy paid glowing tribute to the politician who stood staunchly against the prevailing sentiment of colleagues and public. A year before his inauguration, Kennedy delivered a speech to the National Press Club which borrowed heavily from Sidney Hyman's charismatic school of presidential interpretation. A good president must place himself in the very thick of fight, and must be willing to incur the momentary displeasure of the people for their long-run good.

During the spring and summer of the election year, Kennedy was drawn to Richard E. Neustadt's *Presidential Power,* which presented the image of a successful president as one being power conscious. Such a president would effectively draw to himself the strings which would control the executive and legislative branches of government. Thus a president should make policy choices, employing the criterion of how the particular policy will implement his power, and power in a democracy can be interpreted to mean short-run popularity, even though it may conflict with the long-run good. Such a view of the presidency—while it sacrifices the quality of "courage"—can be seen to have all the more appeal for a president who had won by such a narrow margin and who was confronted by no great crisis which would have added several dimensions to his discretionary power. During the opening months of the Kennedy administration, author Neustadt was spending half of every week in the Budget Bureau counseling on the proper relationship between executive departments with the objective of implementing his theory of presidential power.

A sober reappraisal of the dynamic theory of leadership was forged on the crucible of experience. Theodore Sorensen, the President's counsel, gave two lectures at Columbia University in spring, 1963, entitled "Decision Making in the White House" in which the complexity of leadership was stressed. A president often finds that events or the decisions of others, Sorensen declared, limit his freedom of maneuver. Any choice a president does make may well close the door behind him and he may find himself in a one-way tunnel, or in a baffling maze, or descending a slippery slope. He cannot see ahead, and yet he must act.

The lesson the President and his staff had begun to learn after the catastrophic Cuban invasion, was that a number of decision-making components seriously restrict the rationality of the ensuing action. Indeed, the very decisions the President makes are as much a matter of chance as they are an ordered process; a controversy looming large in the press will capture his attention; a conflict between departments, or the fickle personal interest of the President may all determine the issue. Once the issue comes to the President, his decision may well depend upon how it is presented to him by his advisers, and by the following important restraints which will limit the range of alternative courses of action available to him: (1) the extent to which Congress, other nations, or international law would approve the decision; (2) the cost of the decision in terms of money, manpower, time, credibility, patronage, and other tools at the President's command; (3) the proper timing of the decision; (4) the President's previous commitments, exclusive of party platforms and campaign promises (President Kennedy commenced his review of the Soviet missile crisis in Cuba by reading copies of all his earlier statements on Cuba); (5) the lack of information which is even greater on the world than on the domestic scene.

President Kennedy was to be preoccupied with foreign policy during the course of his two years and ten months in office. Sooner or later this is the fate of all presidents; foreign affairs are more urgent and interesting, and the President has more power to act in foreign as compared to domestic affairs. It was also true that the so-called urgency of foreign issues had been in part the creation of the young Democratic candidate himself. He had defined world problems in the harshest possible terms both during the campaign and in his Inaugural Address. Yet only eighteen days after Kennedy took office, his Secretary of Defense, in an off-the-record press conference, declared that the "missile gap between the U.S. and the Soviet Union" (of which the Democrats had made much during the campaign) was nonexistent. The world in crisis, however useful for campaigning purposes or for augmenting the decision-making role of the President, could not be long sustained on a rational basis.

The new President brought a new style of operation to the White House. Compared to Eisenhower's "football team"—elaborate planning, extensive co-ordination, interminable time spent in huddles—the Kennedy team was more along the lines of basketball. As Douglass Cater noted, everybody was on the move all the time and nobody had a very clearly defined position. The President had a habit of throwing the ball in any direction and he expected it to be kept bouncing.

The stars of this basketball game were more ephemeral than in the previous administration. Thus neither the wagon-wheel model (with all relevant information from Treasury, Defense, State, and White House staff flowing to the President, who represented the hub of the wheel), nor the quadrangulation theory (with Treasury, Defense, State, and White House staff each in its equal corner making their respective decisions) adequately characterized the decision-making process—although both theories were projected.

Symbolic of the new organization was the early decision (February 19) to abolish the Operations Control Board. The previous administration had established the OCB to supervise and co-ordinate the execution of policies which had been determined by the National Security Council. At one time the OCB had proliferated into 45 interdepartmental committees and it was precisely this morass of committees against which Kennedy and his intellectual mentors like Neustadt had inveighed. It was the committee which, instead of recommending courageous policy decisions, merely achieved the lowest common denominator of agreement. It was the committee that enabled timid officials and departments to escape responsibility for decisions. Committees, as Robert Lovett (who had turned down the position of Secretary of State for reasons of health) had declared, "were the foul-up factor in policy making." Senator Jackson's Subcommittee on Government Operations gave congressional support for this view in its publication February 5, entitled *The Department of State.*

One top-secret committee of the OCB, known as the Special Group, was not abolished. This committee controlled much of the secret operations of the four-billion-dollar intelligence community. Meeting once a week to make decisions which were too sensitive or too divisive to be entrusted to the United States Intelligence Board (representing all the intelligence agencies), the Special Group launched the secret activities of the CIA.[9] McGeorge Bundy became the key man on this committee during the Kennedy administration, and he was joined by McCone, McNamara, the Deputy Secretary of Defense, Gilpatric, and the Deputy Under Secretary of State, U. Alexis Johnson. The Special Group regularly met in the Situation Room, a restricted command post deep in the White House basement. The room was supplied with top-secret maps, electronic equipment, and communications outlets.

Kennedy sought to prove that his organizational innovations would help a president who wished to take his foot off the brake and give a firm push on the gas pedal. For a president who wanted to act decisively, to innovate, and who possessed a sense of urgency and adventure, the tidiness of the Eisenhower organization was expendable. In his own person, Kennedy wanted to concentrate all relevant information and to control all important decisions. One of his first acts as President was to install a complicated telephonic apparatus, permitting him to call rapidly the lower officials in the State Department and elsewhere for the facts he wanted. As a voracious seeker of information, he did not want to be frozen out and insulated by the White House guard. Nor did he want the information divested of any pungency and character which might well have happened were it subjected to a chain of command. It was generally agreed, furthermore, that the heightened morale of the lower officials, thus flattered by the President's attentions, proved to have a tonic effect throughout the government. The six newspapers Kennedy read daily further insured him against the unwanted isolation, although more importantly they kept him abreast of the public image his administration was creating.

The White House staff, particularly McGeorge Bundy, was nonetheless destined for a powerful, although a differing role, from that of its predecessor. Bundy's predecessors had not been members of the Special Group. Together with his colleagues, Bundy's request for information and/or action to any of the departments or agencies carried all the respect and prestige of the President himself—so much so at first that the staff was criticized for its passion for power rather than for anonymity. But when the OCB was eliminated, some agency had to oversee the co-ordination and execution of foreign policy, to stir respect in the executive departments—especially State, to burrow and bully the way to the problems that lay hidden, and to negotiate gaps between agencies. One lesson learned from the Bay of Pigs disaster, however, was that the White House staff should not be partisan to any decision before it was taken—as Bundy had been. Schlesinger, it was true, expressed doubt about the operation, but without vigor, and Rostow was not involved until the very end. Rather should the staff make certain that the President is confronted with alternatives, ensuring binocular vision of any situation and providing him with multiple choice.

The task-force approach to decision making was a second organizational innovation (the first being the elimination of the OCB). Adolf A. Berle, Jr., who refused the position of Assistant Secretary of State for Inter-American Affairs because it was not upgraded in authority to Under Secretary, did agree to head a separate task force on Latin America. The group included Richard N. Goodwin and Schlesinger of the White House staff (neither could be rated knowledgeable in Latin America in any professional sense) together with career foreign service officers, but it was quite autonomous from and superior to the Inter-American bureau of the Department of

State. The Bay of Pigs disaster administered it a crushing blow from which it did not recover, and Berle shortly thereafter retired from government service. A second task force on the Berlin crisis of 1961 was headed by former Secretary of State Dean Acheson. It was another indication of the distrust the President had for the State Department, although not for its higher officials. When, however, this task force refused to accept the hard-line recommendations of Acheson, including mobilization of troops, refusal to negotiate, and rejection of UN consideration of the problem, Acheson left Washington for an extended vacation.

Whatever the Kennedy administration may have said about the role of the Secretary of State (he was to be first among equals in the formulation of foreign policy), it was clear that this was not to be the case. By personality and inclination, Dean Rusk preferred to execute policy which was presidentially determined. Rusk was in no position to run a tight shop with many of his key deputies chosen by the President and with the President appealing directly to them for information and advice. The vigor of the White House staff, the inroads on State Department authority made by the task forces, and the control of foreign, covert, and military operations by the CIA and the Defense Department with their vast budgets, all contributed to the erosion of State Department authority. Even abroad, as a candidate, Kennedy promised to give full power to ambassadors over all personnel in the Embassies including military, CIA, and economic assistance. Kennedy did so empower all ambassadors on May 29, 1961, but it was clear to the Senate Subcommittee on Government Operations by late 1962 that ambassadors were still unable to give orders to the local CIA agents or to stop an agency operation. "The primacy of the ambassador," the report said, "is a polite fiction."

The Kennedy administration boast that a disorderly administration must be judged on the creativity of its results—that a creative government must always be out of channels, that confusion and meddling always discomfit officials whose routine is disturbed and whose security is threatened—met its first test in the Bay of Pigs decision and was found wanting. The original boast itself was subjected to knowledgeable doubt.

Nowhere were the weaknesses of the early Kennedy administration more glaring than in the Latin American area. The State Department role as chief co-ordinator of foreign policy had been abandoned: the former Under Secretary of State, Douglas Dillon, had taken his experts on Latin America to the Treasury Department, and the irascible Adolf Berle, having rejected the Assistant Secretary post as being impotent (the post of Assistant Secretary was not to be filled for five months, when U.S. Ambassador to Chile, Robert F. Woodward, was drafted after twenty-one others had refused the position), was running his own task force independently from the Department's Inter-American bureau.

Berle's task-force report on Latin America came to the President before the inauguration. It was kept secret because it dealt with Cuba and Communist infiltration, but it was generally appreciated that Berle's approach to these problems could be characterized as "hard," "realistic," and generally favoring right-of-center regimes. Berle had little respect for legal solutions in foreign relations and he associated himself with those who recommended active intervention in the accomplishment of hemispheric objectives. His sandpaper personality irritated careerists in the Department, whom he often found to be timid and fearful of any action. He was more of one mind, therefore, with defense and intelligence officials involved in Latin affairs than he was with either the State Department careerists, or the so-called White House experts.

Neither the 29-year-old Richard Goodwin nor Arthur Schlesinger, Jr. had more than a superficial knowledge of Latin problems, but their visceral responses were liberal as Berle's were conservative. While neither wanted to appear "soft" (Schlesinger went along with the Bay of Pigs decision, although he correctly questioned CIA's estimate of guerrilla strength inside Cuba), both reflected a sensitivity to, if not a sense of guilt for, the unfortunate imperialistic record of the U.S. in Latin America. After his appointment as Deputy Assistant Secretary of State under Woodward, Goodwin seized the opportunity (in the absence of his superior), early in August, to instruct the United States Ambassador, Joseph Farland, in Panama, to inform the Foreign Minister that the United States would undertake immediate negotiations for a new Panama Canal treaty. The 1903 treaty, as amended, no doubt symbolized for Goodwin the weak link in hemispheric relations. He would subsequently realize that the largest number of Panamanian beneficiaries of any renegotiated treaty were those groups which most strenuously resisted economic and social reform. In any event, more experienced hands amended Goodwin's instructions the next day to the effect that the United States was prepared to discuss the *possibility* of negotiations. Along with Adlai Stevenson, both Schlesinger and Goodwin favored collective to unilateral action; preferred the untidy and sometimes chaotic democratic regimes to military dictatorships, and believed that the spread of communism could best be checked by the adoption of social and economic reforms.

The decisions which led to the Bay of Pigs[10] largely reflected Berle's approach to hemispheric problems—but only to a point. The image-conscious planners—including the President himself, would not permit the overt use of the United States military and would restrict the covert bombing missions when American involvement became apparent.

President-elect Kennedy was first officially informed of the extensive preparations for the overthrow of the Castro regime on November 18, 1960. During the previous spring the Eisenhower administration had entrusted to Richard Bissell, CIA's Deputy Director for Plans, the responsibility for a long, slow build-up of the underground within Cuba with exiles whom CIA agents had trained in Guatemala. For this purpose the CIA had built a $1.2 million air base in Guatemala. The CIA, however, failed to get a secure and effective underground operating in Cuba, and on November 4, Bissell had decided that there must be a late fall landing in Cuba of four hundred well trained and well supplied men to serve as a focal point for other guerrillas. The Nicaraguan government secretly agreed to let the United States use the air base and post at Puerto Cabezas as a staging area for the invasion. By the time Bissell first briefed Kennedy about the plan, it had acquired a life of its own and Bissell had become an apologist and salesman for its adoption.

More than a dozen meetings and conferences on the Cuban invasion were held in Washington between November 29, 1960, and April 12, 1961. The Joint Chiefs of Staff were briefed on the operation for the first time in January. The guerrilla movement within Cuba had completely collapsed and plans now called for a full-scale invasion (which was to number 1,400 men). The military at first agreed that a proposed landing at Trinidad had an even chance of success, but during the course of the next three months, the Joint Chiefs had become an unhappy lot. Some of them were bewildered by the informality and lack of procedures after the accustomed strict discipline of the Eisenhower administration. Admiral Burke in particular was disturbed by the way the plan was being constantly modified. On April 10, at a White House meeting, the military were asked to approve a change in the landing site from Trinidad to the Bay of Pigs; the latter site was uninhabited and invasion forces would therefore run less risk of shooting civilians, as well as giving the appearance of a smaller and more spontaneous operation. The Joint

Chiefs went along with the change, but they gave it less than an even chance (they were doubtful that the establishment of a beachhead would prompt an uprising).

One last opportunity for Kennedy's advisers to have scotched the ill-conceived CIA invasion plans was at a meeting in the new State Department building April 4. Bissell and Lemnitzer (chairman of the Joint Chiefs) of course were there, together with Robert McNamara, Douglas Dillon, Dean Rusk, Thomas Mann (not yet replaced as Assistant Secretary of State for Inter-American Affairs), Paul Nitze, Adolph Berle, Richard Goodwin, Arthur Schlesinger, Allen Dulles, and Senator J. William Fulbright of Arkansas. Bissell reviewed the Cuban operation, and Dulles declared it would be easier to accomplish than one which overthrew the Arbenz regime in Guatemala in 1954. The President then went around the table asking for the opinion of the others. Only Fulbright spoke up firmly against the operation. Four days earlier he had given the President a memorandum in which he pointed out the immense difficulties of keeping this operation secret, the concern he had that the Cuban exile leaders who had been selected by the CIA would not provide a strong and liberal successor government to Castro, and whether, in the event the exiles' invasion failed, the United States would succumb to using its own armed forces and thereby revive Latin memories of imperialism. At the close of the meeting, however, Fulbright told Kennedy there was more to the operation than he had thought.

Reassured by Bissell that United States involvement could be kept secret, and that the operation would succeed without any direct participation of United States armed forces, Kennedy was less fearful of a negative world response. In addition, the bold plan appealed to the Kennedy brothers—it was risky, to be sure, but it was audacious, glamorous, and new. Were Kennedy to scrap the plans, the thwarted Exile Brigade would accuse him openly, and there would be public charges that the White House amateurs, disregarding expert advice, were soft on Castro and on communism. But even more, the confident Bissell and Dulles had encouraged him to speculate on the rewards of success: Castro would be eliminated without overt United States participation and therefore without tangling with the Soviet Union. Later, with the 20-20 hindsight of an historian, Kennedy was to ask, "How could everybody involved have thought such a plan would succeed?"

It would seem that the CIA officials were less than candid with the President. They were aware of his interest in establishing a liberal successor regime to Castro, yet they selected the most conservative exiles to lead the invasion. An operation of these dimensions could hardly be kept secret; the existence of the Guatemalan base "surfaced" in November, and by the time Schlesinger's "White Paper" on Cuba was released April 3, United States involvement in some imminent plan seemed probable. In an effort to maintain the "cover", Rusk, Stevenson, and other government officials damaged their reputation for integrity by issuing deceptive statements. Stevenson had been briefed by a CIA agent a few days before the first raid of eight B-26's on Cuban territory, April 15 (although he may not have connected this raid with the invasion plans), and again more thoroughly April 17, by McGeorge Bundy, before he issued denials of United States involvement in the operation. The President and Dulles both contributed to the "cover" by leaving Washington over the weekend for innocuous tasks elsewhere.

It was for naught. One of the B-26 pilots was forced to make an emergency landing in Florida. His cover story, that he had defected from Castro's air force, was not only given wide publicity in the Sunday press, but was accepted with more than measured caution. The President was now discovering that it was both difficult and precarious for the government to try to deceive the press and the country to protect a covert operation. The second B-26 strike, scheduled before dawn on the day of invasion (April 17) would be best called off to keep the cover story from dissolving any more rapidly. From the beginning, the President had insisted that the invasion must not jeopardize larger United States interests—as public knowledge of United States involvement could well do. And Kennedy's advisers now told him that the second strike was unnecessary. He cancelled the attack and twice refused to reinstate it, when first Rusk (at Bissell's and Cabell's request) and later Cabell (4 a.m. April 17) raised the possibility in telephone conversations with the President in his summer estate at Glen Ora.

Back in Washington on Monday, as the invasion got off to a catastrophic start, the key decision-makers began to sense defeat. Ten pilots had been killed and ten of the sixteen B-26's lost. Two supply ships with all the supplies were sunk. When the news reached Kennedy, he reinstated the second air strike. But attrition and exhaustion had overtaken the Cuban pilots and the weather had turned bad. Air cover of six bombers for the invading exiles on Tuesday afternoon (April 18) destroyed a Castro convoy on the road to the beach. Despite the presidential pledge that no Americans would participate in the fighting, two of the bombers were flown by American CIA pilots. All but one of the five B-26's were piloted by Americans on the following day.

The feeling of failure that crept into the President's Oval Office on Monday was not to be shaken. Kennedy put in a call to his brother Robert to tell him the invasion was not going well and to return to Washington from Williamsburg as soon as he could. The midnight session on Tuesday with the major men of the government might better not have been held. With Robert Kennedy muttering "We've got to do something. We've got to do something" the decision was made that United States air cover for a final B-26 strike would be provided by the aircraft carrier *Essex*. The one-hour strike would also provide cover while supply ships went in to unload. Confusion over time zones resulted in the B-26's arriving after the American air cover. Four American pilots never returned from that strike.

By noon on Wednesday a seven-hour meeting had begun. Again the same team. It was left to Kennedy to reject the proposals of his military men: sending in the marines to conquer the country; appealing to the Organization of American States for collective action; blockading the country; mounting another rebel force. Time and time again Kennedy stood quietly off from the others, talking to his brother. It was in these talks that the Kennedys began to realize the need for reorganization and personnel changes. More immediately an explanation was owed the American public and the world; Rusk, Bundy, and the Russian expert, Charles Bohlen, met with the President and Sorensen after dinner to pool their collective wisdom in a speech which would be given the following day. The President was to warn Khrushchev that we were prepared to support unilaterally the Monroe Doctrine, and he announced to all that military security is not enough—the United States must struggle in many ways more difficult than war. One of them was the new emphasis given to guerrilla training. A part-time counterinsurgency school in Panama was expanded for the training of the Latin military.

Kennedy would placate the key Republican leaders by flattery and contrite acceptance of full responsibility for the disaster. Lunch with Eisenhower at Camp David was followed by private talks with Richard Nixon, Barry Goldwater, Nelson Rockefeller, and even General MacArthur in the Waldorf Towers. Robert Kennedy had been particularly concerned about the Cuban exile invaders whom Castro had made prisoners. Word went out to Cuba from Latin embassies that the United States President would be forced to take drastic new action against Cuba if the prisoners were executed. They were not. Nearly 1,200 Cuban prisoners were ransomed for $53.9 million in

December, 1962, and flown to the United States. The aftermath of the Bay of Pigs found President Kennedy's popularity with the voting public (as measured by George Gallup) climbing to a stunning 83%.

Among key advisers, the foreign policy "liberals" were not the beneficiaries of the reorganization following the disastrous invasion of Cuba at the Bay of Pigs. It was not that the liberals were responsible, but rather that the failure of the abortive invasion was felt, by an anxiety-ridden administration, to be attributed to weak-willed officials who lacked the necessary fortitude to make the operation a success. The Central Intelligence Agency was chiefly responsible for the operation and its directorate was completely replaced between November 29, 1961, and May 16, 1962.

To replace Allen Dulles, a strong-willed, stern-looking Catholic convert multimillionaire from California, John A. McCone, was selected. His fortune had been made in the ship-building business during the war, and in his previous government service under James Forrestal, and as chairman of the Atomic Energy Commission in the Eisenhower administration, he had gained a reputation as an uncompromising supporter of the Dulles doctrine of massive retaliation, of the hardline strategy against the Soviet Union, and of the Air Force's atomic warfare theories. Robert Kennedy, as talent scout for the administration, was also impressed with McCone's reputation as a hard-nosed executive who could get things done. Liberal complaints that McCone, as trustee of California Institute of Technology, had condemned those scientists who had supported Adlai Stevenson's proposal for a nuclear test ban treaty as "taken in" by Soviet propaganda, went unheeded. (Senator Fulbright, however, voted against his confirmation because the Senate Foreign Relations Committee had not been consulted.)

Three Deputy Directors for the CIA were also replaced. Major General Marshall Sylvester Carter, a close aide to General Marshall in World War II, was to direct the detailed operation of the agency, but there was no doubt about the real director when Carter would welcome old military friends to his office with "Welcome to McConey Island." The new director of plans (Richard Bissell lost his claim to the directorship after the Cuban fiasco) was a 48-year-old Williams College graduate, Richard M. Helms, who had served in the OSS during World War II and had elected to stay with its successor, the CIA. Helms' counterpart as the deputy director for intelligence, Ray S. Cline, 44, was also a careerist in intelligence, with a Ph.D. and Phi Beta Kappa from Harvard. There were those who worried that Cline's shop, which presided over the analyses of the four-billion-dollar intelligence community, would be victimized and imprisoned by its own predictions—a rigidity which could prevent new and more realistic interpretations before an unexpected crisis developed. Cline, however, asserted that just the contrary was true with his staff. His real concern was rather with the maintenance of a modicum of continuity of intelligence estimates. Cline impressed upon his assistants the need to get their intelligence estimates to the key decision-makers— an easy task for them during the well-ordered Eisenhower administration, but one of infinite complexity in the free-wheeling Kennedy administration. The CIA would lose its influence in the formulation of policy, Cline recognized, were this not done.

The Joint Chiefs of Staff and their chairman had also failed the President during the Cuban invasion. General Maxwell B. Taylor, who had resigned from the Eisenhower administration in opposition to the "more bang for a buck" military policy, was brought back to the White House as military adviser and, at the first opportunity, as Chairman of the Joint Chiefs. His book, *The Uncertain Trumpet*, criticized the Eisenhower military strategy for its preoccupation with the ultimate weapon because it deprived the country of flexible military alternatives which had to be used for guerrilla and limited war operations. The Kennedy administration had adopted his strategy.

A stricter system was imposed almost surreptitiously, although resistance to "structure" still remained fierce at the White House. Stung by the criticism that he had not consulted the National Security Council in making his decision on the Bay of Pigs invasion, Kennedy noted that at one time or another he had discussed it with all of them except the directors of the USIA and AEC. Yet biweekly meetings of the National Security Council were reestablished during the last week of October, 1961. It was made clear, however, that the President would retain the ultimate decision-making power, and that the meetings would be chiefly informational in character. It was also clear that the President hoped to allay criticism by informed observers (Kennedy shared with Eisenhower the high respect of the general public, but a lower esteem of professional observers regarding the effectiveness of his administration) by submitting to the routine of these regular meetings. As Sorensen wrote, not the least indispensable advantage of the more regular NSC meetings was the "increased public confidence inspired by order and regularity and the increased esprit de corps of the participants." But it was not until October, 1962, (at the time of the Russian missile crisis in Cuba) that the President fully appreciated the contribution of the NSC to a successful decision. Even then, however, it was the "executive committee" of the NSC, for President Kennedy preferred small to large meetings, and these to include the official views he required (e.g., Secretary of State or Defense) or the unofficial judgments he valued (White House staff, brother Robert, Acheson, Berle).

More than anything else, Robert Kennedy declared, the Cuban fiasco brought home the great truth of the presidency—the enormous complexity and difficulty of making the right decisions on any given questions. It brought home to President Kennedy the care which must be taken in listening to and evaluating advice. It changed the pattern of his work. It made him appreciate the truth of Theodore Roosevelt's old adage—"Experts must be kept on tap but not on top." Schlesinger felt that it also made Kennedy more skeptical of the military, diplomatic, and intelligence establishments and more reliant upon the White House staff. Kennedy's history-making speech at American University in June, 1963, (in which he anticipated a detente with the USSR) was drafted exclusively with the White House staff, and not shown to the Departments of State and Defense until the last days. Kennedy knew the restraints they would caution, but was sufficiently courageous to present his own conception of what should be done.

To restore the trustworthy image of a United States genuinely dedicated to economic and social development in Latin America, Kennedy asked Stevenson to make a good-will tour of South America. Stevenson had long held the respect of Latin leaders, and it was felt that he had not been sympathetic to the Cuban invasion project. During his 18-day trip in June, Stevenson reminded the Latins of Kennedy's 10-year plan for hemispheric development, called Alliance for Progress,[11] which the President had discussed with Latin diplomats at the White House on March 13. An earnest example of United States intentions was the $600 million aid appropriations bill passed by Congress a week before Stevenson's departure.

Stevenson's statesmanlike report to the President and to the public reassured the western world, if not the chauvinistic elements of the American people (powerfully represented by southern and midwestern congressmen with long seniority). Stevenson found the Latins shocked over the abortive Cuban invasion, and he warned that hemispheric "fidelism" would be invested with an aura of martyrdom should the United States continue its unilateral action against Cuba. He further warned those demanding collective action against Cuba (including eleven smaller Latin countries which were conservatively led, resistant to reform, and economically dependent upon the United

States) that it would be "meaningful only if it is supported by two or three of the largest Latin countries—Argentina, Brazil, Mexico—regardless of whether 14 votes (the two-thirds majority required for OAS decisions) could be secured." The larger states, representing more than two-thirds of the Latin territory and population, opposed such collective action. Kennedy had failed in his attempt to persuade Canada to join the OAS (during a visit, May 16) and thereby receive the support of that large country in the regional councils. Having thus argued against a continuing preoccupation with the Cuban problem, Stevenson called attention to the Latin poor by noting the chafing gulf between them and the rich, the uneven progress of social reform, and warned that the poor were no longer politically passive.

The rhetorical skills of the Kennedy administration were again mobilized for the August meeting of the Inter-American Conference of Finance Ministers, held in Punta del Este, Uruguay. Douglas Dillon led the United States delegation, and if there was a difference between the resolutions he initiated and supported at this conference and those of the 1960 Bogota conference (under the Eisenhower administration) it was in the degree of specificity of the stated objectives, and in the greater emphasis placed on social reform. Hailed by Kennedy as "one of the most significant meetings of the Western Hemisphere in this century," the conferees agreed upon a 26-page Charter of Punta del Este. The millenial social and economic goals to be accomplished within a decade included a $2\frac{1}{2}\%$ per capita annual increase in production, six years of schooling for all children, literacy for 50 million illiterates, eradication of malaria, large-scale public housing, and potable water. Agricultural and tax reform were both pledged, but the Latin signatories were in no way committed to implement them. Approximately 20% of this $100 billion program would come from abroad—Dillon promised $500 million annually from public funds and estimated a like sum would come from private investors in the United States.

Kennedy might well have asked the same question about his Alliance for Progress that he had on the Cuban invasion episode—"How could everybody involved have thought such a plan would succeed?" For the success of the Alliance plan depended upon the active co-operation of groups who had not yet been consulted (in Europe) or whose enthusiasm for it was notably restrained (the Latin oligarchies who chose to view it as a hand-out program, together with certain key leaders in Congress and private enterprise). Its success likewise depended upon such tough economic considerations as the mobilization of scarce skills to put the program into operation, and the galloping population explosion to which the social reform provisions of the Alliance contributed. Furthermore, the Latin governments engaging in this vast co-operative project were expected to be democratic and liberal—somewhat in the pale image of the United States itself. The problem was one of striking a balance between the liberalism of political democracy, the costly, short-run humanitarianism of social reform, and the pragmatism of economic development (involving the competing philosophies of private enterprise vs. statism). For Latin America it was a problem of balancing short-run order (which too often degenerated into military dictatorship) with long-run progress, which more often than not fell short of the rising expectations of the people. But early apostles of the Alliance program, like Charles Harley, who was instrumental in drafting the charter for the Inter-American Bank, and Ben Stephanski, United States Ambassador to Bolivia, would be satisfied with the minimal objective which they described as "letting the genii out of the bottle." Once the program alerted the Latin masses to their social and economic rights they would not permit their leaders to neglect them again.

One of the least successful of the Alliance goals, during the course of the Kennedy administration, was the implementation of democratic regimes. It was also the most difficult—the traditional and transitional social and economic structures of the respective Latin countries had little in common with their Anglo-Saxon neighbor. The military tradition and the commanding strength of military groups within the respective countries made them likely successors in power when weak civilian regimes faltered. Even liberal military elements were less tolerant of civilian concessions to leftist groups and of the costly techniques by which these regimes maintained themselves in power—including excessive graft and unbalanced, inflation-producing budgets.

United States military and CIA agents, endowed with substantial secret funds, often shared this concern over disorderly regimes, and with or without the approval of the respective United States Ambassadors, often contributed both moral and/or economic support to the military coup d'etats. Thus, five days after Kennedy's inauguration, the left-wing junta in El Salvador was overthrown by a coalition of army, oligarchy, and what in Latin America was widely believed to be the CIA. The military succeeded to power in Argentina and Peru in 1962, and they ousted four additional civilian regimes in 1963. Hardly seven Latin countries could now be said to be relatively free from excessive military influence. While the Kennedy administration had been able to extract from the Peruvian and Argentine military leaders the promise to hold free elections within a year, it was unsuccessful in obtaining similar concessions in 1963.

The waning influence of such liberals as Richard Goodwin and Teodoro Moscoso (United States director of the Alliance program) may also have accounted for the increasing disposition to accept the new military regimes. Career foreign service officers like Edward Martin, who had succeeded to the position of Assistant Secretary of State in 1962, tended to be "realists." They were predisposed to agree with the Pentagon advisers that at least some military regimes were more likely to impose a degree of order and had already demonstrated a serious interest in developmental projects. In accepting, and on occasion fostering the eclipse of civilian regimes, the Kennedy administration could claim that it was not only countering the hemispheric subversion of Castro (and thereby winning important Congressional support), but also was rescuing the social and economic objectives of the Alliance program. Such claims could not always be sustained, and liberal Congressmen, like Senator Wayne Morse, became as a result fundamentally disenchanted with the entire Alliance program. United States military assistance to Latin America had increased from $54 million to $72 million annually, and had significantly increased the domestic power of the military groups. Significantly, many of the coups were engineered by Latin officers, trained in guerrilla tactics by United States officers in the Panama Canal Zone, and armed with United States weapons.

The promise of social reforms had reached the many but had been realized by too few. Latin population, which was growing by seven million annually, divided the Alliance and outran the Progress. Alliance health programs completed between 1961 and 1963, including 1,500 water and sewage systems, food-for-peace programs benefiting nine million children, the 900 hospitals, and 140,000 homes, were calculated to increase the population and thereby burden even more the educational and employment facilities of the area. Effective land-reform programs had been undertaken only by those countries which had undergone a political revolution (Mexico, Venezuela, and Bolivia) while equitable tax burdens were yet to be legislated and enforced.

Economic development fared no better. In most countries the per capita annual growth failed to keep pace with the increasing population, despite the infusion of more than $1 billion annually in public assistance. Almost half of this amount, however, was used to bring short-run relief to debt-ridden economies in the form of export refinancing or balance-of-payment loans. Another quarter of this commitment awaited precise agreement with the respective governments. That these goverment credits had a peripheral effect on a number of Latin economies was indicated by the fact that Colombia had lost two to three times more income from falling coffee prices than it had received from Alliance credits.

To account for the failure of the Alliance economic and social objectives, Latins were disposed to blame the faulty administration of the program by the United States. While it was true that Teodoro Moscoso had not been accorded the autonomy in handling the program that he had desired, it was also true that he did not have the quality nor quantity of effective assistants he needed. Nor were Moscoso's gifts primarily administrative—he was rather a skilled and much respected advocate of the Alliance program.

But whatever the faults of the United States in the administration of the Alliance program, these were small as compared with the administrative weaknesses within the Latin countries, and the failure of the private sector—both foreign and domestic—to make proportionate contributions. But beyond all this was the millennial nature of the 10-year program. A more experienced Kennedy was to appreciate (by December, 1962) that the exaggerated goals he had set for his administration in Latin America were beset with staggering obstacles.

The failure of the private sector to make its proportionate contribution to Latin development prompted a dialogue between representatives of private business and the Kennedy administration. Two widely publicized reports in March and April, 1963 (by Lucius B. Clay and J. Peter Grace) recommended the concentration of governmental assistance on those Latin governments which encouraged the private sector. Expropriation of United States petroleum investments was threatening in Brazil, Argentina, and Peru in 1963, and it was hoped that these regimes might be discouraged thereby from taking such action. But further discouragement to new investment was the hard evidence that Latin enterprise realized 9% profit (as compared to 15% in Europe), for reasons which could be ascribed variously to rampant inflation, feather-bedded payrolls, and weak governments.

No wonder United States investors were withdrawing more money from Latin America than they invested in it, and the Latins themselves were depositing their capital in Swiss accounts. While the Kennedy administration could do little, by itself, to improve measurably the investment climate, it did conclude—with 23 major coffee-producing-and-consuming countries (September, 1962)—a five-year agreement which assigned quotas and provided for the gradual increase of coffee exports.

New sugar legislation was less beneficial to Latin exporters, however. Although 23 countries, seeking larger sugar quotas, paid more than $500,000 to their respective Washington lobbyists, the Kennedy administration successfully steered its own legislation through Congress. In effect, the legislation reduced the premium price paid to Latin producers (dollar earnings from sugar would be cut an estimated one-third) while a compensating sugar tax collected by the United States would be used to supplement foreign assistance.

Withal, the long-range hemispheric development program was obscured by Congressional and public preoccupation with the Communist-oriented Cuban government. Personally stung by the monumental failure of his administration's unilateral Cuban policy, Kennedy now turned to collective diplomatic action to help erase the public memory of the abortive Cuban invasion. Action of some sort against Castro's Cuba was a political imperative during the Congressional election year of 1962.

DeLesseps Morrison, the United States Ambassador to the Organization of American States, was quick to endorse the Colombian proposal that a conference of foreign ministers be held on the Cuban problem. The Caribbean governments had demanded such action against the communist menace in Cuba; they were the most strategically vulnerable and many of their oligarchic regimes were politically unrestrained by domestic pro-Castro factions. The larger and more democratic Latin governments (Argentina, Brazil, Chile, Mexico), representing two-thirds of the Latin population and territory, however, found the Cuban issue a politically divisive one. These governments, together with those of Bolivia, Ecuador, and Uruguay, maintained diplomatic relations with the Castro regime and were unwilling to risk their tenuous domestic stability, even when confronted with the mounting evidence of Cuba's intimate ties with the Soviet bloc and its subversive activities in Latin America. Privately, their diplomats complained that the United States was undermining their political stability to foster the political interests of the administration.

Punta del Este, the fashionable beach resort near Montevideo, Uruguay, was selected as the site for the meeting. The Kennedy administration engaged its prestige in this Eighth Meeting of Consultation of America Foreign Ministers (January 22-31, 1962) as the United States seldom had done in a hemispheric situation. The United States delegation of 20 included those State Department and White House officials together with four congressmen most closely connected with Latin problems. Dean Rusk was successful in persuading the Caribbean countries from leaving the conference when their recommendations for strong action against Cuba were not supported. Two critical votes were required to secure the necessary two-thirds majority (14 votes) to oust Cuba from the OAS. Uruguay provided one of them and the corrupt and tyrannical Duvalier regime of Haiti sold its vote, after being given assurances that its economic and military assistance would not be discontinued.

Kennedy had reason to believe that the conference results might placate a concerned public opinion. Except for Cuba (who voted against them all), there was unanimous support for five of the eight declarations which were approved by the foreign ministers: the principles of communism were declared to be incompatable with the Inter-American system; Cuba was removed from the Inter-American Defense Board; elections were encouraged; the Alliance for Progress was supported. A five-member advisory committee of experts on Communist security was established. With the exception of Argentina, the larger Latin countries abstained from approving the immediate suspension of trade in arms with Cuba.

While reaping the domestic rewards of the conference results, Kennedy was not unmindful of the costs in Latin America. Violent political clashes between the extreme right and left were unleashed in Uruguay, Chile, Ecuador, Brazil, and Argentina, thereby reducing the effectiveness of the moderate forces in these countries. Military groups, antagonistic to their government's position at the Punta del Este meeting, forced the Argentine and Ecuadorian presidents first to sever diplomatic relations with the Castro regime and subsequently to abandon office altogether. Powerful Brazilian business and military interests were alarmed at President Goulart's lack of support for the United States; they would, within two years, get the necessary cues from former Harvard professor, Ambassador Lincoln Gordon, and others, that the United States would recognize a successor government brought about by a coup d'etat.

Kennedy was not sanguine about the prospects for his party in the congressional elections of November, 1962. It was traditional for the party in power to suffer off-year losses in Congress. But this year the Republicans—Capehart, Bush, Goldwater, and Keating among the Senators—had found a campaign issue in Cuba which, they felt, would prove irresistible. The Republican campaign committee had declared that Cuba would be the dominant issue of the campaign, and opinion polls revealed an increasing impatience with American policy toward communist influence in the Caribbean. In Chicago, where he was to give his last campaign speech, in mid-October, Kennedy was greeted with the sign "Less Profile—More Courage."[12]

The Kennedy policy towards the Castro regime had been one of economic harrassment, surveillance, and propaganda — measures hardly strong enough to satisfy the public. When the President confirmed on September 4, 1962, the massive Soviet military aid received by Cuba since the last week of July, the American public regarded it as the boldest challenge yet to the Monroe Doctrine. The 1823 doctrine declared that the United States would consider any attempt by European powers to extend their system to any portion of the Western Hemisphere as dangerous to its peace and safety. President Kennedy, however, characterized the new military strength of Cuba as "defensive" in nature. But he had warned Cuba that the United States would use whatever means might be necessary to prevent aggression against the Panama Canal, the Guantanamo Naval Base, or Cape Canaveral, and to protect itself from offensive missile bases.

There were measures calculated to assuage the public. Raids on Cuban vessels and shores from U.S. territory by Cuban exile groups were countered by mild disapproval and little interference. There were attempts to persuade the western allies to discontinue all commerce with Cuba. But these half measures lacked the vigor with which the Castro regime seemed to be pursuing its objectives. Cuba was the training base in subversion for Latin youths. Six powerful transmitters were broadcasting communist propaganda throughout the continent 22 hours a day. A projected Soviet "fishing base" would surely be used as a Communist submarine port.

In the meantime, the intelligence establishment had increased its air surveillance of Cuba after a short-range ground-to-air missile (SA-2) had been spotted there August 29. However, the weekly, CIA-operated, U-2 flights furnished no visible evidence that offensive weapons had been introduced into the country by October 4. While CIA director McCone had private misgivings about the massive Russian build-up in Cuba, he did not make them official CIA policy nor did he share them with the White House. The agency produced a National Intelligence Estimate (September 19) which stated that it was highly unlikely that the Soviet Union would send offensive missiles to Cuba because of its awareness of the violent reaction such an action would provoke in the United States. State Department Russian experts, Charles E. Bohlen and Llewellyn E. Thompson, both agreed with the estimate, which was attributed primarily to Sherman Kent.

A day after this estimate was made available—September 20—Ray Cline, CIA's deputy director for intelligence, received an eyewitness report of an offensive missile in Cuba. Checking its files, the agency concluded that the missile had arrived in a shipment of Soviet cargo on September 8. But CIA believed it to be a short-range missile, and besides there was no photographic evidence. McCone, at an urgent meeting of the United States Intelligence Board on October 4, noted that there had been no new pictures of the western sector of the island for a month. Responsibility for the U-2 surveillance flights was now transferred to Defense's Strategic Air Command, because the introduction of the SA-2's into Cuba made them too vulnerable. The next mission over western Cuba, however, was delayed until October 14 to make sure that the flight plan avoided unnecessary risk to the pilot and the U-2. The photographs from this mission were to produce some of the tensest moments in the Kennedy administration.

Word of the mobile medium-range ballistic missiles which had been photographed in Cuba October 14 was carried to the President in his bedroom shortly before nine o'clock October 16 by McGeorge Bundy. Kennedy named the officials he wanted to consult—they were later to be called the Executive Committee (Excomm) of the National Security Council. They included Robert Kennedy, Lyndon Johnson, Rusk, McNamara, Gilpatric, Bundy, Maxwell Taylor, CIA's Carter (McCone was brought in when he returned from the West Coast), Sorensen, Dillon, Under Secretary of State George Ball, and Edwin M. Martin. Stevenson joined the group in the afternoon and Dean Acheson and Robert Lovett were called in later in the week.

To give this group time to weigh all alternatives and to maximize the surprise effect of the final decision, secrecy had to be maintained. Press releases from the Department of Defense throughout the week denied any knowledge of the missile bases and the key officials kept their regular appointments (Kennedy left Washington on scheduled campaign trips October 17 and 19) so as not to raise the suspicions of the press. It was also true that the press was preoccupied with the campaign and its normal curiosity about foreign affairs was therefore lessened.

Kennedy came to the first Excomm meeting with two alternatives: destroying the missiles with an air strike, or appealing directly to Khrushchev. The alternatives were weighed during the next four days by the Excomm with a resulting consensus on October 20, favoring the establishment of a blockade and warning the Soviet Union that if the missiles weren't withdrawn, direct military force would be applied. Robert Kennedy strongly influenced this decision—he opposed the air strike, which he feared would outrage the world, and he did not want his brother to go down in history as the American Tojo. Stevenson was reported to have favored direct representations to Khrushchev, or at least to confront Gromyko with the evidence when the latter was scheduled to see the President October 21. Stevenson also encouraged the group to give consideration to the long period of negotiation which would probably follow the removal of the missiles—he felt too much attention was being given to the detailed technical analyses of what kind of surveillance and inspection would be required to ensure the removal of the missiles. Once the missiles were out, Stevenson proposed that the U.S. might trade its promise not to invade Cuba and the withdrawal of its missiles from Turkey (which had already been decided) for the removal of all Soviet troops from Cuba.

Kennedy himself set the style for the committee discussions. He relentlessly demanded more information. He encouraged open discussion of all possible alternatives. He welcomed the reports of heated arguments over the relative merits of a proposed policy during his absence, and proposed to absent himself again if the group felt less constrained without him. Each alternative course of action was tested against the question—What will be the reaction of the Soviet Union? But Kennedy first had to satisfy himself with an answer to the question—Why did the Soviet Union place the missiles in Cuba? He finally was convinced that Khrushchev had gambled heavily to upgrade the relative power of his country. Khrushchev knew, as did Kennedy, the overwhelming superiority of United States power.

There were several considerations which accounted for the final decision. One was the image which members of Excomm thought the world, and in particular Khrushchev, had of the Kennedy administration. This was felt to be "soft," "vascillating," "an easy push-over," "reluctance to act." A second consideration was the image the American public had of its President in an election year, and paradoxically enough, this corresponded with that of Khrushchev. These two considerations alone ruled out direct representations to Khrushchev, and were reflected in Kennedy's remark, "The worst course of all would be to do nothing." If the President's earlier warnings to the Russians and Cubans about offensive weapons were to be meaningful (and Kennedy had begun his review of the crisis by calling for all his earlier speeches on the subject), some action was called for.[13]

Among the other alternatives, the one involving the lowest level of violence was selected. It would be dramatic enough to reflect the administration's grim determination and yet allow the Soviet Union to take the desired action without serious loss of face. A blockade, however illegal, would sound sinister; yet could be enforced without provocation—as indeed it was determined that the first Soviet vessel enroute to Cuba and accosted on the high seas would not be boarded, for fear that its captain had not yet received the message. Nicholas Katzenbach in the Department of Justice obligingly came up with an opinion that such a blockade was legal under international law (an opinion challenged by such international law experts as Quincy Wright), while Leonard Meeker, Deputy Legal Adviser in the Department of State, declared the action would be "more legal" if it were first endorsed by the Council of the Organization of American States. The latter procedure was accepted by the President.

The most acute danger of escalation began with Kennedy's television address to the nation October 22.[14] Key congressional leaders, former presidents, and the heads of allied governments had been briefed earlier in the day. The United States, the President declared, would pursue the following course of action: (1) impose a "strict quarantine" around Cuba to halt the offensive Soviet build-up; (2) increase surveillance of Cuba; (3) meet any nuclear missile attack launched from Cuba with a full retaliatory response upon the Soviet Union; (4) reinforce Guantanamo naval base; (5) call a meeting of the Council of the OAS to endorse the quarantine; (6) call for an emergency meeting of the United Nations. The President also stated that additional military forces had been alerted for any eventuality, and on the following day he issued an executive order which mobilized the reserves. Some of his advisers had wanted Kennedy to place the North Atlantic Treaty forces on maximum missile alert, which meant putting American-controlled nuclear warheads on the NATO-controlled missiles. General Norstad, NATO's Supreme Command, objected successfully on the basis that such preparations were more likely to bring war by way of the "self-fulfilling prophecy."[15]

In an unprecendented demonstration of unanimity, the OAS Council endorsed the blockade on October 23, and it was put into effect at 10 a.m. the next day. A fleet of 25 Soviet ships was nearing Cuba at the time and there was no evidence throughout the day that they would turn back. Erection of the missile sites in Cuba proceeded at full speed. It was not until October 25 that a break came in the chain of events leading to an apparently imminent confrontation. Twelve Soviet vessels turned back in mid-Atlantic. On Friday, October 26, a Soviet-charted freighter was searched without incident and allowed to proceed to Cuba. Khrushchev accepted UN Secretary U Thant's appeal to keep Soviet ships away from the blockade area for the time being, and Kennedy replied to U Thant that the U.S. would try to avoid any direct confrontation at sea in the next few days. While concern among the members of Excomm was high—work on the missile sites continued—Kennedy was not about to rush Khrushchev into an irrevocable decision. It was agreed that the U.S. would slow down the escalation of the crisis to give Khrushchev time to consider his next move. A sign in the briefing room of the State Department stressed this point. It read. "In a Nuclear Age, nations must make war as porcupines make love—carefully." In addition, there had been no demand which the Soviet Premier could not understand, none that he could not carry out, and none calculated to humiliate him unduly.

———————

Shortly after midday Friday, October 26, John Scali,[16] State Department reporter for the ABC, received an urgent call from a ranking official of the Soviet Embassy asking for a meeting at the earliest possible moment. The Russian wondered whether Scali might sound out some highly-placed friend in the State Department about the acceptability of the following compromise: the Soviet Union, under United Nations supervision, would remove the missiles and would promise not to slip them in again. For its part, the United States would publicly promise not to invade Cuba. Should Adlai Stevenson pursue the compromise proposals with the Russian Ambassador Zorin, he would find fertile ground for these ideas. Roger Hilsman and Rusk were immediately informed. Some hints to this effect had been dropped that morning at the U.N. Rusk decided the offer was genuine and instructed Scali to report that the United States was interested in it but that time was of the essence. When Scali gave this message to his Russian contact that evening, the Russian tried to "up the ante" (trade inspection of Cuban bases for inspection of bases in Florida). Scali spoke for himself when he said it was not only unacceptable but would inject a new delay into the situation.

At the White House, a secret message from Khrushchev was then being decoded. It indicated a willingness to negotiate and, together with the unofficial formula proposed to Scali, encouraged Rusk. "John," he said to Scali, "you have served your country well. Remember when you report this—that eyeball to eyeball, they blinked first."

But before the members of Excomm had had time to consider the response to this initiative, there were distressing indications that the conflict was about to escalate. First of all, that Saturday morning, Khrushchev broadcast a demand that U.S. missiles be removed from Turkey as a condition for the removal of Soviet missiles from Cuba. The new mood (did it mean that the hard-liners in the Kremlin, backed by the military, had taken over? Excomm members asked each other) was emphasized by the shooting down of a U-2 over Cuba. Still later an American U-2 was caught over Soviet Siberia. Did the Russians believe the United States was about to attack?

Scali felt he was played for a fool. In cold rage he met his Soviet contact and demanded to know "what kind of a stinking double-cross" was going on. The Soviet diplomat hinted that the latest Khrushchev demand might be due to a delay in communications, but had not Walter Lippmann suggested the Turkey-Cuba trade? Scali exploded upon hearing these excuses. He was then reassured that the original compromise proposal had been sincere and an effort would be made to get a quick response from Moscow.

Scali then briefed the members of Excomm at the White House. On the basis of this information, Robert Kennedy proposed that the Turkey-Cuba swap be ignored, and that a letter to Khrushchev specifically refer to his original compromise and declare that it was generally acceptable. Another channel was then used (it could well have been Stevenson at the UN) to make clear once again the sense of urgency and seriousness felt in Washington. Sunday morning the Kremlin broadcast its acceptance of Kennedy's proposals. Scali was later told that his "explosion" on Saturday had helped Khrushchev make up his mind quickly. Both Kennedy and Rusk were effusive in their thanks to him.

The Kennedy response was distinguished for its flexibility and its self-disciplined restraint in the use of power in the pacing of events, by giving the Soviet Union time to think. And given this time, Khrush-chev chose to define the situation in terms of a cold-war, Russian-American dispute. Khrushchev refused to tie his policy to that of a weaker ally—Cuba. One of the most intriguing aspects of the crisis—the role played by Scali—highlighted another element vital to suc-cessful diplomacy—effective communication between the disputants. That the leading antagonists must believe each other's threats and proposals is vital to any discussion leading to an agreement. The settlement of the missile crisis, furthermore, may well have paved the way for a detente between the two largest world powers.

But Kennedy was highly favored by conditions surrounding the missile crisis which would not accompany every critical situation. He was given a full week to consider the situation—unhampered by the press and the public.[17] He had caught the Russians, as Hubert Humphrey declared, in an embarrassing position, "with their rockets down and their missiles showing." The Russians had underestimated the intelligence and strength of their opponent, and they were pre-pared to withdraw their missiles under circumstances which were not humiliating.

Adlai E. Stevenson had delayed his acceptance of the position of Permanent Representative to the United Nations until the new Sec-retary of State as well as the President had assured him of his deci-sion-making responsibilities. At the State Department he had a friend in Harlan Cleveland, Assistant Secretary for International Organi-zation. Stevenson, unlike his predecessor Lodge, didn't have to worry about a Secretary of State who jealously guarded his own decision-making authority. Arthur Schlesinger, his speech writer during the 1952 and 1956 campaigns, was on the White House staff. With the President, Stevenson carried the public image of a senior statesman who could not be ignored and whose supporters provided the crucial margin of votes, in the big cities, which the Democrats needed. If the number of reporters attending briefings were the yardstick for measuring power and influence, it was noteworthy that Stevenson consistently outdrew Dean Rusk.

Stevenson brought an outstanding group with him to the U.S. Mis-sion to the United Nations. Francis T. Plimpton, 60, a Wall Street lawyer, whose New England exterior covered a brilliant mind and sparkling wit, was appointed Deputy Representative. Charles W. Yost, career foreign service officer, was assigned to the Security Council, and a Chicago acquaintance and businessman, Philip M.

Klutznick, was entrusted with United States representation on the Economic and Social Council. Jonathan B. Bingham, son of the former senator from Connecticut, and Charles P. Noyes as counsellor completed the new staff.

The U.S. Mission under Stevenson, even more than under Lodge, was to become something of a second foreign office—a state of affairs deplored by some experienced diplomats like Robert Murphy. But if this had to be the case, Murphy preferred the system which raised no question as to who was in command on United Nations matters. To maintain this status, however, it became apparent in April, 1961, that Stevenson would have to be kept fully informed on all decisions made in Washington. He had not been told of the CIA cover story on the bombing mission which preceded the Bay of Pigs invasion. Stevenson's forceful and eloquent denial of U.S. involvement was easily exploded by the Cuban foreign minister before the General Assembly's political committee. When Stevenson learned of the story, he was understandably furious—some credit him, together with Rusk, in convincing the President to call off the second bombing mission in view of the damage it would do to the United States image.

Stevenson's role in the Cuban missile crisis better illustrated the effective co-ordination of his personal counsel in the decision-making process and in the execution of the decision at the United Nations. Stevenson later declared, "It was a classic example of UN performance in the manner contemplated by the Charter. The Security Council provided for public discussion of our complaint. It provided a means of focusing public attention on the facts and the threat to peace and security, and it provided through the Secretary General the means of consideration, mediation, and negotiation." On that occasion, Stevenson's own dramatic confrontation with the Soviet representative—challenging him to deny the missile emplacements in Cuba—contributed significantly to this objective.

The successful UN role in the missile crisis stilled some, but not all, of the growing skepticism regarding the central place which Washington had accorded the United Nations. The problem arose from the rapid growth in membership of the so-called Asian-African, "anti-colonial" group. When Stevenson arrived at the United Nations in 1961, there were 99 members—by December, 1963, membership had grown to 113 and about half of them belonged to the Asian-African group. Under these circumstances, the fear grew that the United States and Western point of view would be drowned out. It was not only the radical right that echoed this fear. Respected senators including Fulbright, Henry Jackson, and Mansfield declared early in 1962, that too heavy reliance was being placed on the United Nations (they were thinking of the Congo problem) and raised the question of weighted voting so that American influence might more closely correspond with its financial contribution to the organization (about one-third of the budget). The violent antagonism towards the United Nations that characterized a limited section of the American public was evidenced on October 24, 1963, when Stevenson was spat upon and assaulted by a small group of extremists in Dallas, Texas.

Stevenson arrived at the United Nations at a time when that organization was experiencing a "crisis of confidence." At no time since its origin had it been so plagued with serious problems. At the heart of the matter lay the UN policy in the Congo. The Eisenhower administration had successfully championed the cause of a UN peace-keeping force being sent to that African country in 1960. But the international force had now become involved in an internal struggle whereby the wealthy Katanga area, under the Belgian-oriented Moïse Tshombe, was fighting for its indepedence.

The UN involvement was violently opposed by the Russians, who had hoped to capitalize on their support of popular nationalist leader, Patrice Lumumba. The murder of Lumumba, apparently by government troops, brought an outburst from the Russians and it included a general attack on the United Nations. In preparing his response to Khrushchev on February 15, 1961, Kennedy found the statement prepared by Rusk too tough. The President wanted to answer the Soviet threat of intervention firmly but not harshly, and to keep open the delicate lines of communication between himself and the Russian leader. Accordingly, he got Adlai Stevenson on the phone and for more than an hour they hammered away on the statement. Kennedy would express serious concern for what appeared to be a threat of unilateral intervention and would reaffirm United States support of the United Nations presence in the Congo.

The importance of the Congo to both the United States and Soviet Union was sufficiently little to deter them from flaunting UN authority in the area. During the course of the next two years, UN officials were to bring about a reunified government, thereby eliminating the principal cause of strife in the Congo.

But in the meantime, Khrushchev's dissatisfaction with the decision to send a UN force to the Congo prompted him to put forward his "Troika" plan for reorganizing the United Nations Secretariat.

Leadership within the United Nations in recent years had fallen to the vigorous Secretary General, Dag Hammarskjöld (the Security Council was Soviet-vote bound, and the General Assembly had become unwieldy). To deprive the United Nations of the advantages of this unified executive direction, the Russians were now aggressively advocating the substitution of three Secretary Generals for the present one—one each for the Communist, Neutralist, and Western worlds. All decisions would be made jointly.

The sudden death of Hammarskjöld while on a peace mission in the Congo in September, 1961, seemed to provide the opportunity that the Russians were seeking. The Soviet Union, however, did not carry obstruction to the length that originally seemed probable and lines of agreement emerged after negotiations between Stevenson and his Russian counterpart, V. A. Zorin, in October. A representative from a neutralist country, U Thant of Burma, was selected as Acting Secretary General, and he in turn appointed eight Under Secretaries (one each from the Soviet Union and the United States) as his representatives. By November 30, 1962, the Russians were sufficiently satisfied with U Thant and somewhat reconciled to the emerging Congo situation. They now agreed to designate him for the full term as Secretary General and therewith dropped their demand for the troika reorganization.

Having opposed sending the peace-keeping force to the Congo in the first place, the Russians were not about to help pay for the expensive operation. Two UN forces, one in the Middle East and the other in the Congo, were costing each year $19 million and $120 million respectively. The Soviet Union was joined by France and some of the Arab states in its refusal to make contributions for this purpose. With United States initiative, the question of whether member states were obliged to make these contributions, and whether, failing to do so, their voting privileges would be suspended when they fell two years in arrears, was submitted to the International Court of Justice. An advisory opinion on July 20, 1962, provided an unqualified "yes" to both questions asked.

In the meantime, money had to be found for the UN operations. Again upon the initiative of the United States, the General Assembly voted a $200 million bond issue, half of which would come from private banks in this country. Kennedy subsequently persuaded a reluctant Congress to endorse the plan (with modest reservations). By 1963, the threat of bankruptcy still overhung the United Nations. A special session of the General Assembly in May approved a complicated formula which brought temporary relief, but the decision would yet be made on the suspension of delinquent members.

Apart from the Congo problem, the question of the admission of Communist China provided an annual debate in the General Assembly. Stevenson noted the growing international sentiment favoring admission but he also recognized that were this to be the case, American public confidence in all UN activities would be shaken. As a result of an energetic campaign to keep China out—he won the good will of many African states by agreeing to the admission of Mauritania and Mongolia, and he got a favorable vote ruling the question of admission "important" and thereby requiring a two-thirds majority —Stevenson was able to defeat the proposal 37 in favor and 48 against. The cause of Communist China fared no better in 1962 with a vote of 42 to 56. As the Sino-Soviet conflict became more bitter in 1963, Albania replaced the Soviet Union in introducing the customary resolution on China and this time there was one less favorable vote and one more negative vote than the previous year. Favored by developing events and an intelligent and able team, Stevenson had done well in representing United States interests on cold war issues.

The General Assembly was convened on September 17, 1963, in an atmosphere of hope and optimism. Kennedy recalled the dire forebodings that prevailed in 1961, and in the spirit of the day proposed a joint expedition to the moon. Soviet diplomacy was characterized by broadly conciliatory stance calculated to disarm criticism without necessarily weakening the Soviet position on what Moscow considered fundamental—for example, financing the peace-keeping activities. Outer space was one area in which agreement could be reached, and indeed progress had been made in this field even during the troubled year of 1961.

The General Assembly unanimously agreed on the last day of its 1961 session to convene its Committee on the Peaceful Uses of Outer Space within three months. It resolved, furthermore, that international law applied to outer space, that the area was free for exploration and use but not subject to national appropriation, colonialism in outer space was ruled out, and hereafter the UN would be notified of all space launchings.

The following year brought a long-sought-for agreement with the Soviet Union on a co-ordinated program of scientific research, which in turn would be integrated with that of the UN and would focus on the use of satellites for meteorological observations and the study of the earth's magnetic field. Of a more spectacular nature—and perhaps a second milestone on the long road toward containment of the nuclear threat (the first being the test-ban treaty)—was the unanimous declaration of October 17, 1963, prohibiting nuclear weapons in outer space. The "Spirit of Moscow" again made itself felt with final agreement on the additional principles regarding outer space: non-government activities in space would be subject to government control; there would be consultation in advance of potentially harmful space experiments; radio frequencies for space would be allocated; a formal treaty incorporating all these principles was envisaged.

Progress was noted in the field of atomic energy when the Soviet Union relaxed its opposition to a system of safeguards designed to ensure that peaceful atomic processes were not abused for military purposes. It was agreed on October 1, 1963, that the International Atomic Energy Agency would operate the system. For its part, the United States reversed its ten-year-old policy against signing treaties for the promotion of human rights. Kennedy submitted three UN treaties, dating from 1953, to the Senate for ratification in July, 1963. These dealt with the abolition of slavery, abolition of forced labor, and political rights of women. "The fact that our Constitution already assures us of these rights does not entitle us to stand aloof from documents which project our heritage on an international scale," the President declared.

The revitalization of the United Nations came at a time when regional organizations—whether they be the Warsaw Pact, NATO, OAS, SEATO, or CENTO—were being torn by divided counsel if not immobilized by apathy. The change could be viewed with optimism, for it was the larger organization alone that could provide a bridge between the large and competing power blocs. If Kennedy were disappointed by the failure of the regional organizations, he now knew that there were limits to his country's capacity to change the policies of other governments.

Kennedy was ill prepared for the formidable task of economic policy-making.[18] Once in office, however, the President was faced with the problem of dwindling gold reserves and the threat of Europe's Common Market to American exports. And these, in turn, were related to the domestic economy which was just emerging from a recession. Kennedy would have to rely on able counsel for policies he adopted in the arena of economics. Walter Heller, University of Minnesota, was appointed Chairman of the Council of Economic

Advisers. Douglas Dillon, with whom Kennedy quickly developed a close association, played a vital role in all major economic decisions. And as the White House staff liaison responsibilities with the various executive departments grew, Sorensen assumed major responsibility as co-ordinator for Heller's and Dillon's recommendations, and Sorensen's assistant, Mike Feldman, carried the ball for the Department of Commerce.

As his first year in office was coming to an end, an analysis of the foreign economic situation had been fairly well firmed up and a consensus had developed as to what should be done.[19] The chronic deficit in United States balance of payments had assumed serious proportions. In the years since 1958 the United States had paid out annually from $3.5 billion to $3.9 billion more for its imports, foreign aid, investments, and overseas defense than it took in from its exports of goods and services.

To meet the problem the United States would have to curtail its overseas expenditures, and increase its income from abroad. But it was determined that there would be no sacrifice in the basic military and economic assistance—the savings would come from the elimination of "non-essentials" and by tightening up the efficiency of the operations. Most reluctantly, and only after the Berlin crisis (during the summer of 1961), did Kennedy agree to reimpose Eisenhower's ban on overseas travel by dependents of U.S. military personnel, and he rescinded this ban in April, 1962. Sacrifices from the private sector were demanded; duty-free tourist purchases of $500 were limited to $100 in 1961 and measures were imposed to make U.S. investment in developed countries less attractive.

To increase the income from American exports and services, a "visit U.S.A." program was inaugurated, and a "buy American" policy was reaffirmed for the expenditures involved in American military and economic assistance programs. A vigorous export expansion program was announced. This program stressed the need for competitive prices and was the reason Kennedy risked the ill will of the business community in his strong reaction to the steel price rise in the summer, 1962.

A final effort in brightening the credit side of the U.S. balance of payments was that of discouraging the flight of American short-term capital funds attracted by the higher levels of economic activity and higher interest rates prevailing in Europe. Interest rates were raised to rival those in Europe, and speculators who would capitalize on the devaluation of the American dollar (which they foresaw with the continuing depletion of Treasury gold stocks) were alerted to a $6 billion increase (of which the United States contributed $2 billion in October, 1962) in the stabilizing capital with which the International Montetary Fund was prepared to guarantee the integrity of the dollar.

The entire program was not an unqualified success. While the balance-of-payments deficit fell to $2.5 billion in 1961, and again to $2.2 billion the following year, it was up again in 1963; and in the past five years had aggregated to almost $16 billion. Perhaps the most successful of the various projects was the curtailment of the flight of short-term capital. The executive director of the IMF declared after the program was in operation that the global money markets were gratifyingly calm and singularly free from disturbing rumors—even the stock market crash did not unsettle the capital flow. It was not clear, however, how the program would assist the U.S. and its European partners (who had agreed within the Organization for Economic Co-operation and Development (OECD) in 1961, to raise their combined gross national product by 50% in the decade of the 60's) in the accomplishment of their own developmental goals.

The outflow of gold continued at an even higher rate in 1963, although some economists argued that the complete depletion of the U.S. gold stock would not harm U.S. economy. And higher interest rates limited the availability of developmental capital for an expanding domestic economy. Altogether the program, viewed in the light of Kennedy's 1963 request for an income tax reduction (which promised to increase the budget deficit to over $10 billion), could be interpreted as an international pump-priming project. Kennedy would ask a Yale University audience to join him in entertaining unorthodox economic views (his father, after all, had been listed by *Fortune* in 1957 as the 12th richest man in the United States—between $200-$400 million dollars—and had gained his wealth by ignoring orthodox economic principles). Perhaps (it was argued) an inflationary (and, therefore, debt-ridden) budget was as useful internationally as it had proved domestically. The theory, however, would not be tested much longer; a restless Congress authorized $3.6 billion for foreign aid in 1962 when $4.5 billion had been requested by the administration, and subsequently appropriated only $3 billion in 1963.

Directly related to the balance-of-payments problem was the question of exports. Any increase in U.S. exports would lessen the deficit with which the country had been burdened. But there already existed a strong export surplus—$5.3 billion in 1961 and $4.4 billion in

1962, and heavy tariff bargaining would be required to realize additional surpluses. The four-year-old European Economic Community (Common Market), composed of six increasingly prosperous and self-confident nations, furthermore, presented a threat to existing United States markets. Unless the administration were armed with more flexible authority in negotiating tariff cuts, this country might find itself systematically excluded from an area which purchased almost one-third of its total exports. Under the present extension of the Reciprocal Trade Act, which was due to expire in 1962, an item-by-item and country-by-country approach resulted in long and unnecessarily complicated haggling in Geneva.

There were those who viewed the Common Market and with it the western alliance as the greatest single challenge for the United States in the 60's. Former Secretaries of State Acheson and Christian Herter argued in favor of a virtual membership in the Common Market as a desirable step towards Atlantic unity. In determining its course of action, the Kennedy administration chose not to go that far, but rather to request from Congress the most extensive delegation of tariff-making authority ever granted a President of the United States. Once decided, the question next arose as to timing—when should the request be made? George Ball in the Department of State wanted to wait until 1963, at which time the effects of the Common Market would be known and could be incorporated in the new act. Kennedy, in this instance, chose to take the advice of his congressional assistant, Larry O'Brien, who argued that if the administration waited for a year, it would look as if it feared Congress.

The decision thus made in the fall of 1961 would demand the full resources of the Kennedy administration.[20] Protectionist demands of sickly as well as powerful industries were particularly insistent in congressional, business, and labor circles. The requested legislation would come before Congress in a by-election year when these demands would be accorded greater respect—although O'Brien probably felt that the projected Democratic losses in Congress would make the new 1963 Congress no easier to deal with.

There were three approaches Kennedy and his advisers chose to employ. One was the direct contact with individual congressmen. Another was the skillful use of concessions to powerful domestic interests which would be affected. A third approach, and it appeared to be the main thrust of the campaign, was an unprecedented speechmaking effort involving practically everyone from Kennedy, Rusk, Howard C. Peterson (the President's special assistant on trade matters), to desk officers in the Department of State.

The O'Brien approach was direct, hard-hitting, ad hoc, and pragmatic. His charts and files were complete with detailed personal information on each member of Congress. The appeals and blandishments to each would differ with the varying needs and personalities. Campaign support for a Democrat, a promise not to support the Democratic opposition of a key Republican vote, not to mention all the other inducements and threats which the power of the President could muster, were employed for the occasion. There was but one criticism of O'Brien and his staff—lacking substantive knowledge of the legislation they were backing, and therefore less able to argue the merits of the case, they too often employed favors and patronage. O'Brien could claim that he had cut the negative Southern Democratic vote from 66 out of 99 in the House during New Deal days, to an average of 45 in 1961 and 35 in 1962. But had he debased the currency in the process, and would future congressional victories be more difficult to come by? Kennedy's next and last year in office would indicate this to be the case.

For the self-interested industries which would be affected by the new tariff legislation, Kennedy demonstrated a sensitive regard. Written into the proposed legislation was assistance for companies which were adversely affected, together with benefits for farmers and workers involved. In addition, Kennedy saw to it that the sickly textile industry would receive protective treatment in a special agreement which was cleared through the General Agreement on Tariffs and Trade (GATT) in Geneva during the year. U.S. tariffs on woven carpets and sheet glass were increased in March (only to prompt EEC retaliation on U.S. chemical products), and the President went out of his way to assist the ailing lumber and shoe industries.

Under Secretary of State Ball initiated the speech-making campaign for the tariff legislation on November 1. Kennedy himself addressed the National Association of Manufacturers, December 6 (stressing the balance-of-payments problems) and the AFL-CIO the following day, when he noted that exports help full employment and promised transitional aid for those negatively affected. Former presidents Eisenhower, Truman, and Hoover, together with national leaders from both Republican and Democratic parties publicly endorsed the legislation.

The House passed the bill with a bipartisan majority of 298-125 on June 28. Less than three months later the Senate with a 78-8 vote produced an even more decisive majority. As finally passed, the legislation gave the chief executive authority for five years to enter into trade agreements with foreign countries which would reduce tariffs as much as 50%. Should the countries—or group of countries (e.g., Common Market) and the U.S. collectively account for 80% of the free world's export, duties on that item might even be eliminated. Such industrial items might well be numerous were Great Britain to join the EEC, but very few if Britain did not. There were escape clauses for threatened industries like zinc, lead, and petroleum, and the President was given broad powers of retaliation against unreasonable restrictions of other states—as for example the exclusion of American agricultural products. Kennedy signed the bill October 11, with the remark, "This is the most important piece of legislation, I think, affecting economics since the passage of the Marshall Plan."

The trade extension act was an integral part of the "grand design" which the Kennedy administration had elaborated for Europe. Kennedy had alluded to it in his July 4, 1962, address when he called for "Atlantic partnership." This was envisioned to mean an increasingly unified Western Europe (including Great Britain), increasingly intimate relations between Western Europe and North America, and finally the strengthening of ties between these two areas and the rest of the world. The outline for this broad association existed in NATO on the military side and in the 20-nation OECD on the economic.

The Kennedy plan to reinvigorate the military and economic areas called for the broadening of the Common Market, first by the inclusion of Great Britain and later by the other Western European nonmembers. The trade extension act gave the President authority to deal with them as a group. On the military side, Kennedy secured Prime Minister Macmillan's support for a multilateral nuclear force (MNF) with the warhead to be controlled by the United States.

The Kennedy design conflicted with that of the French President, Charles de Gaulle. His concept of a Europe-centered world, in which state sovereignty would not be replaced by a supranational organism, suggested a "third force" which was not aligned with either the Anglo-American or Soviet systems. Specifically, De Gaulle did not trust the U.S. to come to the aid of Europe in a crisis, thereby exposing vulnerable American cities to the Russians. He had been insulted by the United States offer to supply Polaris missiles without warheads or submarines to carry them. De Gaulle left no doubt where he stood and left Kennedy's Grand Design in ruins with his historic press conference on January 14, 1963. In a vehement repudiation of the Anglo-Saxon powers, he declared that Britain did not belong in Europe and were she admitted on her terms it would be an entering wedge for American influence. The French would not entrust their defense to the United States and rejected MNF out of hand. France would, however, continue to tighten its bonds of co-operation with West Germany. Just two weeks later, January 29, the French foreign minister disbanded the EEC Council of Ministers meeting at Brussels. No formula for the admission of Britain to the Common Market would satisfy the French.

In an effort to restore the waning momentum of Western affairs, Kennedy journeyed to West Germany in June. But it was already clear that prosperity and a diminishing fear of Communist aggression had unravelled the invisible cords that held the Western Alliance together. Dim prospects were held out for the "Kennedy round" of tariff cuts in the spring of 1964. The Western world, like the Communist world, was speaking with many voices—and there were those who welcomed the developing multilateralization of power as contributing to world stability, and to lowering world tensions. In such a world, presidential leadership was likely to be more successful on the home scene than it was abroad—as the Trade Expansion Act so dramatically demonstrated.

President-elect Kennedy had directed his first worried thoughts toward the problem of Southeast Asia[21] in mid-December, 1960. It was then that the Soviet airlift of arms to the Laotian neutralist leader, Prince Souvanna Phouma, had started. Before the first of a chain of major decisions on the area was made in mid-March, the President would be prodding his advisers for answers to questions about Laos. On the day before his inauguration, Eisenhower had apologized to Kennedy for leaving him the Laotian "mess." The very first meeting of the National Security Council, January 21, considered the problem, and twice-daily intelligence briefings brought reports of warfare in that country.

Kennedy was soon to learn that there was indeed no easy solution for this problem. The right-wing military government of Phoumi Nosavan, a creature of the CIA and Pentagon, had received $300 million in aid from the United States. It was Secretary Dulles's intent to create in Laos a military bastion against communism. But Dulles had not reckoned with a Buddhist, peace-loving population and General Phoumi's reluctance to do battle with the left-wing Pathet Lao.[22]

If the Communist Pathet Lao were to be kept from overruning the capital, Vientiane, and the Mekong River Valley separating Laos from Thailand, Eisenhower had told Kennedy, U.S. troops would have to be employed. But Kennedy found the U.S. armed forces unequipped for small fights in Laos, and he worried that direct involvement, including massive air power and the use of tactical nuclear weapons on southern portions of Communist China would produce another Korea, if it did not unleash World War III. It was finally decided on March 9 to prop up the Phoumi government with more and better supplies and improved troop training and deployment. Word of the new decisions failed to encourage Phoumi, and the Communists continued their successful engagements across the country. Kennedy blamed his military planners for advice which so ignored the quality of leadership and the fighting morale of the Laotian soldiers.

When the Russian foreign minister, Andrei Gromyko, failed to respond to Dean Rusk's stern plea for a neutral Laos, Kennedy believed quiet diplomacy would have to be abandoned. His Security Council agreed that a strong public statement would have to be made. In a nationally-televised news conference on March 23, there was the clear implication that the United States was prepared to intervene with military force. Kennedy's words were far more stern than his intentions but they stirred up some desired results. A meeting with British Prime Minister Harold Macmillan at Key West resulted in the reluctant commitment of a Commonwealth force if necessary, and a White House meeting with Gromyko permitted the President to emphasize the seriousness with which he viewed the matter. The mighty U.S. Seventh Fleet moved into the South China Sea, giving further evidence of U.S. determination.

The Soviet Union, wary of a direct confrontation with the United States, agreed in principle to a British-United States proposal for a cease fire, to an eventual coalition government for Laos, and to an immediate fourteen-nation conference. A tenuous truce was concluded May 3 and the conference was convened in Geneva.

Fourteen months of tedious negotiations finally resulted in the Geneva Accords of July 23, 1962. Credit for the agreement, to a very large extent, could be attributed to the Kennedy administration. To bring about a neutralist coalition government, under the leadership of Souvanna Phouma (a cheerful, pipe-smoking, French-educated engineer) it was necessary to secure the consent of the U.S.-financed Phoumi faction, as well as the Communist Pathet Lao. Phoumi refused to relinquish the Defense and Interior Ministries, as the Geneva conferees had decreed, and he had reasonable expectations that if he held out long enough, the Pentagon and CIA would again come to his rescue as they had in 1960. When Phoumi ignored Kennedy's private rebuke, Averell Harriman (who was charged with the negotiations) requested that the CIA agent who was attached to Phoumi and who had saved the Laotian General once before—Jack Hazey—be ordered out of the country early in 1962. Neither this nor the termination of the $3 million monthly assistance from the U.S. in February convinced Phoumi, although it may have prompted him into military action, which for him was as rare as it was unfortunate. For his large-scale reinforcement of an outpost, provocatively close to the Chinese border, brought strong retaliation from the Pathet Lao, sending Phoumi's troops in wild retreat in May. It was now Kennedy's concern that the Pathet Lao would take over the country; he ordered 5,000 U.S. troops to take up positions in Thailand near the Laos border on May 15. The action halted the Communist advance and agreement was reached at last.

The Geneva Accord which Assistant Secretary of State for the Far East Averell Harriman signed was not the kind of iron-clad arrangement Kennedy would have wished, and the free, independent, and neutral Laos which it guaranteed could be assured only by the continued observance of the agreements by all the signatories. The first big test came on October 7, when all foreign troops were to be out of the country. The United States withdrew its 666 military advisers and began the withdrawal of 1,800 marines in Thailand. But Communist North Vietnam failed to comply—on March 30, 1963, its 5,000 troops supporting the Pathet Lao launched a new offensive which brought much of the Plain of Jars under their control.

Kennedy responded as he had before: the Seventh Fleet was ordered off the coast of Vietnam, 3,000 U.S. troops commenced war games in Thailand, and Harriman flew to Moscow to consult Khrushchev. The Russian leader reaffirmed his support of a neutral and independent Laos, but it was also clear that he had lost control of the situation to Peking and Hanoi.

As Kennedy was now viewing the situation, only Vietniane and the Mekong Valley seemed strategically valuable. Were the neutralist government to collapse completely, a modest American force would be moved to Vietniane as a diplomatic test of the Geneva Accords. Failing this, Kennedy was prepared to strike against North Vietnam as evidence that the U.S. would risk a major war to protect a neutral Laos. The President had come to appreciate De Gaulle's estimate of the Laos situation in 1961, that the Russians were competing, rather than co-operating with the Chinese in the area. He could admit privately that U.S. expenditures of nearly half a billion dollars in

Laos for the past decade had done little to improve the security and political stability of the area. Yet the situation that he left for his successor in Laos was far better than he had found it and the formula of neutralism was one which could be applied elsewhere with the co-operation of the Soviet Union. Thus Cambodia's neutrality was recognized in 1962, and both De Gaulle and Khrushchev were to urge Kennedy to adopt a similar policy for Vietnam.

In his concern with the Laotian problem, Kennedy had by no means overlooked the plight of South Vietnam. Walter Rostow, who had headed the Southeast Asia Task Force, had presented a report on Vietnam to the President in February, which provoked the comment, "This is the worst one we've got." South Vietnam was clearly the primary target of Far Eastern communism, and, in contrast to Laos, its government was prepared to fight the Communists.

As with Laos, however, Kennedy had inherited "hard line" CIA, military, and diplomatic advisers who had been responsible for selecting and then keeping in office President Ngo Dinh Diem. More than $1 billion of U.S. military and economic aid had flowed into the country, and optimistic military advisers, including the commander of the Seventh Fleet, Admiral Harry D. Felt, had convinced Kennedy that the Communists could be defeated and U.S. forces withdrawn by 1965 or 1966.

The situation in South Vietnam which the President found so discouraging, was one in which the Diem regime controlled no more than a third of the country, while the Communist Vietcong forces and their North Vietnam allies controlled the rest. Since 1959 the Vietcong operations had greatly expanded—Diem apologists in Washington declared that the Communists did not want Diem to bring off his economic miracle while others claimed that the Communists were capitalizing on the wide-spread disaffection from Diem's repressive regime.

Kennedy's first step was to send Vice-President Johnson to Saigon in May.[23] There Johnson agreed to underwrite the cost of an increase in the Vietnamese army from 150,000 to 170,000 men, to equip and support the entire 68,000-man armed police, and the 70,-000 Self-Defense Corps. The Communists continued to advance, and in October, Kennedy turned to Maxwell Taylor to make "an educated military guess" as to what would be needed to salvage the situation. This time Diem requested American troops, as well as more weapons and training programs. Taylor so recommended, but he also saw an imperative need for reform within the army.

A massive build-up for what later became an undeclared war began in December, 1961.[24] Within a year there were 11,000 U.S.
troops in South Vietnam and by July, 1963, some 16,000. Total
U.S. aid to the country since 1955 had reached $3 billion and was
running $1.5 million daily.

Two special projects within the country were also begun in 1961.
The first was the relocation of 90% of South Vietnam's 15 million
population into 11,000 fortified villages. By the end of 1963, all but
15% of the Vietnamese peasants were living in these villages, but
many of them had been forced into the program against their will
and the forts were easily penetrated by the Communists. A more
dubious CIA program involved the training of primitive mountain
tribesmen as scouts and border guards to cut the Communist supply
routes from North Vietnam. At a cost of $4.5 million, the project
achieved considerable success in sealing the border, but there were
those who worried that the trained tribesmen—10% of whom were
Communists—would turn against their countrymen.

But it was the political leadership the U.S. had chosen to support
in South Vietnam which proved to be the weak link. Diem's popular
support was rapidly disintegrating in 1963; the repressive treatment
of Buddhists by the Roman Catholic leader brought private warnings from Washington. When the warnings were ignored, it was clear
that Kennedy had to make their meaning loud and clear for the Diem
regime. Henry Cabot Lodge, the Republican vice-presidential candidate in 1960, was sent to replace Ambassador Frederick Nolting
who had been closely identified with the regime. It was a politically
deft appointment insofar as it involved a leader of the opposition
party in the administration with a foreign policy which was threatening catastrophe as the election year approached.

Lodge was unable to persuade Diem to remove his brother, Ngo
Dinh Nhu, from his powerful position as Defense Minister. Nhu
had been responsible for many of the most unpopular actions of the
regime. The CIA, therefore, discontinued its $250,000 monthly
subsidy for the Special Forces and recalled its agent, John H. Rich-
ardson, who had been close to the administration. It was clear to
any disaffected military officer in Vietnam that the United States
would support a new regime which would enjoy popular support and
could direct all its energies to winning the war against the Communists.

Kennedy was not unprepared for the military coup in South Vietnam on November 1, 1963. U.S. military officials in the country had
been appraised of its imminence. Yet it was of sufficient importance

that McGeorge Bundy awakened the President at 3 a.m. to report the news. A gathering of Southeast Asia advisers at the White House the next morning at 10 a.m. followed the dispatches as they came in from the American Embassy. There were Dean Rusk, Averell Harriman, Roger Hilsman (now Assistant Secretary of State for the Far East), John McCone, and Maxwell Taylor. Even the hardliners among them recognized that American objectives could be obtained either by Diem changing his policies—which he failed to do— or by his removal. The group, nevertheless, was distressed to learn that Diem and his brother, who, for so long had been the agents of U.S. policy in that area, were both assassinated.

The South Vietnam problem was not of Kennedy's making, nor was it one for which he had found a solution. Together with Cuba it was destined to loom large in an election year. The President may have been misled by his military advisers who promised success against the Communists following a massive military build-up in Vietnam. The build-up, as it developed, contributed to the escalation of the warfare in that area, and even more in the minds of the American public. Increasingly, the administration lost flexibility in selecting alternative policies, as the public in an election year would demand nothing less than absolute victory.

———

Relations with the strongest American adversary, the Soviet Union, were crucial to Kennedy.[25] From the beginning he set himself the task of understanding the country and, in particular, Premier Khrushchev. It was inevitable, perhaps, that he should not have been immediately successful—in spite of his expert Russian advisers like Charles Bohlen and former Ambassador Llewellyn Thompson, his intelligence reports, and his meetings with Russian leaders—since Khrushchev's actions themselves would reflect his estimate of Kennedy.

By midsummer, 1961, Kennedy had concluded that Khrushchev viewed the United States administration as being soft, as well as inexperienced. Perhaps the Americans should not have made the effort not to offend Khrushchev at Vienna in June, Kennedy now thought. Certainly the administrative indecision reflected in the Bay of Pigs episode reinforced this feeling. It was important, therefore, that the Russians be alerted to the firm positions the United States would indeed take on Berlin and elsewhere. To do this Kennedy could not count on verbal threats and statements alone—there would have to be meaningful action as well.

Since their meeting in Vienna, Khrushchev had been pressuring the United States to settle the German question by agreeing to recognize East Germany and according some international status to a united Berlin. The Russian threats and warnings, accompanied by an increase in the Soviet military budget, impressed Kennedy that a firm response was in order. In one of the toughest peacetime speeches ever made, on July 25, the President called for partial mobilization, for $3¼ billion increase in the military budget, and for an extensive fallout-shelter program.

At home the speech did have the effect of ending the prevailing national apathy on civil defense, but as Sorensen subsequently noted, it also unleashed an emotional response which grew to near hysterical proportions. In the future—as in the Cuban missile crisis—Kennedy would remember that the task of arousing public opinion was delicate.

Khrushchev, however, was undeterred and the order was given to erect a wall around West Berlin to prevent the mass flight of 1,500 East Germans daily. An action response from the United States was called for. American troops numbering 1,500 moved across the East German corridor to West Berlin—thereby testing the crucial right of access to the city. Tension mounted during the course of the next week (August 13-20) and in the White House the feeling prevailed that the action could escalate. It did not, and the ceremonial welcome the troops received in West Berlin on August 20 by Vice-President Johnson reassured the Germans.

Ten days later, however, word reached the White House that the Russians would resume nuclear testing in the atmosphere. Having two hours' notice before it was made public, Kennedy conferred with Rusk, Dulles, and Bundy, and decided that the United States would have to resume testing also—although it would at first be underground only. The announcement of the American response would be delayed until the Russians had had an opportunity to reap all the unfavorable world opinion and after a piously-worded message to Khrushchev (signed also by Macmillan) to call off the testing brought no answer. During the course of the next months, Kennedy's military and scientific advisers began pressuring him to resume atmospheric testing—a pressure which became irresistible when a National Security Council report indicating that the Soviet Union was now ahead of the United States leaked to the public in November. The resumption of atmospheric testing in April, 1962, however, prompted a reappraisal of the dangers of atomic fallout by a significant group of scientists who had heretofore underestimated its seriousness.

During 1962, the scene of Russian-American struggle shifted to

Cuba, with consequences which have been noted. In one sense the missile showdown marked the end of the first era in Khrushchev-Kennedy relations. Two years of action and response had given each a measure of the other. There would be no diplomatic successes for either without concessions by both. If Kennedy had found Khrushchev unmoved at Vienna in 1961, when he suggested that both countries soften their position a little to avoid the danger of nuclear war, the Russian Premier was now writing him that if each of them relaxed their grip on the two ends of the rope they were pulling, the knot in the middle would be easier to untie.

New patterns of world power reinforced the emerging accommodation between the United States and the Soviet Union. Western Europe, no longer fearing Soviet aggression, and enjoying a growing prosperity, could indulge its independence from United States leadership. A De Gaulle-led France encouraged the dissolution of the Western Alliance and pointed the way to a third force in Europe, exclusive of Great Britain and the Commonwealth. The very success of post-war American policy—including joint efforts in defense and economic development—had contributed to this result. By January, 1963, even the most ardent proponents of western alliance, like Dean Acheson, began to appreciate that Kennedy's grand design for the West would founder on a De Gaullian rock. International experts who feared the instability and high world tensions resulting from the two power blocs welcomed the change.

For its part, the Communist bloc was also changing. The most formidable ideological change in Soviet communism had come with the replacement of the doctrine of the inevitability of war with that of peaceful coexistence. The new doctrine recognized the catastrophic horror of thermonuclear war, and it was more congenial to a maturing society, secured by the socialist states which flanked it. Paralleling the progressive mitigation of the harshness that had characterized Soviet internal life, the strict control of the European satellites by Moscow gave way to a more elastic system that tolerated greater local autonomy. Kennedy had inherited a policy which discriminated between the differing faces of communism—both Poland and Yugoslavia were indeed receiving United States assistance.

But the most important feature of the emerging Communist world, was the now open cleavage between China and the Soviet Union. On the ideological side, the quarrel concerned the new doctrine of peaceful coexistence which the Chinese leaders refused to accept. By the end of Kennedy's first year in office, the two Communist giants were vying for allies. With exceptions like Albania and Outer Mongolia, the division tended to take the form of a split between European Communism headed by the USSR, and an Asian Communism headed by the Chinese. The split worsened in 1962, when the Soviet Union supported India at the time that country was attacked by China, and again when Khrushchev agreed to withdraw Russian missiles from Cuba, despite the vigorous protest of Mao Tse-tung. While Khrushchev proposed in January, 1963, that there should be a truce to polemics so there might be time for the wounds to heal, the fragile armistice was irreparably broken by the Chinese in June.

Withal, the Soviet Union in recent years had not been enjoying the economic growth rate which was considered desirable. Poor weather and administration accounted for severe agricultural shortages, and the need to meet minimum consumer demands, if indeed to live up to his own boasts, pressed Khrushchev to review allocations in a budget which had given priority to the military.

Kennedy was not unaware of these changing patterns. Sometime during late spring he decided the time was ripe to make a "peace speech." The idea of the speech was kept within the confines of the White House. Bundy and Sorensen worked with Kennedy on the first draft. Subsequently others, including Schlesinger, contributed to later versions. The Departments of State and Defense were not given drafts until the Friday before the Monday, June 10, 1963, when it was given as a commencement address at American University.

The speech, proposing a nuclear test-ban treaty, called for a reexamination of the United States attitude toward (1) peace, (2) the Soviet Union, and (3) the cold war. In considering peace, Kennedy deplored the pessimists who thought war inevitable. He emphasized the common interests which the Soviet Union and his country shared—both hated war, they had never been at war with each other, and both had a mutually deep interest in halting the arms race. The President cautioned nuclear powers in the cold war to avert those confrontations which bring an adversary to a choice of either a humiliating retreat or a nuclear attack. Peaceful competition and the strengthening of the United Nations were specifically endorsed.

The speech was timed to counteract pressures building up on Khrushchev to adopt the tough line of talk and action demanded by the Chinese. Foreign response was enthusiastic. The Russian press printed the text, while others in Western Europe were quick to call it the best Kennedy had yet given. It quickened the hopes of those who were pressing for disarmament and it provided a checkpoint for the inauguration of a new era in relations with the Soviet Union, should this be the case.

A continuous East-West dialogue on disarmament had been reopened in 1962. But the discussions in the 18-nation Disarmament Committee, which included Western, Communist, and Neutral governments, had revealed no areas of mutual agreement. Kennedy had been most disappointed by the virtual collapse of prospects for an early nuclear test-ban treaty. "Personally, I am haunted by the feeling that (without a test ban) by 1970," Kennedy declared, "there may be 10 nuclear powers instead of four and by 1975, 15 or 20. I regard that as the greatest possible danger and hazard." He had been heartened by Khrushchev's belated agreement with his and Macmillan's appeal of April 24 to get the test ban going.

Now there were to be small but encouraging signs before the exploratory test-ban talks would get underway in Moscow. The Soviet Union suddenly stopped jamming Voice of America broadcasts and, following a series of technical discussions, a Soviet delegation agreed to establish a direct Washington-Moscow communications link or "hot-line" on June 20. Later Kennedy agreed with Adenauer to defer action on the proposed nuclear multilateral force which had incurred the particular opposition of Khrushchev.

The spirit of test-ban treaty negotiations as they got under way July 15, with W. Averell Harriman representing the United States, was suggested by Khrushchev's remark, "We begin immediately with the signing." The Russians would not, as the United States feared, tie the treaty to an unacceptable NATO-Warsaw Pact nonaggression treaty. There were no problems of inspection, because underground testing would not be banned. The only obstacle related to the provision for withdrawing from the treaty—3 months' notice for impelling reasons, or immediately if violated by another party. The Russians argued that these provisions were unnecessary because it was a well-recognized rule of international law (*sic*) that a state may withdraw from a treaty whenever it is in its interests to do so. The negotiators initiated the treaty draft July 25. Parties to the treaty (and there were 100 when the treaty went into effect October 10) renounced further nuclear tests in the atmosphere, outer space, and underwater. The U.S. Senate approved it in a rousing vote of 80 to 19. Both France and Communist China rejected it.

"Why did they sign it?" an incredulous Allen Dulles asked Harriman. It was indeed, as Kennedy said, the first concrete result of eighteen years' effort by the United States to impose limits on the nuclear arms race. Harriman suspected there were two important reasons. Khrushchev had shown him a sizeable budget which would be taken from military appropriations and diverted to consumer goods once a general disarmament agreement could be reached. Harriman thought that Khrushchev would make this shift whether or not a disarmament treaty was reached, but the existence of the latter would make it easier for the Russian Premier to convince his military. After all, Harriman noted, the Russians have their Pentagon problem, too. Furthermore, Harriman was reassured by the new direction these measures indicated for the Soviet Union. It is good for the country to become a fat cat, he said, because fat cats don't fight. A second reason for Russian interest in the treaty was the embarrassment it would cause Communist China with the unallied nations of the world.

The "fat cat" allusion assisted Kennedy in taking what was to be his last step in furthering the accommodations with the Soviet Union. The President disclosed, on October 9, that he could find no legal or security obstacle to the sale of several million tons of surplus wheat to the Soviet Union. The failure of Khrushchev's agricultural program had forced him to turn to the West to make up Soviet deficiencies. "While limited in scope," the President declared, "this sale demonstrates United States willingness to relieve food shortages, reduce tensions, and improve relations with all peoples."

The new relations with the Soviet Union did at least indicate a pause in the cold war. They might well lead to a detente. But seventeen years of mutual incrimination and suspicions would not vanish overnight. The public mind would be the last to change and this would require inspired direction. In years to come, historians might well record that Kennedy's decision to pursue more cordial relations with the Soviet Union in the months following the Cuban missile crisis, was the key event of his administration.[26] All humanity would be grateful.

Kennedy's appreciation of the real complexity of decision-making had cured him of his over-optimism. This was accomplished soon enough in the shaking of his faith in his advisers (the Bay of Pigs), in his persuasive powers with Adenauer and De Gaulle (he talked with both), and in his power of moderation in his Vienna talks with Khrushchev. He learned that arousing public opinion is a delicate task. Kennedy's speeches continued to be bolder than his action, but this was explained in terms of educating the public rather than alerting foreign governments of forthcoming action. A chastened and experienced administration emerged in Washington; two years had provided the youthful intellectuals with the time to learn; the world situation was viewed more realistically and was recognized to be more diverse; and the interrelation of a need for more careful balance of foreign and domestic policies, and such mutually exclusive foreign policies as peace through military strategy vs. peace through international law was finally perceived. But there were only months remaining before the nation would be deprived of its leader by a tragic assassination.

Perhaps more than his post-war predecessors, President Kennedy aspired to greatness. For this, he would have to establish the image of strong leadership. His choice of key associates and of organizational procedures reflected the ambitious goal he had set for his administration. Essentially it would be a government of action-oriented decisions which could be attributed directly to the President.[27] Because committees inhibited such decisions, they were dispensed with whenever possible. Even the National Security Council was not convened with any regularity until the disastrous Bay of Pigs episode, and thereafter the NSC meetings were held more in deference to the public regard for orderly governmental processes than in the utilization of the committee process itself. Kennedy's administrative, like his social style, was relaxed, informal, and personal. With the new telephone system he had installed in the White House, Kennedy had quick and direct access to a wide range of consultants including Assistant Secretaries and even desk officers in the Department of State. But no one quite knew when the next call or the next assignment from the President would come.

The personnel of his administration, accordingly, was more important to Kennedy than organization. While few of his key advisers on foreign policy were experienced men, many of them were distinguished for their intellectual attainments. None possessed, nor did they seek a wide scope of decision-making authority such as Secretary of State Dulles had enjoyed in the Eisenhower administration. Their relative influence changed with time and with the situation, but Kennedy himself was always ready and willing to assume responsibility for the final decision. He wanted this decision, however, to result from a full and frank consideration of all relevant facts and rational alternatives. This, of course, was not the case with the Bay of Pigs decision. Kennedy's respect for Douglas Dillon in Treasury was always great—yet he could thank Dillon for no one spectacular success of his administration. History might well record that two men, more than all others, shaped Kennedy's final decision on any given foreign policy matter. These two were his brother, Robert, and his counsel, Theodore Sorensen. Both men had dedicated their lives to the President's career, and John Kennedy fully appreciated that fact. Of the two, Robert Kennedy was the more aggressive and independent, while Sorensen was more self-effacing and retiring. Were John F. Kennedy himself to write the history of his administration, he might well record that Sorensen was the greatest influence of all.

Of the general conditioning forces which influenced Kennedy's foreign policy, by far the strongest was domestic public opinion. The narrow margin by which he had been elected restrained presidential action in the foreign field, although his speeches suggested bold and forthright policies.[28] Schlesinger had declared that the speeches were intended to "educate" the public during Kennedy's first term in office and that as a result the President would be re-elected with a much larger majority and with stronger Congressional support. Major accomplishments in the foreign as well as the domestic fields would wait until the second term, while the first was being used to attract wide public support. It is true that the American system, more than that of any other major world power, enhances the role of public opinion in the formulation of foreign policy. But Kennedy, perhaps more than any of his post-war predecessors, was sensitive to the public mood.

Because effective foreign policies depend upon the responses of other governments, specialists have noted that conditions abroad should account for at least 60% of any particular decision. The fact that the American system does not easily permit the President to so divorce himself from public opinion—except in times of crisis— has always limited United States effectiveness in the game of power politics. In times of public indifference, public support for a particular policy must be mobilized before action can be taken. Alternatively, when the public is deeply involved in foreign problems, the President finds it exceedingly difficult to maintain certain policies of restraint which would be calculated to maximize the country's position in a given situation.

Kennedy had inherited an over-alerted public. This inhibited the influence of those foreign conditions about which policy was being formed, in at least two ways. In the first place, the interpretation of foreign conditions may well have been unduly influenced by the public stereotype. The failure to recognize the growing cleavage between the Soviet Union and Communist China would be a case in point. Secondly, the public mood propelled the administration into adopting activist policies (which also suited the temperament of Robert Kennedy), whatever restraints may have been counseled by conditions abroad. After the Bay of Pigs, Kennedy found it virtually impossible to maintain his non-intervention policy towards Cuba for this reason. His policy of acting through the Organization of American States in ousting Cuba from the regional organization was calculated to appease the American public, but at the expense of political stability in the Latin countries. Were conditions abroad more important to Kennedy, he would not easily have undertaken a policy of projecting an American neurosis upon the unstable Latin countries, when it was precisely those Latin countries and groups which most strongly endorsed the Alliance for Progress objectives that were most bitterly opposed to the Cuban policy.

Since World War II, the United States had given far less attention to its traditional policies in the formulation of its foreign decisions than it had in earlier periods of history. The rapidly-changing world had long since removed such policies as the "open door" from active consideration, and a developing "one world" in a technological sense had tended to internationalize hitherto regional policies. There still remained one such policy—the Monroe Doctrine—to which the public and Congress remained firmly wedded. Kennedy was able to capitalize politically on the defense of this doctrine in the Cuban missile crisis.

A final factor conditioning foreign policy—international law—carried as little influence in the Kennedy administration as it had in the preceding post-war administrations. The Bay of Pigs operation dramatized this lack of respect for the law in the Kennedy administration, however, in an unprecedented manner. The decision to submit the proposed embargo, during the Cuban missile crisis, to the Organization of American States for approval, merely made the embargo "more legal" (or less illegal) in the opinion of the Deputy Legal Adviser, Leonard Meeker. But international law could not be expected to thrive under cold war conditions. If Kennedy would eventually be credited with helping bring about a detente in East-West relations, he would have contributed more to enhancing the future role of international law in the decision-making process than any previous post-war president.

President Kennedy, by virtue of his own youth and vigor, of his desire to be a strong and therefore action-oriented chief executive, and of his aspiration to win the approval of an activist public in the

1964 elections, had equipped himself with a staff and organization that was prepared to make crisis decisions in a bipolar world. But the international situation, as the President had come to recognize it by June, 1963, was diverse and complex; a multipolar system had replaced the rigid bipolar structure. Nationalism and prosperity had reduced Europe's interest in accepting American leadership. Russia and China were vying for control of the Communist world, and countries within each camp were enjoying more autonomy than ever before. Withal, modest progress was noted in Soviet-American relations. Regional co-operation in a more secure world was, at the same time, less necessary and less possible. The tough problems involved in assisting the underdeveloped countries were not about to be resolved by any instant formula.

The President, as a result, was all dressed up with no place to go. He chose not to damage his international image by sending United States forces to overthrow Castro during the Bay of Pigs affair. He refused to take a "hard line" decision in Europe which might jeopardize his developing relations with the Soviet Union. State and Pentagon specialists in NATO problems might complain that the President was a Hamlet when it came to strengthening the Western Alliance— that he vacillated in these decision-making tasks. But the President may have had a more accurate measure of De Gaulle's determination to the contrary, and the European specialists themselves may have been prisoners of their own dated image of that area. Even where he had been most successful—in the Cuban missile crisis— the President was not creating an international situation, but rather responding to it in a commendably limited way. The time had passed, if indeed it had ever existed, for the world to be remade in the American image in seven days.

In such a world the kind of leadership the United States had been exercising since the war was no longer possible. And by September, 1963, while on a political speech-making tour of the middle and far western states, Kennedy sensed that another kind of leadership was popular with the people. It was a leadership related to the test-ban agreement and a leadership by example. By extending civil rights, by reducing poverty, by increasing employment, and by improving educational facilities at home, the United States would best convince other nations that its system of government and its policies were worthy of emulation. But Kennedy did not live to see this done.

V.   Lyndon B. Johnson: Extensions of Power

Line Engraving from Continuous Tone Negative. Photograph by United Press International

President Johnson offers to Negotiate on Vietnam

★ V ★

Lyndon B. Johnson: EXTENSIONS

OF POWER

by EDGAR E. ROBINSON

WHEN VICE-PRESIDENT JOHNSON succeeded to the presidency on November 22, 1963, he inherited the foreign policies of his predecessor. These he acknowledged as his own and pledged there would be no alteration, especially in attempting to ease cold war tension. He took the place that rulers of other states had for three years identified with President John F. Kennedy. In the eyes of the world President Lyndon B. Johnson now embodied the incalculable power of the United States in international relations. World rulers and their representatives wondered what this power would prove to be as they came to Washington to attend the funeral ceremonies for John Kennedy.

Although he arrived in the presidency suddenly and unexpectedly, Lyndon Johnson was not without preparation. He had observed the four occupants of that office at close hand in Washington for a quarter of a century (1937-1963). He had been a member of both House and Senate. He had served as minority leader of his party in the Senate and then as majority leader until his elevation to the vice-presidency in January, 1961.

Nothing like this preparation had existed in the experience of previous successors to the presidential office. Truman and Kennedy came from the Senate, as did Harding, but it was Johnson who had been the most conspicuous of all presidents as leader in American politics prior to occupation of the presidency. Furthermore, he had

199

visited thirty-four countries during his term as vice-president and had just returned on November 9 from a trip to the Benelux countries in Europe, reporting that the United States hoped to expand trade with the Common Market nations.

Johnson inherited the staff in the various executive departments of the government that had implemented the Kennedy policies. Cabinet officers, particularly Secretary of State Dean Rusk and Secretary of Defense Robert S. McNamara, were given prominent parts in Johnson's presidential announcements henceforth. Both operated effectively in supporting the new President's program. The President directed that they should co-ordinate their schedules to prevent, whenever possible, their absence from Washington at the same time.

As was to be expected, the approach of the President to the Congress was direct, personal, and urgent. He attained immediate success in this relationship. Early in this period of change from Kennedy to Johnson, James Reston could comment:

> "Presidents Truman and Kennedy were also Capitol Hill men, and their first presidential speeches to the Congress were also a kind of homecoming. But Johnson is something different in the congressional mind. He ran the place . . . Also Johnson talks in their own idiom . . . Congress does not adore intellectuals, and vice versa. But Johnson is not an intellectual, not a man of thought but of action, not a critic but a champion of the Congress. . . . The whole psychology of the capital city . . . has been changed by the cruel events of the last week. The program is the same. President Johnson did not alter a single line . . . but the mind and spirit of the city have been transformed. This is the terrible paradox and tragedy of the moment, for President Kennedy apparently had to die to create a sympathetic atmosphere for his program."

Lyndon Johnson (with the exception of Woodrow Wilson, who left the South at an early age) was the first Southerner to occupy the presidency since Andrew Johnson left that office in 1869. This fact at once promised a new relationship between the executive office and the southern members of Congress. Lyndon Johnson's southern friends in Congress were naturally opposed to items in his presidential program (for example, the civil rights bill sponsored by predecessor Kennedy), but would have to account for their opposition to leadership that had suddenly veered southward from New England.

Johnson's point of view as to the operation of the government under his guidance is seen in his immediate actions, pronouncements, and program. Press relations were gradually changed until the country accepted the informality and the generality of the press conferences. Sometimes they were conducted while the President walked about in the rose garden at the White House; sometimes, at his ranch in Texas. Like Kennedy, who, however, knew professionally the International News Service, Johnson made his talks with newsmen part of his policy-making. Talking to a reporter to push a view *is* policy-making; talking in friendly but at-arms-length fashion is using the press as an independent agent of government by public opinion. The results of course depend on what the reporter knows, or is capable of knowing and understanding; and, dangerously, on the bias of the newsman. The personal element is all-controlling in this situation. It was said that "Johnson took the press too seriously," however informally he treated it.

The new President's early action was an indication of what the remaining year of the interrupted Kennedy administration would reveal. Prior to the Kennedy funeral, on November 24, Johnson had met with Ambassador to South Vietnam Henry Cabot Lodge, who had just returned from a "strategy" meeting in Honolulu on November 20. This was an attempt, conducted by Defense Secretary McNamara, to assess the situation in South Vietnam.[1] After meeting with Lodge, Secretary of State Rusk, McNamara, McGeorge Bundy, State Undersecretary George W. Ball, and CIA Director John A. McCone, President Johnson pledged continuance of United States policy toward South Vietnam as established by President Kennedy.[2]

On November 25, Johnson held his first personal conference with chiefs of state and foreign representatives at a reception by the State Department following the funeral ceremonies for President Kennedy. In the full view of the nation, by television, the new President's reserved greeting of each guest was indicative of his realization of his grim confrontation with world leaders. After the State Department's reception, Johnson met with many of the 220 representatives of 92 countries. Among these, he talked with President Charles de Gaulle of France, Prime Minister Lester B. Pearson of Canada, Prime Minister Hayato Ikeda of Japan, Emperor Haile Selassie of Ethiopia, British Prime Minister Sir Alec Douglas-Home, President Diosdado Macapagal of the Philippines, Premier Ismet Inönü of Turkey, Soviet First Deputy Premier Anastas I. Mikoyan, and Chancellor Ludwig Erhard and President Heinrich Lubke of West Germany.

To West Berlin's Mayor, Willy Brandt, the President gave assurance that United States policy toward Berlin would not be changed. The White House announced on December first that Chancellor Erhard and Douglas-Home would return to Washington soon for "working visits" with the President. Johnson's first public foreign policy statement was, however, addressed to 100 representatives of Latin American countries who met at the White House and heard the President reaffirm the Alliance for Progress.

On November 27, in an address to a joint session of the Congress, President Johnson pledged himself to maintain the military strength of the nation against enemies to peace. Expressing his determination "to continue the forward thrust of America" begun by President Kennedy, in his "dreams" of conquering space, of partnership across both the Atlantic and Pacific, and of a world-wide Peace Corps, Johnson pledged that the nation would "keep its commitments from South Vietnam to West Berlin" and would not cease in the search for peace. He added that the United States "must recognize the obligation to match national strength with national restraint" and "must be ready to defend the national interest and to negotiate the common interest." Johnson rededicated the nation to support of the United Nations and to honorable and determined execution of its commitments to our allies with strength second to none. He announced his intention of preserving the stability of the dollar, of expanding our foreign trade, and of reinforcing our programs of mutual assistance and co-operation in Asia and Africa as well as the Alliance for Progress in this hemisphere.

In addressing the Congress, Johnson had urged passage of the foreign aid bill. He was not altogether successful in obtaining the sum he had asked for and warned that, with the reduction contemplated, the United States would provide for Latin America "less than the Soviet Union is putting ino Cuba alone." And, said the President, "this was no way to combat communism in Latin America." In signing the $3.6 billion authorization bill on December 16, which was to be cut down in subsequent appropriation bills of the Congress, the President said the reductions reflected a growing tendency "to hamstring executive flexibility with rigid legislative provisions wholly inappropriate and potentially dangerous in a world of rapid change." In his fiscal 1965 total budget for $97.9 billion, which the President called a budget of economy and progress, there was a reduction of $1.1 billion in defense expenditure including military foreign aid, although defense still claimed $51.2 billion, or more than half the total budget.

On December 17, Johnson called on the United Nations to help instigate a "peaceful revolution" that would wipe out hunger, poverty, and disease all over the world. In reaffirming support of the United Nations, he warned that this effort to transform the world was feasible only if United Nations member states succeeded in preserving peace. And "Peace," said the President, "is a journey of a thousand miles and it must be taken one step at a time."

United States Ambassador to the United Nations, Adlai E. Stevenson, had announced before the General Assembly's Political Committee on December 2, that President Johnson had reaffirmed the proposal of President Kennedy of a joint United States-Soviet expedition to the moon. Only 10% of United States space spending was directly involved in the lunar program as a part of outer space exploration. Stevenson's renewal of the lunar proposal was made during the opening of debate on the report of the UN Committee for the Peaceful Uses of Outer Space. Progress was signalized by Soviet-U.S. agreement on a compromise draft declaration of legal principles governing activities in the exploration and use of outer space, to be carried on "for the benefit and in the interests of all mankind," inasmuch as "outer space and celestial bodies are not subject to national appropriation by claim of sovereignty, by means of use or occupation."

On December 17, President Johnson criticized as "undesirable in principle," congressional prohibition on the use of any money in the current space appropriation for a joint-manned lunar landing with the USSR or any other nation. Of course, the President admitted, no such expedition would take place in the current fiscal year! Later, in his State of the Union Address to Congress in January, he reaffirmed U.S. "pre-eminence in the peaceful exploration of outer space, focusing on an expedition to the moon in this decade, in cooperation with other powers, if possible, alone if necessary."

The new President found his most urgent problem in areas beyond our borders in the alliance of the fifteen NATO countries. The influential Ninth Annual Conference of Parliamentarians from the NATO countries held in Paris November 4-8, had urged that steps be taken to establish a system of joint control over the nuclear forces currently at the service of the Atlantic Alliance. Changes were recommended to insure "all member nations . . . real participation" in the full nuclear strategy of the alliance. Pending such progress, the conference said it was "logical" to leave in the hands of the President of the United States the authority to fire nuclear weapons; but in the event of a Soviet attack on Europe, western forces should be committed to the use of tactical nuclear weapons at the beginning, and nuclear arsenals of NATO in Europe should be increased to insure fulfillment of this commitment. Although the conference was an advisory body whose recommendations were not binding on the North Atlantic Council (the alliance's supreme policy-making body), the great interest of the European community in the problem of their defense was destined to bring forth an incisive declaration from President Johnson, which was thought to be a distinct departure from the Eisenhower and Kennedy policies. The question of the American President's exclusive control of the nuclear weapons of the United States was destined to play an important part in the forthcoming presidential campaign.

In his State of the Union Address to the Congress on January 8, 1964, President Johnson said that he would maintain the defense of the United States and use it "as John Kennedy used it in the Cuban crisis and for the test-ban treaty," to demonstrate both the futility of nuclear war and the possibilities for lasting peace. On the other hand, Johnson declared he would "take new steps" toward control and eventual abolition of arms. He advocated an increase of the "use of our food as an instrument of peace."

Favoring expansion of world trade, the President promised continued progress toward balancing U.S. international accounts, preserving at the same time the gold value of the dollar. Hoping the nation would become better neighbors with the "free states of America," Johnson said we should achieve a "more rigorous" administration of foreign aid and increase the role of the private investor abroad. Strengthening the Atlantic and Pacific partnerships, the President would not only strengthen the United Nations, but develop with our allies new means of bridging the gap between East and West, "facing dangers boldly wherever danger exists, but being equally bold in our search for new agreements which can enlarge the hopes of all while violating the interests of none."

The day following the expression of these hopes for mankind, a serious crisis took place in Panama. Both Secretary Rusk and U.S. Army Secretary Cyrus R. Vance charged that Castro Communist agents were involved in instigating the riots, which were accompanied by Panamanian severance of diplomatic relations with the United States. Later investigations seemed to indicate that the United States, for fifty years in treaty agreement with Panama upon operation of the Canal, had not been an aggressor and that the riots had not been instigated by Castroites. In any case, the incident was seized upon by the Communist governments in China and the Soviet Union and energetically exploited. It was not until April 3, 1964, that agreement was reached between the United States and Panama to postpone negotiations on a new treaty until after presidential elections had been held in both countries. But in all of his references to this conflict, the President reiterated his willingness to consider carefully all of the elements involved.

Johnson, in office, but not yet elected as President, had assumed a "holding" position in foreign affairs. Having inherited the problems of all three administrations that preceded his in the period following the end of World War II, he was definitely not belligerent. He stressed the idea of joint action everywhere; stressed our purposes and methods as "friendly"; exhibited strength and persuasion where there was conflict. Of this there was considerable throughout the period in which he was carrying out the Kennedy policies, that is, until November 3, 1964. After that, he was to have his own "mandate," if elected to presidential office.

Political explosions and violent overthrow of government in several Latin American countries; the crisis in Panama; the quarrel with Cuba over water supply to the U.S. base at Guantanamo; the flaunting of the U.S. quarantine of Cuba by a number of our European allies—all of these situations were met by the President and his aides with full awareness and calmness, at least on the surface of relations.

Throughout the eleven months prior to the election of 1964, the constant irritant was the problem of United States policy in Southeast Asia. This was not only an indication of a long period of frustration (in which Johnson had had a part, when as vice-president he visited South Vietnam) but also a reminder of the larger struggle against communism in all of Southeast Asia, as well as in East Germany and the Caribbean.

In addition to crises in various parts of the Caribbean, Latin America, and Southeast Asia, the year 1964 witnessed a great game of international chess, in which the President of the United States was called upon for defensive strategy. The United States advanced certain declarations of principle that might be called rules of the game.

The first was Dean Rusk's statement of United States policy calling for a fundamental revision of United Nations machinery for keeping the peace. This statement was developed in an address prepared for the second Dag Hammarskjöld Memorial Lecture, which

Rusk was to deliver at Columbia University. Detained by the Panamanian crisis, Rusk had his address read by Assistant State Secretary Harlan Cleveland. Representing a major turn in United States policy toward the United Nations, the statement was based on the fact that the growing number of smaller UN member states had altered the internal structure of the UN in such a way that a two-thirds majority made up primarily of smaller states could recommend a course of action for which other nations would bear the primary responsibility and financial burden.

It was the United States position that an answer to this problem must be found that would assure financial support for UN peace-keeping operations on a fair basis. The UN membership had grown from 51 in 1945 to 113 members and a prospect of 125-150 nations ultimately. Stated Rusk: "The rapid and radical expansion of the General Assembly may require some adaptation of procedures if the United Nations is to remain relevant to the real world and therefore effective in that world." The continued refusal of the Soviet Union to pay toward the peace-keeping function of the UN organization created a mounting conflict between the United States and the Communist nations, but there was every indication in the closing months of the year that President Johnson intended to call for enforcement of the original provisions of the UN charter, depriving unpaid member states of votes in the General Assembly.

On January 18, 1964, Johnson replied to a Soviet bid for a treaty outlawing territorial aggression among nations. Accepting the central idea of the Russian proposal, he appended to it suggestions for strengthening and broadening the proposed treaty to cover forms of aggression utilized by the Soviet bloc since World War II. Rejecting the time-worn Russian proposals (1) that Taiwan come under Chinese Communist control, (2) that West Germany be subjected to special restrictions, and (3) that the United States liquidate its system of foreign military bases, Johnson called on Khrushchev to stop "emphasizing our well-known disagreements" and to join the United States in supporting, at the impending Geneva Disarmament Conference, proposals to reduce the risk of nuclear war. But the President also made counter-proposals to Khrushchev's position which Johnson said were "even broader and stronger" than Khrushchev's.

The Soviet Union, however, had another old chestnut on hand. A disarmament proposal by the Soviets, at the eighteen-nation Conference at Geneva on January 28, called on the nations of the world to join in destroying all their bomber aircraft, even in advance of an agreement on general disarmament. This was acceptable "in principle" to the United States, said William C. Foster, Director of the United States Arms Control and Disarmament Agency. The Russian memorandum called again for liquidation of all foreign military bases, the signing of an East-West non-aggression pact, inspection to guard against surprise attack in Cenral Europe, and machinery to halt the spread of nuclear weapons.

The Russians warned that the United States-sponsored plan for a multilateral Western nuclear force would have to be "swept away" before there could be any agreement curbing the spread of atomic weapons. Tsarapkin, USSR chief negotiator, made clear that the USSR believed a Western nuclear force would put such weapons in the hands of nations not currently possessing them, even if none of these nations legally had authority to launch them. If West German "militarists" were able to obtain nuclear weapons directly through the proposed Western force, "they would not hesitate to unleash atomic war." Perhaps the knowledge of such pressures on United States policy was to influence the President in his insistence throughout the forthcoming presidential campaign that he and he alone controlled the nuclear power of the Western world.

The French recognition of Communist China had brought forth a statement from the State Department on January 27, 1964, that the French action was "an unfortunate step, particularly at a time when the Chinese Communists are actively promoting aggression and subversion in Southeast Asia and elsewhere." The statement added that the United States would "stand firm by its commitments" to Nationalist China, South Vietnam, and other countries that might be affected by the French move. This was Johnson's view, and Rusk added in Tokyo on January 28, "We will never abandon the twelve million people on Taiwan to Communist tyranny. We support the Nationalist government of Taiwan, recognize it as the legitimate spokesman of the Chinese people, and will continue to support it in the United Nations and elsewhere."

As Rusk interpreted the relationship of the Chinese problem to American obligations in Southeast Asia, it became clear that, as he said, "When China has a government which is prepared to renounce force, to make peace, and to honor international responsibilities, it will find us responsive." But, said he, Communist China had proved itself to have "nothing but contempt for the most elementary condition of peace," and was not worthy of recognition.

Meanwhile, Defense Secretary McNamara had told the House

Armed Services Committee that the United States still hoped to withdraw most of its 15,000 troops from South Vietnam before the end of 1965. The major military assistance program to South Vietnam had begun in 1961 and, said McNamara, it was "reasonable to expect that after four years of such training, we should be able gradually to withdraw certain of our . . . personnel."

Against this background of circumstances, on February 21, President Johnson warned North Vietnam of the possible consequences of its support of the Vietcong in South Vietnam. The USSR, on February 25, in turn warned the United States that it would not stand idly by if the United States extended the Vietnamese war to North Vietnam.

President Charles de Gaulle discussed his proposal for the neutralization of Southeast Asia at a news conference on January 31, at which he revealed the implications of France's recognition of Communist China. This was part of a French plan for a settlement of the continuing crisis in Southeast Asia, particularly in Vietnam, Laos, and Cambodia, states formerly comprising French Indochina. The French plan of negotiation on Southeast Asian neutrality with Communist China was rejected by President Johnson, as he announced during his first formal press conference. Johnson said that as long as the present Communist-inspired unrest of South Vietnam persisted, "I think that the present course we are conducting is the only answer." And, said Johnson, "I think that the operations should be stepped up there." He added, "I do not agree with General De Gaulle's proposal. I do not think that it would be in the interests of freedom to share his view."

With characteristic optimism, the President on February first cited "progress" in seven areas of world tension: Panama, Cyprus, South Vietnam, the Indonesian-Malaysian dispute, East Africa, East Germany, and even in the French recognition of Red China. "It is not our desire or in our interest," said the President, "to create an air of emergency about these or other events." He added, "Our work proceeds both day and night, quietly, steadily, I believe confidently, and I think the American people have every reason to share in that confidence." In his opening remarks on this occasion, Johnson noted the reduction in defense costs, because of a "business-like basis" and "real unification" achieved in the Defense Department and "improvements" in the missile arsenal.

From the contemplation of Russian fear of the possibility of atomic weapons in West Germany, and French efforts to bring about "neutrality" in a Southeast Asia threatened by Communist China, President Johnson had to turn to the more immediate problem in the Caribbean. Whereas the President later remarked of the suspension of water supply by Cuba to the Guantanamo base early in February, that "We have dealt with the latest challenge and provocation from Havana without sending the marines to turn on a water faucet," he could scarcely conceal a vigorous disagreement over Britain's sale of 450 buses and other industrial goods to Castro.

On February 21, at a Charter Day anniversary celebration at the University of California in Los Angeles, President Johnson reviewed his foreign relations problem, saying: "In South Vietnam, the struggle is first and foremost a contest to be won by the government and the people of that country for themselves." He hinted that "outside enemies" who direct and support the terror and violence "would do well to be reminded and to remember that this type of aggression is a deeply dangerous game." He remarked that "Larger than the troubles I have stated is the spreading civil war among the Communists." He added that larger still is the steadily growing strength of the worldwide community of freedom. "The power of the free community has never been greater. . . . We are interested in the deeds of our adversaries and not in their creeds. Let them offer deeds of peace and our response will be swift."

President Johnson took occasion, on February 27, to state that it was essential to maintain a defense "shield so powerful that no aggressor dares try its strength." Such strength permitted exploration of the policy that "reducing the danger of nuclear holocaust" was also in the national interest of the Soviet Union. "But patiently following this thread of mutual interest we may yet find a way out of the tortuous maze of hostility and conflict," said the President hopefully.

Two days later, Johnson sought to dispel reports that the United States was planning an extension of the war in South Vietnam. As he said, "The plans (for possible widening of the conflict) that have been discussed in the papers are not plans that have come to my attention or that I have approved." He added that he felt that "no good purpose . . . would be served by speculating on the military strategy of the forces of the South Vietnamese." Secretary of State Rusk had asserted, shortly before this, that an extension of the war to North Vietnam would not "suddenly transform or eliminate the problem in South Vietnam." He testified before the Senate Foreign Relations Committee on March 3, 1964.

The American people had an opportunity to hear from the President concerning his policies when an interview taped on March 14 was broadcast by the three national television networks the following day. "I may not be a great President," he said, "but as long as I am here, I am going to try to be a good President and do my dedicated level best to see this system preserved, because when the final chips are down, it is not going to be the number of people we have . . . or the number of resources that win; the thing that is going to make us win is our system of government."

Equally vigorous was his explanation of United States foreign policy as he saw it, for he said, ". . . as long as we are living in a world with 120 nations . . . we have got to realize that we have got 120 foreign policies. . . . We have discouraging incidents from time to time and . . . sometimes the role of the peacemaker is not a very happy one . . . for that reason, we have to do things that we don't want to do sometimes and are rather irritating—and sometimes we are abused because we do them, and sometimes we are misunderstood. But if the final result is good, then our action is justified." The President appealed for understanding of new nations "coming in without experience." For, said he, "They have their pride, and although it looks a little odd for the prime minister of a new country (Zanzibar) to come in with a pistol in his hand and arrest an American chargé d'affaires, we have to be prepared . . . and try to provide leadership that will keep us from getting in deeper water."

Speaking of the Guantanamo crisis in retrospect, the President reported that "reflection, evaluation and study" had preceded action there. He spoke out against those "who feel that all we need to do is mash a button and determine everybody's foreign policy." And he added: "I have no doubt but what for centuries to come . . . we will be a leading force in molding opinion of the world, and I think the better they know us the more they will like us."

A little later in the month, one of the President's most influential critics, Chairman J. William Fulbright of the Senate Foreign Relations Committee, rebuked the administration for its policies in the Caribbean. He called the Treaty of 1903 with Panama "in certain respects obsolete," and urged redressing Panama's grievances against the treaty as it now stands. Fulbright said he considered there were three possibilities in the Cuban situation: (1) invasion, which he admitted was not feasible; (2) political and economic boycott, which he thought had been a failure; and (3) acceptance of the Communist regime as a disagreeable reality, because Castro's regime was not on the verge of collapse and "not an insuperable obstacle to the accomplishment of our objectives in the hemisphere."

President Johnson, at an unscheduled press conference at his Texas ranch, said these views did not represent the policy of the administration. On April 16, the President announced that the United States and Colombia had agreed to study the feasibility of a sea-level canal through Colombia that would link the Atlantic and Pacific oceans. Johnson said he hoped "to make similar arrangements" with other countries later.

After a White House meeting in late March, 1964, with the President and Secretary of State Rusk, increased military and economic aid to combat the Viet Cong and to oppose neutralization proposals was reaffirmed by Defense Secretary Robert S. McNamara. This was "to help the South Vietnamese (1) to save their country for themselves; (2) to help prevent the strategic danger which would exist if Communism absorbed Southeast Asia's people and resources; and (3) to prove that the free world can cope with Communist 'wars of liberation' as we have coped with aggression at other levels." McNamara admitted that the situation in South Vietnam had worsened. In Vietnam the United States "was not dealing with factional disputes or the remnants of a colonial struggle against the French but rather with a major test case of communism's new strategy . . . of sabotage, terrorism, and assassination on an unprecedented scale." The prime aggressor in South Vietnam was North Vietnam, "encouraged on its aggressive course by Communist China." Neutralization would be "an interim device" permitting Communist consolidation and "eventual take-over."[3]

A month later at an April 21st news conference, President Johnson said, "I think that our position there (South Vietnam) is something like what it was ten years ago, in 1954, when then-President Eisenhower wrote the then-President of South Vietnam and said, 'We want to help you to help yourselves'. . . . that is what we are trying to do there now."

The President made this statement on South Vietnam in reply to mounting criticism in Congress. Within two weeks the White House announced, on May 3, that Senator Fulbright would fly to London, Athens, and Ankara to express United States concern over the civil war on Cyprus and to seek for President Johnson Greek and Turkish views on the island's future. This mission included no proposals for settling the dispute, but was for the purpose of inquiring into a situation in another part of the world which was as difficult and baffling as that in South Vietnam.

Meanwhile, the condition in Southeast Asia prompted the President in a special message to Congress on May 18, to urge an additional $70,000,000 in economic aid (defense support) and $55,000,-000 in military assistance to combat the Viet Cong. This was to be added to the $500,000,000 appropriation for South Vietnam in the 1965 fiscal year starting July 1. The request was prompted by two major changes in Vietnam since the President had presented the 1965 budget to Congress in January: (1) the Viet Cong guerrillas, under orders from the Communist North, had intensified terrorist actions against the peaceful people of South Vietnam; and (2) a new government under Prime Minister Khanh had come to power.

The crisis was so severe that Ambassador to the United Nations Adlai Stevenson, was called from Europe and on May 21 he made a major policy address to the United Nations Security Council. He expressed the opposition of the United States to the convening of a new meeting of the fourteen-power Geneva conference, to consider the deteriorating political and miltary situation in the former Indo-chinese states. Cambodia charged repeated acts of aggression by the United States-South Vietnam forces against Cambodia. "The United States cannot stand by while Southeast Asia is overrun by armed aggressors," declared Stevenson. "As long as the peoples of that area are determined to preserve their own independence and ask for our help in preserving it we will extend it."

On May 22, Secretary Rusk warned that "if the Communists persist in their course of aggression in South Vietnam the war there could be expanded." He warned further that United States withdrawal from Southeast Asia "would mean not only grievous losses to the free world in Southeast Asia but a drastic loss of confidence in the will and capacity of the free world." Withdrawal by the United States would also bring us "much closer to a major conflagration," said Rusk.

President Johnson, in an address at the 102nd Commencement of the University of Michigan, proposed the "Great Society"[4] for the American people, and on the following day made an equally bold proposal on behalf of American interests in Europe. This suggestion was made, appropriately, at the dedication of the George C. Marshall Research Library at the Virginia Military Institute in Lexington, Virginia, on May 23. The President declared that identity of interest and the prospects of progress for Eastern Europe lay in a wider relationship with the West. He reasserted "our unalterable commitment to the defense of Europe and to the reunification of Germany" and "our belief that wise and skillful development of relationships with the nations of Eastern Europe can speed the day when Germany will be reunited." For, said the President, "there is no longer a single Iron Curtain. There are many. Each differs in strength and thickness, in the light that can pass through it and the hopes that can prosper behind it."

In talks with Chancellor Ludwig Erhard of West Germany on June 12, President Johnson restated the determination of the United States to carry out fully its commitments with respect to Berlin, "including the maintenance of free access to West Berlin and the continued freedom viability of the city." Chancellor Erhard on his part assured the President of his certainty that the Germans would not aspire to national control of nuclear weapons.

Meanwhile, in a message to Turkish Premier Ismet Inönü on June 4, President Johnson warned Turkey not to invade Cyprus on behalf of the Turkish elements involved in the civil war with Greeks. Reportedly, this warning averted the invasion with a huge Turkish fleet. The President's appeal, according to a White House statement, was "only the latest step in a continuing pattern of consultation among allies." The United States realized that the role of peacekeeping and mediation on Cyprus belonged to the United Nations. However, acting on United States government orders, General Lemnitzer of NATO flew from Paris to Ankara. The Turkish government abandoned plans to land forces in Cyprus "for the time being." United States Undersecretary Ball visited Athens June 10 and Ankara June 11 to voice American concern over a possible Greek-Turkish conflict resulting from their dispute over Cyprus. The White House announced June 13 and 15 that Premier Inönü and Greek Premier Georgios Papandreou had accepted President Johnson's invitation to come to Washington and discuss Cyprus with him separately.

On June 1 and 2, 1964, a conference meeting in Honolulu had been called by President Johnson to map United States strategy to cope with the deepening crisis in Southeast Asia, because of strong Communist pressures in Laos as well as in South Vietnam. Secretaries Rusk and McNamara met with Ambassador to South Vietnam Henry Cabot Lodge, Chairman of the Joint Chiefs of Staff General Maxwell D. Taylor, C.I.A. Director John A. McCone, State Undersecretary George W. Ball, and McGeorge Bundy, special assistant to the President on international security affairs.

Prior to the meeting in Honolulu, Secretary Rusk had met with various foreign diplomats on his way through India and Thailand, and William P. Bundy had met with British Foreign Secretary Butler. After the meeting in Honolulu, the President announced that as a result, United States policy was predicated on four basic themes: (1) America keeps her word; (2) the issue is Southeast Asia as a whole; (3) "our purpose is peace"; and (4) "this is not just a jungle war but a struggle for freedom on every front of human activity." Johnson referred to President Eisenhower's commitment in 1954 and said: "Like a number of other nations we are bound by solemn commitments to help defend this area against Communist encroachment." However, there were no plans to extend the war in South Vietnam to North Vietnam.

The President took occasion on June 3, in an address before the 78th graduating class of the United States Coast Guard Academy in New London, Connecticut, to assert that the military strength of the United States was greater than that of "any adversary or combination of adversaries" and greater than "the combined might of all the nations in the history of the world." And, said the President, "We, as well as our adversaries, must stand in awe before the power our craft has created and our wisdom must labor to control." He continued, "This staggering strength" was built "not to destroy but to save, not to put an end to civilization but rather to try to put an end to conflict." He added, "Those who would answer every problem with nuclear weapons display not bravery but bravado, not wisdom but a wanton disregard for the survival of the world and the future of the race."

On June 22, the State Department issued a general statement on United States policy in Southeast Asia. This was to the effect that "there can be little doubt in the minds of the Communist leaders... that we are prepared to help the Vietnamese repel Communist aggression. Our support to Thailand is equally clear. We have provided military assistance to Thailand for some time, while also helping the Thai government build its military capacity. Our position with respect to Laos is equally clear." The United States determination to prevent a Communist take-over of Southeast Asia was reported to have been conveyed to President De Gaulle of France, to the leaders of Communist China, and to Soviet Premier Khrushchev. This was an unlimited commitment to bar Communist aggression in Southeast Asia, similar to the United States position on defending West

Berlin, and it was clear that the United States was strengthening its position in Southeast Asia.

Ambassador Lodge, resigning on June 23 because, as he said, he believed it his duty to help Governor William W. Scranton of Pennsylvania win his contest for the Republican presidential nomination, was replaced by presidential appointment of General Maxwell D. Taylor. In a policy statement, President Johnson said the United States "seeks no wider war," but "is determined to use its strength to help those who are defending themselves against terror and aggression." "We are a people of peace," said the President, "but not of weakness or timidity."

South Vietnamese Premier Nguyen Khanh called, on July 19, for a full-scale military attack on Communist North Vietnam. This was opposed by the United States, although in the realm of contingency planning, and the attitude of General Taylor and of the State Department was non-commital. Five days later President De Gaulle proposed that the United States, the USSR, Communist China, and France agree to leave the Indochinese peninsula and guarantee its neutrality and future political independence. President Johnson rejected this proposal in a prepared statement read at his press conference on July 24. He urged instead the honoring of existing agreements. "We do not believe in conferences called to ratify terror," said he, "so our policy is unchanged."

On August 2 and 4, North Vietnam PT-boats attacked two U.S. destroyers in international waters in the Gulf of Tonkin. President Johnson had issued a warning of retaliation after the first incident, but when the attack was repeated, United States Navy planes bombarded North Vietnam coastal bases, patrol boats, and installations along 100 miles of coastline. In a period of five hours 64 sorties destroyed or damaged 25 PT-boats (about half of the North Vietnam navy), and an oil storage depot representing 10% of the oil storage facilities of North Vietnam. Two planes failed to return, one lost at sea and the other believed shot down by North Vietnam anti-aircraft. Reinforcements were sent in the event of more trouble and Secretary McNamara said, "We are prepared for any action they may take." The President announced that the retaliation was ordered by him and that "repeated actions of violence against the armed forces of the United States must be met not only with alert defense but with positive reply." And, said the President, "this new act of aggression aimed directly at our own forces, again brings home to all of us in the United States the importance of the struggle for peace and security in Southeast Asia." The President added that, although the "full commitment" of the United States to South Vietnam "will be redoubled by this outrage . . . our response for the present will be limited and fitting." He instructed Secretary Rusk to make it totally clear to friends and to adversaries and, indeed, to all, that "We still seek no wider war." President Johnson had preliminary discussions of the handling of this incident not only with congressional leaders of both political parties, but also with Republican presidential candidate Barry Goldwater.

The following day, in a speech at Syracuse University, the President asserted, "There is no threat to any peaceful power from the United States . . . but there can be no peace by aggression, and no immunity from reply. And that is what is meant by the actions we took yesterday." The President reminded his audience that "The challenge that we face in Southeast Asia is the same challenge we have faced with courage and that we have met with strength in Greece and Turkey, in Berlin and Korea, and in Lebanon and Cuba." And, said the President, "Let no friend needlessly fear, and no foe vainly hope that this is a nation divided in this election year."

U.S. Ambassador to the United Nations Stevenson requested an emergency meeting of the Security Council on August 5, to explain the position of the United States on the Gulf of Tonkin incident. The United States Congress not only supported the President's action, but approved a resolution giving Johnson its advance approval for any actions he might have to take in the Southeast Asia crisis. The House vote was 416-0; the Senate vote, 88-2. The resolution also approved in advance "all necessary steps, including the use of armed force," that the President might take to help any nation that requested aid "in defense of its freedom," under the Southeast Asia Collective Defense Treaty. Ex-Ambassador Lodge was designated by the President to tour capitals in Europe to explain to allied leaders the situation in South Vietnam and the position of the United States.

Reaction to the Gulf of Tonkin incident in Europe varied from the British response that the United States had "every right on the high seas to defend themselves against their assailants," to that of the French government, which urged acceptance of President De Gaulle's repeated calls for an international conference on Southeast Asia. The majority of the NATO members supported the United States position after it was explained.

Meanwhile, civil unrest and political revolution were reaching a point in South Vietnam at which the newly formed regime (August 16) of President Nguyen Khanh resigned after anti-government riots by students and Buddhists, who charged the new constitution gave Khanh dictatorial powers. The ruling military council announced it had voted to rescind the constitution and to elect a new leader. A single leader was replaced on August 27 by a triumvirate of three generals, including General Khanh. Khanh resumed his position as premier on September 3, after two weeks of violent anti-government demonstrations. The interim government of Khanh faced widespread political unrest as it sought to consolidate its position and pave the way for a civilian regime that Khanh said would take power on October 27.

During this chaotic period in South Vietnam, Lyndon B. Johnson was accorded the Democratic presidential nomination on August 26—as had been expected—and on September 7 opened his campaign for election with an address in Detroit. On September 16, he spoke in Seattle of the horror of nuclear war and the necessity for sole control by the President of the United States over the use of its nuclear weapons. He pledged that he would "never let slip engines of destruction because of a reckless and rash miscalculation about our adversaries." He said his administration had "taken every step man can devise to insure that neither a madman nor a mal-function could trigger nuclear war."[5]

However, in response to the sending of Communist Chinese planes to North Vietnam after the United States retaliatory raid, President Johnson was reported to have ordered "hot pursuit" of Communist planes by American fighters across the Communist Chinese border if necessary, in event of attack upon United States warships off the Vietnam coast.

Significantly, speaking to the Research Institute of Japan in Tokyo on September 29, Assistant Secretary of State (for Far Eastern Affairs) William P. Bundy said the United States did not "aim at overthrowing . . . North Vietnam but rather at inducing it to call off the war it directs and supports in South Vietnam." Measures the United States was considering to halt contacts between North Vietnam and the Viet Cong in South Vietnam included the bombing of Communist staging bases in Laos and in North and South Vietnam.

On the eve of the most bewildering crisis of the year in mid-October, President Johnson delivered a warning speech on the state of the world at an Alfred E. Smith Memorial dinner in New York City. "Almost all general statements about the world are wrong" he said. "They are not necessarily false. They are just inadequate. It is true, for example, that communism is a danger. But Russia is a different kind of danger from Yugoslavia. A small Communist party in Africa is different from the government of Red China. These different dangers require different policies." This speech had been prepared, presumably, before the President could have known what was to follow, but it contained the admonition, "Beware of those who come to you with simple explanations. Theirs is the path of peril and not of peace."

Within two days it was known all over the world that the Communist Chinese had detonated their first nuclear device (as Secretary Rusk had foretold two weeks earlier), and Nikita S. Khrushchev had been deposed and Aleksei N. Kosygin made chairman of the USSR Council of Ministers (equivalent to premier). The sudden removal of Khrushchev was apparently as surprising to everyone as it was disconcerting, and President Johnson announced that he would report to the people on a nationwide television and radio broadcast, October 18, on the implications of these two disquieting events, as well as the change to a Labour government in Britain.

The President said that Khrushchev, from the Soviet point of view, had been "guilty of dangerous adventure" in foreign affairs, apparently, for example, in the Berlin and Cuban crises. But, said the President, Khrushchev had "learned from his mistakes" and "in the last two years his government had shown itself aware of the need for sanity in the nuclear age."

As examples of Russian actions favoring peace, Johnson mentioned Soviet agreements on the Nuclear Test-Ban Treaty, the Moscow-Washington "hot-line" of communication as a precaution against accidental nuclear attack, and the fact that outer space had been kept free of nuclear weapons.

"We do not think it was these actions that led to Khrushchev's removal," said the President. But he added that the upheaval meant at least four things: (1) "The men in the Kremlin remain dedicated Communists. A time of trouble among Communists requires steady vigilance among free men—and most of all among Americans. . . . (2) There will be turmoil in the Communist world . . . . (3) This great change will not stop the forces in Eastern Europe that are working for greater independence. Those forces will continue to have our sympathy . . . . (4) Our own course must continue to prove that we . . . are ready to get on with the work of peace."

The President was able to give assurance that the Soviet government had officially informed him through Soviet Ambassador Anatole Dobrynin that "it plans no change in basic foreign policy." Johnson said he made it clear to the Soviet government that "We intend to bury no one, and we do not intend to be buried." The President's reaction to the Communist Chinese nuclear explosion that it was "no surprise" to the United States government, was coupled with the reassurance that the "military significance of the atomic blast" was not to be over-estimated, as China was still a long way "from having a stockpile of reliable weapons with effective delivery systems."

Two days after its nuclear explosion, the Chinese government released the text of a note in which Premier Chou En-lai called on the world leaders to join in a summit meeting to ban nuclear weapons. The State Department made it clear that President Johnson had received the note and that the Chinese proposal, in view of the existing Test-Ban Treaty, was unacceptable to the United States.

Thus, in part, appeared the world that Johnson faced after his election, by a record plurality of 15,951,244 votes, on November 3. His 43 million votes constituted 61% of the total votes cast. This the President called "a mandate for unity." As he said, "We have voted as many, but tonight we must face the world as one." Foreign reaction to the election was overwhelmingly favorable.

It was not yet certain, however, that the President, now *elected* to that office, would proceed to handle his foreign relationships in the manner of the preceding eleven months. Perhaps hints of his forthcoming policies could be discerned from his campaign statements. In view of the incautious and at times conflicting statements on foreign affairs of Johnson's opponent, Senator Barry Goldwater of Arizona, in the presidential contest, what Lyndon Johnson said of the subject was naturally of absorbing interest not only to the American people but to the peoples of the world.

The President could stand before the American people as a successful arbiter of disputes between two European nations—Greece and Turkey over Cyprus; as formulator of a strong policy in South Vietnam; as successful solicitor of foreign aid funds from Congress; and as recipient from Congress, after a long battle, of a bill to provide Civil Rights throughout the nation, thus furnishing an example to other nations struggling against the evils of inhumanity to man.

The presidential campaign had forced the President to discuss his problems in foreign relations and, in general, he proclaimed his purpose to follow the course of conciliation and negotiation maintained on the whole during the administrations of Truman and Eisenhower as well as of Kennedy.[6]

In the period 1945-1963, the United States played a leading role in the world. The decisions of President Roosevelt had laid the basis for such leadership in foreign affairs. There was violent opposition to it throughout Roosevelt's term of office (1933-1945) and there were remnants of this opposition in every year of his successors— Truman, Eisenhower, Kennedy, and Johnson. But nothing seriously weakened this trend as the vast army of participants in the formulation of American foreign policy carried on the process of education through conference, publication, and campaign. There was thus created a political atmosphere and a code of political conduct that made attempts to return to the isolation of earlier years attractive to only a minority of the population.

Not expected to initiate changes in the basic bi-partisan foreign policy of his predecessors since World War II, President Johnson had outlined his objectives during the presidential campaign as follows: (1) the strengthening of the Atlantic alliance, admittedly in growing need of repair; (2) increased resistance to Communist threats throughout the world; and (3) improvement of the world economic situation to combat the kind of unrest that breeds violence.

Johnson's announcement, on September 16 in Seattle, that use by NATO of tactical nuclear weapons would be only by his own decision, had led to the central issue of the campaign. Despite reasonable and pertinent questions raised by presidential candidate Goldwater and former Vice-President Nixon as to Johnson's conception of his personal control of all nuclear striking force, the President did not clarify his often-reiterated statement that he and he alone "controlled" the nuclear power of the United States. This position appeared to be at variance with the policy toward the Atlantic alliance advocated by Presidents Eisenhower and Kennedy.

The Republican nominee for president had asserted that an aggressive role was needed, that our policies in Vietnam and in Berlin, particularly in matters of nuclear control, were weak and ineffective. Such declarations gave notice to both allies and foes that an alternative to existing policies would follow the elevation of a Republican president to power and American leadership of the international situation would be changed—in control, method, and intention. As far as could be shown in the heat of a political campaign, this was the choice presented to the people.[7]

The growing crisis in Vietnam was illuminated for all the world by Communist China's nuclear blast. The reaction of the Soviet Union could be seen in the simultaneous deposing of Khrushchev and the elevation of a regime presumably more reconciled than he to the ideological pressures of the Red Chinese. Recalling French President Charles de Gaulle's anti-American campaign in Latin America and the inroads of Chinese Communist influence there earlier in the year, Johnson might reasonably have betrayed a critical anxiety to the American people. In addressing them in the midst of the presidential campaign in mid-October, he had assured them that he would hold the line of American security and peace in the world.

The preceding May, the President had decided to increase American aid to halt communism in its destruction of self-government in South Vietnam and had indicated that the United States would, if necessary, stand alone and firm in its commitment. Throughout the remaining days of the campaign no further light was shed by the President upon the enormity of the confrontation with an altered Communist line-up and its possible effect upon our commitment in South Vietnam.

The campaign of 1964 had emphasized the power of the President in international affairs. Although he does not have the constitutional power to declare war—the power reserved to Congress—yet without the Congress the President can do much by action and by word that may lead to war and call for expenditure of funds, supplies, and men in defense of his policies. These policies, although decided by him, are formulated by his staff, his advisers and his appointees, and never until after the event may such policies be given a chance of approval or disapproval by the American people. For example, it was Johnson as Commander-in-Chief who ordered attack on the Communist PT bases in North Vietnam when Communist PT-boats fired on U.S. destroyers in the Gulf of Tonkin. The permissive congressional resolution came later.

The concentration of attention, in choice of a President, upon his "power" as Commander-in-Chief, means in essence that in a democratic society the people (the soldiers) are voting who should be "captain" of the company. This runs counter to the idea that has grown, with the advent of weapons other than fists, to a belief in the expert—the man who knows more from study and experience than his fellows.

Johnson's capacity in foreign relations had been attested by his ability to maintain the policies of the preceding two decades with emphasis upon (1) security—through defense; and (2) peace—through negotiation. Both policies had been criticized by the opposition in the presidential campaign.

Furthermore, the opposition claimed that President Johnson had failed: (1) to remove the Cuban menace; (2) to settle the war in South Vietnam; (3) to remove the Berlin Wall. In each case, the people involved were not the President's constituents. They were foreigners and they were not on American soil. In short, the President's power in foreign relations does not include removing problems beyond our borders. Johnson had no solution for any one of these problems. He could not take possession of Cuba, nor take ownership of South Vietnam, nor choose to govern Germany!

The final judgment upon the President's conduct of foreign relations must be seen, however, not only in the response of his own people but as well in the attitude toward the United States of other peoples, and in particular the attitude of leaders of great powers. Since the time of the Kennedy funeral in Washington, when Johnson met the visiting statesmen of other nations, he had appeared as the symbol of American strength and intention. In every action in the ensuing eleven months this prestige grew and became more tangible. Disagreements as to policies—within and without his political party—had to be based on presidential leadership. Never more evident was it that the President of the United States enjoyed the power of a prime minister and the prestige of a monarch.

The first year of Johnson's presidency must be judged also in terms of the unusual political situation. Johnson had been Kennedy's choice as vice-presidential candidate in 1960. Johnson in turn—in taking over the office on November 22, 1963—pledged himself to the Kennedy program. And he carried out this pledge in his activities in every area of presidential power. It might have been quite otherwise, and the results of a lukewarm assertion of interest in the Kennedy program would have resulted in a divided Congress, a hopelessly split Democratic party, and a bewildered constituency. It should be added that Johnson was aided in his task by a tremendous wave of support for the Kennedy program because of his own assertions. Even after the political conventions of July and August had made their decisions, the essential lines of Kennedy-Johnson leadership had remained intact.

Viewed in the light of this background, all of the President's decisions—and in particular his pronouncements—had built a conception of leadership of the country in foreign as well as domestic affairs that was distinct and clear.[8]

The outcome of the presidential campaign seemed to indicate to foreigner as well as American that presidential power would be exercised during the new term of office in a manner similar to Johnson's action, utterance, and explanation during his previous eleven months in office. This meant emphatically: (1) use of the United Nations; (2) dependence on the State Department and Department of Defense; and (3) close co-operation with Senate and House majorities. A government was assured within constitutional provisions of long standing.

Yet what this President had done and had said during his first year in office had changed the whole aspect of the duty of the President in directing the attention of the electorate to his objectives in foreign policy. President Johnson approached a question or an issue as something very familiar and dealt with it in language that the voter could easily understand. So it seemed. He was not truculent; he was not vague; and he spoke as if foreign relations could be dealt with as could domestic relations. However hackneyed, "come, let us reason together" is persuasive. We may not have given sufficient importance to the role of the preacher in presidential conduct of international affairs. To exhort and to raise hopes—follow easily upon assertion of moral principles. A conflict of moral principles involving unexpected adversaries is a conflict to enlist support.

Once in his stride, Johnson during that first year in office had provided a personal leadership that has had no precedent. Other presidents have been active, mentally or physically—far beyond their contemporaries. Wilson might be an example, and Truman, another. But no other—not FDR nor JFK—has been in a position to assert a leadership that would not be denied. It cannot be said that this was possible merely because of new means of revealing his leadership as Johnson had done with the aid of television and radio.

Johnson's leadership appeared to be leadership of the *mass*. However much he used individuals—chosen by him or representing interests involved—he was ahead of them, not by denunciation, not by argument, but by the forcefulness of his position. Never was the power of the President so clearly personified. This might be reversion to the authority of the chieftain, but it was not. It was forcefulness of a high order and did not rely upon system or procedure. The President appeared and the whole situation took on the character that he desired!

How had he expressed this leadership in his "trial" year? Very soon the press conference,[9] altered in plan, timing, and purpose, became the forum from which the foreign policy of the administration was elaborated. Not since the early days of Woodrow Wilson had a president used public announcement of executive plan so pointedly as did Lyndon Johnson. We must realize that, like Woodrow

Wilson rather than Theodore Roosevelt, President Johnson used announcement as *action* in the direction of his foreign policy, and, like Wilson, constantly identified his own policy as that of the United States government. No president, not even Franklin Roosevelt in his Fireside Chats during World War II, had expressed so emphatically the judgment of the Executive in international affairs, as did Johnson, even in his first year in office. Constitutional provisions were the basis of this expression, but it was use of every aid—personal and mechanical in preparation and conference—that provided the elaborate setting of a sovereign.

The great vote of confidence that Johnson won from the American people in the autumn elections of 1964 introduced the second phase of his presidential leadership. Following, as it did, upon the threat of catastrophic changes in the balance of world power symbolized by the appearance of Communist China's nuclear bomb, this election invested the President of the United States with all the constitutional power that could be his in the succeeding four years. For several months after the election, while he was formulating plans prior to the inaugural ceremonies to take place on January 20, 1965, President Johnson's future foreign policy was obscured by his own silence.

There were some Americans in positions of political responsibility who thought in early 1965 that it was not too late to withdraw military aid from South Vietnam. Senators Wayne Morse of Oregon and Frank Church of Idaho hammered away at the mistakes they said the United States government had made and continued to make in Southeast Asia. Senate minority leader Everett M. Dirksen proposed that President Johnson call a conference to decide whether the United States should continue to aid the government of South Vietnam in its struggle against its enemies. Senate majority leader Michael Mansfield called for a full-scale debate in the United States Senate on U.S. policy toward Vietnam.

Secretary of State Dean Rusk said firmly on January 3, that the United States would neither pull out of South Vietnam nor expand the war there. The State Department was more concerned about disunity in the South Vietnamese government than it was about the course of the war.

This concern was well founded, for South Vietnam's mounting government crisis remained unresolved at the beginning of the year 1965. A military ouster of the civilian High National Council at Saigon on December 20, 1964, was followed by three weeks of negotiation on the part of South Vietnamese civil and military leaders and U.S. officials. The result was the restoration of the civilian regime. But violent nation-wide Buddhist demonstrations (January 23-27) prompted military leaders in South Vietnam to overthrow the civilian government. A month later, the South Vietnamese Armed Forces Council voted unanimously to oust Lt. L. Nguyen Khanh as council chairman and armed forces commander. Former Vice-President Nixon warned on January 26 that the United States might now be losing the war in South Vietnam.

In the midst of this political confusion in South Vietnam and accompanying uncertainty in the United States, the President had spoken softly in his State of the Union message to Congress on January 4. He said that we were in South Vietnam because a friendly nation had asked us for help against Communist aggression. Ten years ago we had pledged our help and three Presidents had supported that pledge, and we would not break it. Even more softly he said that "our own security is tied to the peace in Asia. Twice in one generation we have had to fight against aggression in the Far East. To ignore aggression would only increase the danger of a larger war. . . ."

But the cloud of uncertainty that had hung over the nation ever since the incidents of the preceding August in the faraway Gulf of Tonkin were not dispelled by anything either the President or the Secretary of State had said.

As often happens when such abstract issues as "aggression" are confusing to people, a concrete incident clarifies the situation and Americans understand the role that has been assumed by their government. In this case, a Viet Cong attack upon U.S. barracks at Pleiku, where eight Americans were killed and 126 others wounded, was sufficient to seem to justify a strike-back at North Vietnam when U.S. and South Vietnamese planes bombed North Vietnam military bases for the first time on February 7.

The following day, Democratic and Republican leaders voiced strong support of President Johnson's decision to order substantial strikes against North Vietnam. On February 17, a statement issued by the joint Senate-House Republicans rejected "negotiations" with North Vietnam while infiltration of South Vietnam continued from the North, and President Johnson reaffirmed U.S. determination to defend South Vietnam against Communist aggression.

As the President said later, in a review on April 27 of the crisis in Vietnam: "For the next six months (after the bombing of North Vietnam in retaliation for the attack on U.S. warships in the Gulf of Tonkin in August, 1964) we took no action against North Vietnam. We warned of danger. . . . Their answer was attack and explosion and indiscriminate murder (in South Vietnam). So it soon became clear that our restraint was viewed as weakness. . . . We could no longer stand by while attack mounted and while the bases of the attackers were immune from reply. And, therefore, we began to strike back (at military targets)."

With the flight of American planes into enemy territory on that day in February, 1965, came the President's order for evacuation of 2,000 dependents of U.S. personnel in South Vietnam.

Henceforth, a series of "firsts" ensued on the military front. On February 18, U.S. piloted jet planes for the first time directly attacked Communist Viet Cong guerrillas in South Vietnam without participation by South Vietnamese. Another air attack by U.S. B-57 bombers and F-100 fighter-bombers on February 24 signalized departure from previous U.S. policy that American military personnel merely "advise and assist" Vietnamese government troops and fight only in self-defense. The State Department said this was consistent with the August 7, 1964, congressional resolution approving and supporting the determination of the President to prevent further aggression, and was in accord with the government's stated policy of continuing action that is "appropriate, fitting, and measured." For the first time the Viet Cong were assembling in large formations away from villages.

Furthermore, a U.S. "white paper," released by the State Department on February 27, charged that "massive evidence" indicated that North Vietnam was assisting the Viet Cong guerrillas in South Vietnam. Since 1959, nearly 20,000 Viet Cong officers, soldiers, and technicians had entered South Vietnam through North Vietnam's infiltration pipeline under orders from Hanoi.

Speaking with less reticence than either the President or Secretary Rusk, in an annual defense review for the House Armed Services Committee on February 18, Defense Secretary Robert S. McNamara said: "The choice is not simply whether to continue our efforts to keep South Vietnam free and independent, but rather whether to continue our struggle to halt Communist expansion in Asia. . . ." McNamara predicted that eventually China would "produce long range ballistic missile systems and arm them with thermo-nuclear war-heads." Ten days later, Communist China charged that the U.S. had long been busy inventing excuses and preparing for new aggression against North Vietnam.

On March 2, two North Vietnamese military bases were bombed

by more than 160 U.S. and South Vietnamese planes in the heaviest air raid of the war thus far. This attack was followed by an air strike March 3 by more than 30 U.S. jets against undisclosed targets in eastern Laos, presumably the Communists' Ho Chi Minh Trail supply route. The March 2 attack was the first that was not in direct retaliation for Viet Cong guerrilla assaults on U.S. installations in South Vietnam.

A U.S. State Department statement on March 3 explained why the U.S. was becoming increasingly involved in the fighting in Vietnam without a declaration of war. "The fact that military hostilities have been taking place in Southeast Asia," explained this document, "does not bring about the existence of a state of war, which is a legal characterization of a situation rather than an actual description." The U.S.-South Vietnam air strikes against North Vietnam were characterized as "collective defense against . . . armed aggression," and as sanctioned by the United Nations charter and the August, 1964, Congress-approved Southeast Asia resolution, which empowered President Johnson to take necessary military action against aggression in that area.

March 8-9, 1965, marked the arrival of the first U.S. combat troops sent to Vietnam. These were marine contingents to guard the strategic U.S. Air Force Base at Danang, used by U.S. and South Vietnamese planes to carry out air strikes on North Vietnam and Laos. The U.S. Defense Department announced that the South Vietnamese government had requested the marines, who would have a limited mission.

At the same time the State Department announced it had informed United Nations Secretary General U Thant that it was opposed to his plan for a seven-nation peace conference on Vietnam (involving the U.S., Britain, France, the Soviet Union, North and South Vietnam, and Communist China) until North Vietnam should indicate a desire to halt its aggression. Several days later (March 13) President Johnson reaffirmed that North Vietnam must halt military intervention in South Vietnam as the precondition for the U.S. to enter negotiations on the Vietnamese war. He said that U.S. policy in South Vietnam remained fixed "although the incidents have changed, in some instances the tactics, and perhaps the strategy in a decision or two has changed. . . . To any armed attack our forces will reply. To any in Southeast Asia who ask our help in defending their freedom we're going to give it. . . ."

But Secretary McNamara, before the House Foreign Affairs Committee on March 11, had said: "The choice is not simply whether to continue our efforts to keep South Vietnam free and independent, but, rather, whether to continue our struggle to halt Communist expansion in Asia. If the choice is the latter . . . we will be far better off facing the issue in South Vietnam."

It was not long (March 25) until Communist China announced that it was ready to intervene militarily in the Vietnamese war if the Viet Cong guerrillas asked it to do so. This was Peiping's first public declaration that it was prepared to enter the conflict. Soviet Foreign Minister Gromyko was reported by *Tass* (March 24) to have informed Hanoi that Moscow was taking steps to bolster North Vietnam's security against "the armed piracy of U.S. imperialism." It should not have been surprising to the forewarned American public that missile base sites were later discovered in North Vietman by U.S. reconnaissance planes.

It was in an address at Johns Hopkins University in Baltimore on April 7, that President Johnson revealed the broad policy of the United States government toward the mounting hostilities on both sides in Vietnam:

> "The confused nature of this conflict cannot mask the fact that this is the new face of an old enemy. . . . And the object of that attack is a friend to which we are pledged.
>
> "Over this war—and all Asia—is another reality: the deepening shadow of Communist China. The rulers in Hanoi are urged on by Peking. This is a regime which has destroyed freedom in Tibet, attacked India, and been condemned by the United Nations for aggression in Korea. It is a nation which is helping the forces of violence in almost every continent. The contest in Vietnam is part of a wider pattern of aggressive purpose. . . .

Immediately following this pronouncement, Communist China, North Vietnam, and the Soviet Union rejected President Johnson's offer of unconditional talks to settle the Vietnamese war and as well of a massive United States-financed Southeast Asia economic development program.

The confrontation with Communist China was not all that the President visualized. To Southeast Asia he was willing to export as much as possible of the Great Society that he had visualized for his own country.[10] Those who were doubtful of his own role in this unprecedented project could meditate on what he said of "power," for he reflected: "We often say how impressive power is. But I do not find it impressive. The guns and bombs, the rockets and warships, are all symbols of human failure. They are necessary symbols. They protect what we cherish. But they are witness to human folly." And those who thought he was delinquent in initiating peaceful negotiation were confronted by his simple exclamation: "Every night before I turn out the lights to sleep I ask myself this question: 'Have I done everything that I can to help unite the world, to try to bring peace and hope to all the peoples of the world? Have I done enough?' "

Ten days later (April 17) President Johnson declared "there is no human power capable of forcing us from Vietnam. We will remain as long as necessary . . . whatever the risk. . . . If the price of ending aggression is blood and men, we are ready to pay that price." In an affirmation of the President's statement, Secretary McNamara some days later (April 26) announced that U.S. combat deaths in the war in South Vietnam had thus far numbered 348. The war effort there was costing the United States about $1½ billion a year.

In addition $700 million for fiscal 1965 was asked of the Congress by the President on May 4, in order to meet mounting military requirements in Vietnam. Congress immediately began affirmative action on this request and Johnson said those supporting his request were "also voting to persist in our effort to halt Communist aggression in South Vietnam." Thus, said the President, it would be obvious to the world that the Congress and the President were standing united in a joint determination that the independence of South Vietnam be preserved and Communist attack thwarted. The House passed the appropriation bill by 408-7 vote and the Senate by 88-3 vote on May 6. The President's bid for full congressional backing was somewhat dimmed when certain Senators, including some who voted for the bill, declared during debate that approval of funds was not to be construed as approval of policies leading to escalation of the conflict or to increased military involvement in Vietnam. The ten opposing votes were cast by three Democrats and seven Republicans.

While the President was reviewing the history of U.S. involvement in Vietnam, about 8,000 U.S. Marines were landing in South Vietnam to increase our military force there to more than 42,000 men. Johnson persistently contended that, as he said, wherever we have stood firm, aggression has been halted, peace restored, and liberty maintained—as in Iran, Greece, Turkey, Korea, the Formosa Straits, Lebanon, and in Cuba at the time of the missile crisis. "Resistance to aggression, moderation in the use of power, and a constant search for peace," he said, were the ingredients of U.S. policy in the world.

As proof of his interest in restoring peace in Vietnam, the President suspended air attacks on Norh Vietnam in the period May 13-18, repeating his offer of unconditional talks. There was no reaction from Hanoi. Then President Johnson claimed that Communist China apparently wanted to continue the Vietnamese war, since it would be to the interest of North Vietnam to come to the conference table at this time. He interpreted the silence as an indication that Communist China not only intended to dominate all of Asia but to discredit America's ability to help prevent this.

During the month of May, "teach-ins" and demonstrations against American policy in South Vietnam throughout the United States were in ironical contrast with Communist China's announcement on May 14, that another atomic bomb had been successfully exploded within its western borders. Thus began a second traumatic period in world affairs, underlined by the discovery of suspected Soviet missile sites in North Vietnam which had recently been spotted by U.S. reconnaissance planes.

Early in June, the State Department reported that President Johnson had authorized General William C. Westmoreland, Commander of U.S. forces in South Vietnam, to *commit his ground troops* to direct combat against Viet Cong guerrillas, if the South Vietnamese army requested such assistance.

There followed debate in the Senate over the proposal of Senator Jacob K. Javits (R., New York) for a resolution specifically authorizing expansion of U.S. military efforts in Vietnam, as "we have been moving in the direction of a massive bogdown land struggle in Asia without any specific consent by Congress or the people for that kind of war." Senator Ernest Gruening (D., Alaska) reminded the Senate that the August 1964 congressional resolution giving the President discretionary powers in Southeast Asia was sufficient to protect South Vietnam. But Gruening charged that the President's actions in the present situation were unconstitutional because he was waging "undeclared war."

Meanwhile, the crisis in Santo Domingo and U.S. governmental military activity there had raised storms of protest both in this country and abroad. Reviewing the critical period April 24-28 in Santo Domingo a month later, President Johnson said he had had "237 individual conversations . . . and about 35 meetings" with various people at that time. The decision to send U.S. troops there was "a unanimous decision about which there was no difference of opinion either at the Dominican Republic level . . . or the cabinet level here . . . ," said the President. Furthermore, fourteen Latin American nations had been consulted and meetings of the Peace Commission of the

OAS as well as of the OAS Council had been held. More than 5,000 foreign nationals had been evacuated, a cease-fire obtained, and economic aid provided the Dominican people. The President praised the OAS role in the crisis, and said, "We have learned in the Dominican crisis that we can act decisively and together."

Lack of stability in the succession of civilian governments in South Vietnam on the one hand, and continued protest against the American military involvement there were counterbalanced by strong measures within the Administration in Washington. On June 16, Secretary McNamara announced that 21,000 U.S. soldiers, including 8,000 combat troops, were being sent to South Vietnam to counter a continuing build-up of Viet Cong forces. This would bring the number of U.S. troops in South Vietnam to 70,000-75,000 men, of whom 21,000 were combat forces. McNamara estimated the Viet Cong forces at 65,000 regular combat and combat-support, and 80-100 thousand part-time guerrillas. It was supposed that 30,000 Viet Cong were "serving in political and propaganda activities in South Vietnam." McNamara said that during 1960-64, there had infiltrated South Vietnam, from North Vietnam, 39,000 verified combat personnel and possibly more, 10,000 in 1964 alone. South Vietnam's entire force of 574,000 men gave less than 4-1 advantage and "less than the force required to deal effectively with the type of military and terrorist threat" posed by the Viet Cong. Air strikes against North Vietnam had not stopped this infiltration.

In mid-summer, air raids by B-52 bombers from Guam were directed against Viet Cong installations 35 miles northeast of Saigon. Continuing crises in the South Vietnamese government during this period were accompanied by rejection, from the North Vietnam capital of Hanoi, of the proposal of a Commonwealth mission to mediate a peaceful settlement in Vietnam.

President Johnson called upon the United Nations, in a speech on the occasion of the anniversary meeting of that body in San Francisco on June 25, for aid in establishing peace in Southeast Asia. Delegations from 113 members (the Dominican Republic the only member not represented) heard this plea. The sudden death of U.S. Ambassador to the United Nations Adlai Stevenson, on July 14, underlined the necessity for renewed American support of the world organization. This the President gave, unmistakably, in the appointment of Justice of the Supreme Court Arthur J. Goldberg to the United Nations ambassadorship. The reappointment of Henry Cabot Lodge as Ambassador to South Vietnam followed the long anticipated retirement of General Maxwell D. Taylor from service in that capacity.

Lodge's return to Vietnam in July coincided with the Administration's announcement that heavy infiltration of North Vietnamese forces had created new dangers in South Vietnam, against which the United States was prepared to take any type of military action needed.

The State Department had announced on July 6 that two Soviet-type anti-aircraft missile sites in the Hanoi-Haiphong area of North Vietnam were ready for use and two other sites in the same area were close to completion. But Secretary Rusk said U.S. planes had not yet bombed within 45 miles of this area and the missile sites were not yet fully operational and were not interfering with U.S.-South Vietnam military efforts "at this time." But on July 27, at least five American aircraft were lost in the attack of forty-six F-105 jet fighter-bombers on two anti-aircraft missile sites in North Vietnam. One of the sites was destroyed and the other severly damaged, but these were in addition to those earlier reported. And three days earlier, an anti-aircraft rocket had for the first time brought down a U.S. plane over North Vietnam. Thus began a new phase of the war and momentous decisions on the part of the United States.

Throughout July a crisis had been building up in Vietnam. This had been anticipated by the Americans, for the Administration was considering early in the month a limited mobilization of U.S. military manpower to cope with increasing Communist guerrilla pressure in South Vietnam and was prepared to take any type of military acton needed there.

Meanwhile the Soviet news agency *Tass* announced that the USSR had signed an agreement on July 10 with a North Vietnamese delegate for aid "over and above" that now being rendered to North Vietnam by the Soviet Union. Communist China, the Soviet Union, and North Korea were reported to have agreed to provide North Vietnam with defense and economic aid. North Vietnam President Ho Chi Minh said his people would fight another twenty years or longer to achieve victory in the "aggressive war" in Vietnam. In a statement issued on the eleventh anniversary of the Geneva accords on Vietnam, Ho urged Americans to end the conflict, and called on the South Vietnamese government and its soldiers to abandon their America allies.

Defense Secretary McNamara, ending the sixth fact-finding mission the United States had conducted in Vietnam, conceded that the military situation there had deteriorated in the fifteen months since his preceding visit, despite massive intervention by the United States armed forces. "But the Vietnam people continue to be willing to fight and . . . die in their own defense," he reported, and the Viet Cong "are suffering increasingly heavy losses . . ."

Against this background of events, President Johnson on July 28 addressed a nation-wide audience on television with the announcement that he had ordered U.S. military forces in Vietnam increased from 75,000 to 125,000, and would order further increases if such action should be dictated by the course of the war.

This significant change came after weeks of speculation over future military policy in Vietnam and followed eight days of White House conferences in the light of McNamara's recent assessment. The President had discussed his decision with congressional leaders of both parties at a White House meeting on July 27.

The President said he had ordered to Vietnam several military units including the Airmobile (First Cavalry) Division, which would almost immediately raise U.S. military manpower in Vietnam by 50,000. Military draft calls would be raised from 17,000 to 35,000 monthly in the United States, but he would not at present order the recall to active service of armed forces reserve units.

Johnson coupled this announcement with reaffirmation of readiness on the part of the United States to seek a negotiated end to the conflict in Vietnam. Several attempts had been made, but all had been rejected by Communist China and North Vietnam. He appealed for the intercession of the United Nations and any of the member states to bring about peace talks. He said that the U.S. would not unilaterally withdraw from Vietnam and declared that "Most of the non-Communist nations of Asia cannot by themselves . . . resist the growing might and the grasping ambition of Asian communism. Our power, therefore, is a . . . vital shield. If we are driven from the field in Vietnam, then no nation can ever again have the same confidence in American promises or in American protection. . . . We did not choose to be the guardians at the gate, but there is no one else."

To an American public confused by the issue in Southeast Asia and perhaps unmindful of the obligation of their government to come to the defense of any nation that had become a party to the South East Asia Treaty Organization, the President explained:

> "This is a different kind of war. There are no marching armies or solemn declarations. . . . It is guided by North Vietnam and it is spurred by Communist China. Its goal

is to conquer the South, to defeat American power, and to extend the Asiatic dominion of communism."

Johnson recalled that fifteen efforts involving forty nations throughout the world had been made to start unconditional discussions, "with any government, at any place, at any time," and that there had been no answer. "But we are going to persist," said Johnson, "if persist we must, until death and desolation have led to the same conference table where others could now join us at a much smaller cost."

Two days later, on July 30, the United States formally called on the United Nations Security Council to help settle the war in Vietnam. And on August 4, President Johnson asked Congress for an additional $1.7 billion in defense appropriations to help the United States meet war commitments there. Ambassador-at-large Averell Harriman, who had conferred with Soviet leaders on his July 12-22 visit to Moscow in order that he might brief the President, reported in news conferences later that the USSR "sincerely wanted peace in Vietnam" and that both Yugoslavia and the Soviet Union were of the opinion that the 17th parallel should remain the dividing line between North and South Vietnam. The Soviet Union had no intention, however, of acting as mediator in the conflict between the United States and South Vietnam versus North Vietnam.

Informing leading members of the Congress on the Vietnam situation, the President expressed himself also to newsmen, stating that "There is no substantial division in this country, in my judgment, and no substantial division in the Congress" on the Administration's actions in Vietnam. Thus, escalation of the war was being carried on by the President with his full confidence in the general support of the American people.

On August 23, U.S. policy in Vietnam was reaffirmed by a White House pamphlet outlining Washington's commitment and objectives and U.S. conditions for a truce to end the fighting. The statement was explained on CBS television by Secretary Rusk, Ambassador to the United Nations Goldberg, and McGeorge Bundy (special presidential assistant for national security affairs).

Faint voices were raised in dissent by House Republicans who issued a white paper through Representative Gerald R. Ford of Michigan, charging the Administration with a lack of candor, inasmuch as "neither the Congress nor the public is being accurately and fully informed about the nation's involvement in Vietnam," and the changing of "the nature of American participation in the war by committing substantial numbers of American troop units to ground combat with the Viet Cong."

With increasing U.S. air activity in the war and the resumption of widespread raids against the Viet Cong in South Vietnam by B-52 jet bombers from SAC units in Guam, U.S. sources in Saigon reported, on August 30, that these attacks would soon be conducted at the rate of about one a day indefinitely. Since the air strikes had begun on February 7, eighty-five aircraft had been lost over Vietnam.

Although the deepening conflict in Vietnam had obscured from the American public the importance of other aspects of the international situation, there were flurries of apprehension during late summer and early autumn over the hostilities between India and Pakistan over Kashmir. President Johnson disclaimed any responsibility for advice, which he said should be delegated to the United Nations, but it appeared at the time that he must have had considerable interest in the situation, for it involved the gravest of implications for the U.S. position in Southeast Asia. Likewise, the continuing internal struggle for power in the Dominican Republic seemed linked with criticism of the President's policy there by Chairman Fulbright of the Senate Foreign Relations Committee. The President had already explained his position in the Dominican Republic crisis and on September 4 extended U.S. recognition of the provisional Dominican regime, pledging full support in the task of preparing for elections in 1966 and rebuilding the economy with $20,000,000 in American aid.

Unremitting in his pressures upon Congress for foreign aid in general, the President on September 6 signed a compromise $3.36 billion foreign aid authorization (HR 7750), promising that "appropriate studies" would be initiated by his Administration on the future direction of the foreign aid program. He expressed confidence that "next year's legislation will mark a renewal of our long term commitment to assist those people who want to live in peace and independence; a renewal of the program which has been vital to U.S. (interest) around the world, and a renewal of the co-operative relationship between the Executive and Congress which has shaped the great foreign policy decisions of the post-war period."

In a statement prepared to mark the swearing in of Harlan Cleveland as U.S. ambassador to NATO and in reply to President De Gaulle's indication that France would quit NATO by 1970, the President urged the strengthening of that alliance, for it, said he, "is the centerpiece of the worldwide system we have been building for 20 years to protect the free world. . . ." Future NATO goals should be its development into an instrument for political co-operation and for organizing joint nuclear defense.

By mid-September the size of the U.S. force in South Vietnam was "somewhat larger," according to Secretary Rusk, than the 125,-000-man goal set by the President, and it was clear that the nation was engaged in a full-scale war which, it appeared, might last for years. Into this dreaded "ground war" on the vast continent of Asia, the President had drawn the American people with, he believed, their consensus. The implications of presidential power were now revealed as never before in the history of the United States, and cast a new light upon the development of the nation under powerful presidents preceding Lyndon Johnson.

When we consider the known activities of the President in the first ten days of August, 1965, for example, we observe that almost all of these had to do with the assembling of support for his program—foreign and domestic—as it developed. He explained first to his advisers (official, unofficial, and a large group of experts) what he was doing and why. This briefing was followed by similar meetings with representatives of the press and radio and television; then with special groups of citizens termed leaders in finance, business, education, and public welfare.

The first briefings with advisers were secret, and news releases were meager and stated in terms of general objectives and measures diplomatic and military. Later meetings were televised and the President explained still further in answer to questions. Meanwhile, the government of the nation went forward at home and abroad with its manifold responsibilities under the authority of the President as Chief Executive.

The similarity existing between the position of the President of the United States (Kennedy) in the autumn of 1963, and the position of President Johnson in the autumn of 1965, necessitated renewed consideration of the actual power of the Commander-in-Chief of the military forces of the United States.[11]

"Commander-in-Chief" suggests that the presidential office is a military one. Washington, Jackson, Grant, and Eisenhower had military careers, successful in the minds of their follow citizens, before they entered upon the presidency. But the presidents who have exercised the greatest power as Commander-in-Chief (Lincoln, Wilson, Franklin Roosevelt, Truman, Kennedy, Johnson) have not been military leaders by profession or experience. In his alleged reason for the build-up of military strength in Vietnam—to insure peace at last in a nation divided against itself—Lyndon Johnson, like Ulysses

S. Grant, discussed "peace" as a state of mind of people rather than as a physical actuality in any area of the world.

The Congress had taken no action on policy in Southeast Asia, for it had not been asked to do so. It had voted funds to support the program of the President. The provisions of the Constitution do not anticipate these actions of the President except as he has acted as Commander-in-Chief. The Senate as a body had not been consulted; it had been informed. The Congress had not acted as a co-ordinating branch of the government in formulating policy, determining objectives, and—except for providing funds— had not participated except as the President had called upon individuals or groups of individuals.

Critics of the procedures described above were not silenced. Yet the voices raised in protest in the Congress—and the shouts in the streets—were ignored as far as as we may observe from the word or action of President Johnson. All the prestige of the presidency as it was exhibited to the public, at home or abroad, was based on the intangible influence of the chosen representative of the people and the tangible effect of his every word and deed. The "elected King" had become a reality.

President Johnson for a year carried out the Kennedy policy of protecting the security of the United States. Then gradually came a shift in that policy, described quite clearly by the President in his Baltimore address of April, 1965. But only gradually did the American people come to realize the implications of the President's policy as the containment of communism in Asia as well as in Europe.

Thus we faced a great war—perhaps a world war—thousands of miles away from the American continent, on terms hitherto avoided in the commitment of ground forces on the mainland of Asia, with no probability of any outcome except unending military engagement. To this war we were committed, as we were told repeatedly, but without the approval of Congress following open debate, and without the *understanding* consensus of the American people.

The existence of "war," in which the United States appeared at home and abroad to be the determining agent by continuing involvement, meant that the President was formulating his own public opinion. Despite what he said of his confidence in consensus, there was no governmental policy except his. The Congress had no policy; the people had none.

Inevitably the debate—if it could be called that—went into the streets where the participants were representative of a small but very persistent element in the population. Some of these were members of the faculties and student bodies of colleges and universities, but it was impossible to characterize the personnel of the "marches" and other demonstrations that occurred, especially in the summer and autumn of 1965.

Consequently, the need of discussion, by members of the government, of the policies of the President—and of the activities of various representatives of the Executive—became more and more evident. The administration had been accused by the press of a lack of candor concerning the nation's commitment in Vietnam. The Presidet's prolonged convalescence from surgery in October, coinciding with the recess of Congress, had produced an inevitable stalemate in political discussion of major issues.

During the autumn and early winter, while public opinion appeared to be confused, irresponsible, and futile, it was evident that the nation was divided not only on the issues, but on a conflict of issues. On the conduct of the war in South Vietnam, many Republicans disagreed with the Commander-in-Chief. They were advocating stronger military measures than had been taken in the limited bombing of targets in North Vietnam. On the other hand, the demonstrators in the streets were protesting the President's policy as Executive in foreign relations. They were disclaiming the necessity for war as an instrument of national policy and were basically opposed to the war in Vietnam. Thus, the President found himself prosecuting a war unacceptable to some, in a manner unacceptable to others.

The fact that the attack upon the President's policy in Vietnam was centered upon his use of the armed forces of the nation meant that the agent of his will was the Secretary of Defense, not the Secretary of State. But both Secretary McNamara and Secretary Rusk had to meet the censure of all opponents of the President's policy and his conduct of the war.

By December first, the record was spelled out by the press so that all could see the steps by which limited commitment had led to war without foreseeable limit. The American commitment had increased by many stages from a small group of "advisers" not engaged in combat activity to a fighting force of nearly 200,000. As one journalist reminded us, "The advisers in Vietnam became 'assistants'; the 'assistants' flew the planes but did not man the guns; then they manned the guns but used them only when attacked; then they 'retaliated' against attacks on our own bases; then they engaged in deep patrols to keep the enemy away from our bases; and finally, they were ordered to 'search and destroy,' to 'find, fix, and fight the enemy'."

At year's end, in December, 1965, came a pause in public discussion. This was natural in view of anticipation that the President's statement to Congress in January would provide definitive information concerning his position on the crises existing in various parts of the world. Suspension of the bombing of North Vietnam in late December did not dispel the gloom reflected in a report by Senate majority leader Mansfield upon the situation in South Vietnam. It was rightly termed a "bleak story" that Mansfield and his senatorial colleagues brought back from Saigon, but it foreshadowed—at last— a full-scale discussion in the Senate, as well as renewed investigation within congressional committees. This welcome development appeared to be more important than the facts of the Mansfield report.

The fully publicized report, though vague and baffling, of what representatives of the President were saying to representatives of nations in Europe and in Asia, as to the "peace offensive" which had often been suggested by the President, did not appear to be reassuring.

In his State of the Union message to the Congress on January 12, 1966, President Johnson summarized his policies, his actions, and the plans that had been developed by him during his administration thus far. "In 1965 alone we had 300 private talks for peace in Vietnam with friends and adversaries throughout the world," he said. The United States position had been made "abundantly clear" to 113 nations "that we have relations with and some that we don't." Said the President, "I am hopeful, and I will try as best I can with everything I've got to end this battle and to return our sons to their desires."

Nevertheless, in a candid revelation of the power of the Executive, he related his position squarely to the commitments of his three predecessors, and the judgment of the American electorate upon critical issues in the period 1945-1965. As President, he was, he said, defending the interests of the United States in an unfriendly, often hostile, and despairing world of nations. He implied that he was confident of tremendous power in the support of the American people. Johnson gave historic setting to his position at the beginning of 1966. It was:

"That conflict (in Vietnam) is not an isolated episode, but another great event in the policy we have followed with strong consistency since World War II. . . . we have defended against Communist aggression—in Korea under President Truman—in the Formosa Straits under President Eisenhower—in Cuba under President Kennedy—

and again in Vietnam. . . . We will stay because a just nation cannot leave to the cruelties of its enemies a people
who have staked their lives and independence on our
solemn pledge—a pledge which has grown through the
commitments of three American Presidents."

It seemed clear at last that adherence to "commitments" needed
to be reassessed in view of changed conditions which might make
such commitments too burdensome to accomplish desired results.

In hearings before the Senate Committee on Foreign Relations,
which were televised for the nation, appeared the conflicting testimony of four experts—General James M. Gavin (retired) former
U.S. Ambassador to France; George F. Kennan, former Ambassador to the Soviet Union; General Maxwell D. Taylor (retired),
former Ambassador to South Vietnam; and Secretary of State Dean
Rusk. This conflict of opinion indicated that when the debate was
resumed in the Senate, attention would be concentrated upon (1) the
wisdom of the original and successive commitments made by the
presidents in the period 1953-1965; (2) the constitutional basis for
these commitments; and (3) the probable effect on world politics of
the proposed course of President Johnson.

The purpose of the Senate hearings, namely, to prepare for a vote
in the Senate on the policies of the President (which Senator Morse
had long insisted upon), was perhaps transcended by the revelation
of certain stark realities of the American system of government. The
conflict between representatives of the people with a grasp of policy
and a sense of immediate political reality, and representatives of
the President possessed of a sense of reality in foreign affairs, and the
relation of these to our national existence could not be easily resolved.

Repeatedly, Lyndon Johnson had talked of our "commitment" in
South Vietnam, sometimes saying that it was to the people of South
Vietnam, sometimes referring to the freedom-loving people of the
world. Obviously he was not speaking of military alliances, nor of
policies adopted by the American government when faced with war
that threatened the existence of the American people.

Ex-Ambassador Kennan was talking of something quite different
when he said: "If we ever incurred such a commitment, how was
it possible to enter into it except through the constitutional processes
of a treaty, ratified by the Senate, or a declaration of war, approved
by Congress?"

The President's answer appeared in the address which he made
in New York City on February 23 (1966). Concluding detailed re-

plies to ten questions that had been asked in the Senate discussions
and hearings, he said:

> "Our men in Vietnam are there to keep a promise made 12
> years ago. The Southeast Asia Treaty promised—as Secre-
> tary John Foster Dulles said for the United States—'that
> an attack upon the treaty area would occasion a reaction
> so united, so strong, and so well placed that the aggressor
> would lose more than it could hope to gain.' But we keep
> more than a specific treaty promise in Vietnam. We keep
> the faith for freedom."

Despite Lyndon Johnson's keen understanding of the will of
masses of Americans, it must be conceded that in proceeding outside
the limits of the constitutional law of the nation, the President had
placed the vital interests of the United States in an exposed position.
The assertion of independent presidential power tended to weaken
us on the field of battle in Vietnam, for the President did not appear to have the united support of the American people. As the war
developed, there was need to clarify the situation at home, where
the governmental position was weakened by opposition of members
of the Senate who believed the legislative branch of the government
had not been properly consulted on the issues at stake. Finally it
was seen that we might soon be at war with Communist China, but
on the President's terms of "defense." It became clear that it was
the President's policy, based upon the policies of his three predecessors, that had brought the nation into an extremely dangerous and
possibly vulnerable position in the Far East.

The most persistent opponents of Lyndon Johnson's program for
"world peace" were those who refused to admit that in the nuclear
age there is absolute necessity of international action supported by
international law and international thinking. In the present emergency, in which the world is involuntarily united by technological advances, there is no recognized international *power* to uphold international law. The United Nations is seemingly as ineffective in this
respect as was the League of Nations.

Into this vacuum, the power of the American President has entered. It was Woodrow Wilson who assumed leadership in bringing
about an international organization in the League of Nations. The
League's failure in lacking implementation led Franklin Roosevelt
to a new concept of international organization in the United Nations.
President Truman accepted the responsibility for its implementation
in Korea.

President Johnson has realized the need of carrying this responsibility in order that international law against international violence (usually in the form of Communist aggression, although not always) shall be upheld. As he has said, there is no one else to guard the gate. As the world "totters on the brink of nuclear disaster," it is obvious that the disinterested defense of freedom by the United States through its President is not a new concept in international politics. Because of the directness and simplicity with which President Johnson has undertaken the defense of freedom in Asia, as well as in Europe, he has not always been understood by those who are suspicious of the combination of political sagacity and idealism that have motivated Lyndon Johnson.

VI. *Presidential Power in the Nuclear Age*

★ VI ★

PRESIDENTIAL

POWER IN THE

NUCLEAR AGE

by EDGAR E. ROBINSON

I N THE TWENTY-YEAR PERIOD 1945-1965, four presidents—using powers granted them in the Constitution and extended by congressional approval and judicial interpretation—have sought to maintain the existence of the United States in a seemingly unending era of "cold war."[1] They have been successful in that no enemy has pressed our gates and the nation continues to live. But the future is uncertain, because the problem of national security has been intensified by the outbreak of revolutionary movements in every part of the hitherto colonial world, and the transformation of these movements into so-called "wars of national liberation" by forces inimical to freedom everywhere. Consequently, the role of the United States among the uneasy nations upon our planet is of deep concern to every American.

Presidential power in the beginning was not of first importance in the foreign relations of the United States. But it is now, and has been for a generation, especially in the years since 1945. The President has the final—as well as the first—word in all contacts, conferences, and agreements, whether the result be declarations or treaties. The foreign policy of the nation is thus the foreign policy of its President.[2] If it is to be changed, he must be crossed successfully by the Congress (especially the Senate), or misinterpreted by the Secretary of State, Secretary of Defense, or Central Intelligence Agency. There is no possibility of real change in the President's foreign policy except by removal of the man in the presidency by death, resignation, or defeat at the polls.

The power of the President is now strengthened by the fact that his action, whatever it may be, has a conclusive character because the people have it right away on television and radio, as well as in vivid newspaper headlines. His words—which constitute action— become part of the consciousness of millions of people at once. Consequently, the effectiveness of that action is amplified millions of times by the miracle of swift communication and is thereby translated into an "act of God" because it defies both time and space.

While the pronouncements of the President are guides to the foreign policy of the United States, individuals sharing this process with the President may be very influential. The President's actions, therefore, are to be judged not only by his declarations but also by the explanations of those speaking for him. Furthermore, the power exercised by the President is to be judged in light of the situation existing at the time in the world beyond our borders.[8]

The division of responsibility in maintaining peace—or in waging war—reflects American conviction of the superiority of the civil to the military office of government. Experience has shown, however, that the necessities of war have often forced upon the Executive action in advance of consent by the Legislative branch. The explanation offered is that a written Constitution with powers clearly defined is ready to reassert the rules once the crisis has passed.

When the Constitution was adopted—and the presidency created with enumerated powers—there was no United States. There were thirteen separate states, loosely organized in a war-time and post-war period of great uncertainty in a world of warring nations. These European nations, out of which Colonies had emerged, had had a history of 300 years of constant strife in commerce, in colonization, and in war. Could the Americans live in such a world? They did live. In commerce they won a place. In colonization, they did. In each case it was done in accordance with constitutional procedures.

In 176 years we fought a half dozen major wars and numerous minor wars. For four years we were torn apart by civil strife. The temporary assertion of supreme power by the President gave us the expansion of continental boundaries in 1803 and again in 1848; saved the federal union in 1865; launched us upon overseas responsibilities in 1898; and enabled us to defend ourselves in 1917 and 1941.

The presidency has survived throughout these years. In the general view of other nations, the President embodies the United States of America. But the powers granted the Executive have been powers shared in the basic law with Congress, Court, and People. Since 1900 and especially since 1940, however, the presidency has tended to transcend the other branches of the government and to dominate them. The question arises: Has this office of President, as provided in the *law* of the land, become obsolete, that is, out of date? Let us examine the role of the President in foreign affairs in light of the following questions:

(1) Has the actual operation of the President's power in foreign relations so altered as to exceed all the powers granted him in the Constitution?

(2) Has the position of the United States in the world so altered since the end of World War II as to make all procedures of the President, as prescribed *or* implied in law, inadequate?

The President's power in foreign affairs appears to have undergone a qualitative transformation. When he uses war as an instrument of national policy, he asserts special powers as Commander-in-Chief of the armed forces. But the use of these powers is now conditioned not only by possession of the nuclear deterrent but by a change in the actual practice of war. The "war of national liberation," as carried on in Vietnam, for example, "confronts us with a bold new form of aggression—which could rank in military importance with the discovery of gunpowder," according to Vice-President Hubert Humphrey, reminding us that it is "a war in which the leaders cannot be located, in which the sources of supply cannot be easily cut off, in which the enemy forces are not outsiders but indigenous troops."[4]

The decisions the President makes concerning military policy in these circumstances are really political decisions. The Constitution has endowed him with both political and military power. But is the power that the President exercises in a crisis the power of the Commander-in-Chief, or is it the power that resides in his leadership of a political party that can win and hold the support of the majority of the American people? In actuality, does the power of the President now lie not in the Constitution but in the practice of self-government that our people have maintained in face of every crisis? This is power born of the willingness of the people to follow the leadership of the President as the expert in government, foreign affairs, and war. Is such power dangerous?

Roots of the development in foreign relations that has transformed the government of this nation may be found in Franklin

Roosevelt's extension of his powers as President. The phenomenal growth of control in the Executive office during his administration lay not so much in legislation influenced by the President and appointments made by him, as in the exercise of personal leadership within other nations as well as his own.

In his role as Commander-in-Chief during World War II, Roosevelt promoted with our allies plans of unprecedented boldness for the future of Europe and Asia. Discovering too late that the Russians were bent on assimilating eastern Europe, Roosevelt left to his successor, Harry S. Truman, the legacy of a new and formidable enemy. At the same time, President Truman found himself possessed of a new and formidable symbol of military power in the first atomic bomb. This he did not hesitate to use to terminate the agony of war against Japan.

The cloud that annihilated Hiroshima was followed by a cloud of communism flung across the world by the Soviet Union as the war ended. Despite Truman's courageous airlift for Berlin, and his aid to Greece and Turkey which halted the spread of communism in Europe, he lost the fight against communism in China. As a Communist government rose to power in Peking, the Nationalist Chinese fled to Formosa in 1949. In American defense of South Korea in 1951, President Truman made a fateful decision; no attack should be made on Communist Chinese territory, even by air. Truman's problem was the conservation of the new power that belonged to the United States, and in this he was successful.

Although Dwight D. Eisenhower, victor on many battlefields, halted the war in Korea, he was able to obtain no more than a truce which was never a treaty of peace. He was reluctant to use the vast power that was his in the nuclear age, but he utilized world-wide fear of American nuclear resources to defend the interest of the United States in the "brinkmanship" of Secretary of State John Foster Dulles. This was presidential power enormously enlarged to defy the spread of communism.

To John F. Kennedy, "Power was not a goal he sought for its own sake. It was there, in the White House, to be used, without any sense of guilt or greed, as a means of getting things done."[5] President Kennedy used this power with some uncertainty at first. As he gained confidence in the position of his nation—and of himself—in the world, Kennedy experimented with the political and material resources at his disposal by increasing the support of "advisers" in South Vietnam; by thwarting the Russians in their exploitation of missile sites in Cuba; and by procuring a Nuclear Test Ban Treaty.

If Kennedy's daring was a component of presidential power, Lyndon Johnson's personal persuasion was another, especially before he was elected in his own right to the office of chief executive. Later, persuasion was transformed into determination. Faced with the defeat of the good offices of the United States in aiding South Vietnam in its resistance to communism, Johnson escalated the responsibilities of the American government there beyond any definable limit. The ending of the "bipolar" world of two decades preceding, and Communist China's nuclear blast did not diminish, but on the contrary increased the responsibility of the United States in the free world. President Johnson accepted this responsibility, and it became clear that the American people were thereby asked to accept a role among the nations without any precedent. There is no one else, said the President, so we must be the keepers at the gate.

If the role of the United States in the international arena is to be that of a unilateral substitute for the United Nations, the Atlantic Alliance, the Organization of American States and the Southeast Asia Treaty Organization—what will be the effect of this gigantic design upon the internal affairs of our own nation in democratic self-government? And what is our relationship to the revolutionary movements now shaking the world?[6]

Thus we return to the inquiry raised at the beginning of this study: "How does the increase of presidential power in foreign affairs affect the future of our republican form of government and our democratic society in the United States?"

In elaborating this question, we might ask:

(1) Does the experience of Presidents Truman, Eisenhower, Kennedy, and Johnson show that the treaty-making power of the President has become crucial because he must have bi-partisan support for his foreign policy?

(2) To what extent has the Executive Agreement or Order bypassed the Senate on important matters?

(3) What limitation, if any, can be placed upon the development of policy by the President as Commander-in-Chief in time of national crisis?

The basic question in our constitutional system is very simple. Does Congress no longer declare war? Reliance upon presidential power to wage war without formal action by Congress means in fact reliance on professional military judgment, as well as upon the advice of the Secretary of State and Secretary of Defense. Does our national effectiveness in war then depend upon adoption of a program by a majority of the people at the polls once in four years?

No congressional vote, no national referendum can win on the issue of war unless it has a substitute for armed force.

It is then evident that the President's powers as Commander-in-Chief of the armed forces are of greater significance than all the other powers prescribed in the Constitution. This is of profound significance, however much discussion may arise over the President's conflicts with Congress, particularly with the Senate,[7] or his relations with his chief appointee in foreign relations, the Secretary of State.[8]

The American people believed they could have a three-dimensional government (executive, legislative, judicial) and maintain an existence on this continent, exercising power—it is true—in the Western Hemisphere. But not since 1900 has this been possible, especially since the role of the United States in the world became what it now seems to be. The growth of the powers of the President of the United States in foreign relations appears to be the most important phenomenon in modern history, inasmuch as the exercise of those powers by four presidents in the past twenty years has determined developments throughout the world.

The presidential office as it now exists needs to be redefined, and the pressure to do this is great because events have outdated the provisions of the Constitution. Drift will not provide a solution to this problem. Yet the decision of the President in protecting the United States depends upon developments outside the nation. Then it may be too late!

The following questions might be considered:

(1) Do we need a new Constitutional Convention to draw up the framework of a government that will meet the needs of our day, and that will give legality and assurance to the exercise of presidential powers that protect our very existence?

(2) If a Constitutional Convention were held now, what powers would be accorded the President?

(3) Should the Constitution be revised to reduce the required two-thirds approval of the Senate for treaties?

As we look more closely at the situation facing the Executive at the present time, further questions present themselves:

(a) Do we need a division of Executive power by providing several vice-presidents with distribution of responsibility?

(b) Do we need an amendment to provide for a referendum of the voters upon a declaration of war, or of steps toward war (as in the case of Vietnam)? It was proposed in 1924 and again in 1938.[9]

(c) Did the disagreement as to meaning and extent of American policy in South Vietnam lead to the conclusion that stages in the development of "commitments" must be judged more exactly as events unfold? In brief, how far can an initial agreement (presidential decision, executive order, or treaty) bind the people of the United States?

(d) How is it possible for a foreign policy to be initiated or developed or defined by any agency of the government except the Executive? Can a legislature or a court deal with such problems in self-government?

(e) To what extent can it be desirable or possible for American policies to be announced, modified, or rescinded because of adverse views expressed by the people or by representatives of foreign nations?

Finally, do we need a new Declaration of Purpose of the United States in world affairs? Do we need to declare, with "a decent respect to the opinions of mankind," as envisaged in the Declaration of Independence 190 years ago, that we support by a vote of the Congress, endorsed by popular referendum, our purpose to act—as in the case of Vietnam—on behalf of order and freedom in the world?

Those who believe in great powers for the President in foreign affairs seem to have won the day. There is no issue—unless it be how best to increase those powers to achieve better results. Those who would limit these powers must offer a substitute that is workable and acceptable to masses of Americans. Any substitute must give consideration to the problem in its historical perspective and assure that adequate government will be provided. In any case, we cannot, on such a brilliantly lighted stage as we now occupy, avoid the problem that confronts us, the problem of presidential power in the nuclear age.

Notes

NOTES

Chapter I. NOTES (pages 3-13)

1. One authority has called these words an invitation to struggle between the President and Congress for the privilege of directing foreign policy. Yet students of American history know that the struggle, if it has been that, has not been between equals. See Edward S. Corwin, *The President, Office and Powers, 1787-1957: History and Analysis of Practice and Opinion* (Fourth Rev. ed., 1957), p. 208.

2. This historical process of growth in the power and prestige of the presidency, especially in the area of foreign relations, has been perhaps the most notable feature of American constitutional development. For details, see Corwin, *op. cit.*, p. 307; Clinton Rossiter, *The American Presidency* (Second ed., 1960), pp. 25-26. Yet, as an English scholar has pointed out, "No legislative assembly in the world rivals the Senate of the United States in its influence in the international sphere." Harold J. Laski, *The American Presidency, An Interpretation* (1940), p. 167. Louis W. Koenig, in *The Chief Executive* (1964), carefully explains the limitations of presidential power. No President, he reminds us, has been able to maintain an important foreign policy without congressional support, p. 8.

3. See George F. Milton, *The Use of Presidential Power, 1789-1943* (1944), p. 23; Wilfred E. Binkley, *The Man in the White House: His Powers and Duties* (1958), p. 18; Rexford Guy Tugwell, *The Enlargement of the Presidency* (1960), pp. 35-36; Arthur B. Tourtellot, *Presidents on the Presidency* (1964), p. 276.

4. See Corwin, *op. cit.*, p. 442, note 123.

5. Herman Finer, *The Presidency: Crisis and Regeneration, An Essay in Possibilities* (1960), p. 51. See C. B. S. Reports, November 23, 1961, quoted in Tourtellot, *op. cit.*, p. 307. For a succinct summary of the facts behind decision-making, see Louis W. Koenig, *op. cit.*, pp. 331-353.

6. Quoted in Louis Brownlow, *The President and the Presidency* (1949), p. 5. See also Donald B. Johnson and Jack L. Walker, eds., *The Dynamics of the American Presidency* (1964), pp. 136-138.

7. See Edgar E. Robinson, *The Roosevelt Leadership 1933-1945* (1955), pp. 298, 305, 317, 377, 386, 406-408. See also Raymond G. O'Connor, "Did FDR Want War in 1941?" in *American Defense Policy in Perspective* (1965), pp. 235-240.

8. San Francisco *Chronicle*, February 23, 1965.

9. See Richard E. Neustadt, *Presidential Power: The Politics of Leadership* (1960), pp. 9-10; and Louis W. Koenig, ed., *The Truman Administration: Its Principles and Practice* (1956), p. 29, and his *Chief Executive*, p. 224.

10. Harold J. Laski, *op. cit.*, pp. 171, 177.

11. Quoted in Tourtellot, *op. cit.*, p. xiii. Koenig maintains that the President does not have enough power in foreign policy, *Chief Executive*, p. 210. See also Louis W. Koenig, "More Power to the President (Not Less)," *The New York Times Magazine* (January 3, 1965), pp. 7, 42-46.

Chapter II. NOTES (pages 17-76)

1. Herman Finer, *The Presidency: Crisis and Regeneration* (1960), p. 119.

2. Harry S. Truman, *Memoirs*, I, *Year of Decisions* (1955), p. 228.

3. Quoted in William Hillman, *Mr. President* (1952), p. 127.

4. Winston Churchill, *Triumph and Tragedy* (1953), pp. 455-456.

5. Jonathan Daniels, *The Man of Independence* (1950), p. 221.

6. Truman, *Memoirs*, I, p. 87.

7. Truman, *Memoirs*, II, p. 473.

8. Truman, *Memoirs*, I, p. 9.

9. Truman, *Memoirs*, II, p. 196.

10. Truman, *Memoirs*, II, p. 1.

11. William Hillman, *Mr. President* (1952), p. 86.

12. John Hersey, "Mr. President," *The New Yorker* (April 7, 1951), p. 48.

13. Harry S. Truman, *Mr. Citizen* (1960), p. 221.

14. *Ibid.*, p. 223.

15. Truman, *Memoirs*, II, p. 192.

16. Quoted in Hillman, *Mr. President*, p. 11.

17. Richard E. Neustadt, *Presidential Power: The Politics of Leadership* (1962), p. 63.

18. Douglass Cater, *Power in Washington* (1964), p. 106.
19. Walter Lippmann, *Essays in The Public Philosophy* (1955), p. 20.
20. Truman, *Mr. Citizen*, p. 74.
21. Cater, *Power in Washington*, p. 225.
22. Truman, *Memoirs*, I, p. 419.
23. Truman, *Memoirs*, I, p. x.
24. H. Bradford Westerfield, *Foreign Policy and Party Politics: Pearl Harbor to Korea* (1955), p. 201.
25. Paul Y. Hammond, "NSC-68: Prologue to Rearmament," in Warner R. Schilling, Paul Y. Hammond, and Glenn H. Snyder, *Strategy, Politics, and Defense Budgets* (1962), p. 363.
26. Arthur H. Vandenberg, Jr., ed., *The Private Papers of Senator Vandenberg* (1952), 518 (entry of September 24, 1949).
27. Quoted in William Hillman, *Mr. President* (1952), p. 150.
28. Wilber W. Hoare, Jr., "Truman (1945-1953)," in Ernest R. May, ed., *The Ultimate Decision: The President as Commander in Chief* (1960), p. 196.
29. Paul Y. Hammond, "Super Carriers and B-36 Bombers: Appropriations, Strategy and Politics," in Harold Stein, ed., *American Civil-Military Decisions: A Book of Case Studies* (1963), p. 468.
30. Samuel P. Huntington, *The Common Defense: Strategic Programs in National Politics* (1961), p. 128.
31. Herbert Feis, *Between War and Peace: The Potsdam Conference* (1960), p. 160.
32. Truman, *Memoirs*, I, p. 546.
33. This letter is printed in Hillman, *Mr. President*, pp. 21-23.
34. See James F. Byrnes, *Speaking Frankly* (1947), p. 238; and James F. Byrnes, *All in One Lifetime* (1958), pp. 400-403.
35. Truman, *Memoirs*, II, p. 106.
36. W. Phillips Davison, *The Berlin Blockade: A Study in Cold War Politics* (1958), p. 149.
37. Robert A. Dahl, *Congress and Foreign Policy* (1964), p. 102.
38. William Hillman, *Mr. President* (1952), p. 249.
39. William L. Clayton, "GATT, The Marshall Plan, and OECD," *Political Science Quarterly*, LXXVIII (December, 1963), p. 499.
40. Truman, *Memoirs*, II, p. 243.

41. Truman, *Memoirs*, I, p. 46.
42. The quotation is from Lincoln P. Bloomfield, "United States Participation in the United Nations," in Stephen D. Kertesz, ed., *American Diplomacy in a New Era* (1961), p. 460.
43. Truman, *Memoirs*, II, p. 331.
44. Truman, *Memoirs*, II, p. 332.
45. Truman, *Memoirs*, II, p. 335.
46. Truman, *Memoirs*, II, p. 338.
47. Courtney Whitney, *MacArthur: His Rendezvous with History* (1956), p. 501.
48. Morton H. Halperin, "The Limiting Process in the Korean War," *Political Science Quarterly*, LXXVIII (March 1963), pp. 36-37.
49. Richard Rovere, "Letter from Washington," *The New Yorker* (April 21, 1951), p. 102.
50. Harry S. Truman, "My First Eighty Years," *Saturday Evening Post* (June 13, 1964), pp. 16-17.
51. McGeorge Bundy, "The Presidency and the Peace," *Foreign Affairs*, 42 (April 1964), p. 357.

Chapter III. NOTES (pages 79-132)

1. This is the theme of Sidney Warren, *The President as World Leader* (1964). For further details see Dean Rusk, "The President," *Foreign Affairs*, XXXVIII (April, 1960), pp. 354-357; Richard P. Longaker, "The President as International Leader," *Law and Contemporary Problems*, XXI (Duke University Law School, Autumn, 1956), pp. 735-752; and Edward S. Corwin and Louis W. Koenig, *The Presidency Today* (1956), p. 63.
2. David B. Truman, *The Governmental Process: Political Interests and Public Opinion* (1958), pp. 398-404.
3. Dwight D. Eisenhower, *The White House Years: Mandate for Change, 1953-1956* (1956), p. 28.
4. The quotation is from Eric F. Goldman, *The Crucial Decade—And After: America, 1945-1960* (Vintage edition, 1961), p. 291.
5. Richard H. Rovere, *Affairs of State: The Eisenhower Years* (1956), p. 17.
6. Quoted in Emmet John Hughes, *The Ordeal of Power: A Political Memoir of the Eisenhower Years* (1963), p. 26.
7. Quoted in A. Merriman Smith, *Meet Mister Eisenhower* (1955), p. ix.

8. The quotations are from Eisenhower, *Mandate for Change*, pp. 13-14.

9. Quoted in Hughes, *Ordeal of Power*, p. 28.

10. Quoted in Norman A. Graebner, *The New Isolationism: A Study in Politics and Foreign Policy Since 1950* (1956), p. 98.

11. The quotation is in Goldman, *Crucial Decade*, p. 221.

12. Quoted in Walter Johnson, *1600 Pennsylvania Avenue: Presidents and the People, 1929-1959* (1960), p. 259.

13. See "The Liking of Ike" in William Lee Miller, *Piety Along the Potomac: Notes on Politics and Morals in the Fifties* (1964), pp. 3-29.

14. He also qualified this point of view, telling an audience in Chicago, for example, "I have no military magic wand to bring that war to an end." Quoted in Smith, *Meet Mister Eisenhower*, p. 48.

15. Eisenhower, *Mandate for Change*, p. 96.

16. Laurin L. Henry, *Presidential Transitions* (1960), pp. 455-703, deals with the transition from Truman to Eisenhower in detail.

17. Robert J. Donovan, *Eisenhower: The Inside Story* (1956), p. 13.

18. Quoted in Henry, *Presidential Transitions*, p. 511.

19. Robert K. Gray, *Eighteen Acres Under Glass* (1962), p. 335. Eisenhower summarized his first brief meeting with President-elect Kennedy for the transition in a seven-page memorandum. It is reproduced in Dwight D. Eisenhower, *The White House Years: Waging Peace, 1956-1961* (1965), pp. 712-716.

20. The full text is in Dwight D. Eisenhower, *Peace with Justice: Selected Addresses of Dwight D. Eisenhower* (1961), pp. 25-33.

21. See Richard E. Neustadt, *Presidential Power: The Politics of Leadership* (1960), p. 165.

22. The quotations are from Rexford G. Tugwell, *The Enlargement of the Presidency* (1960), p. 489; and Herman Finer, *The Presidency: Crisis and Regeneration, an Essay in Possibilities* (1960), p. 183.

23. Eisenhower, *Mandate for Change*, p. 114. For a convenient summary of Eisenhower's concept of leadership and organizational procedure, see W. W. Rostow, *The United States in the World Arena: An Essay in Recent History* (1960), p. 388.

24. Eisenhower, *Mandate for Change*, p. 88.

25. Neustadt, *Presidential Power*, p. 9.

26. Before Eisenhower's time no formal records or minutes of cabinet meetings were kept. Eisenhower did not formalize cabinet procedure immediately; he experimented first. See Richard F. Fenno, Jr., *The President's Cabinet: An Analysis in the Period from Wilson to Eisenhower* (1959), pp. 94-97, 103. James Reston analyzed Ike's staff procedure in the fifth article of a series called "The Presidency," *The New York Times*, June 22, 1956, p. 14.

27. The quotation is from Sherman Adams, *Firsthand Report: The Story of the Eisenhower Administration* (1961), p. 4. Rostow, in *The United States in the World Arena*, p. 397, suggests that this emphasis on consensus stifled leadership. Eisenhower also wanted issues boiled down before they reached him. Fenno, *President's Cabinet*, p. 41.

28. Quoted in Adams, *Firsthand Report*, p. 5.

29. See Edward S. Corwin, *The President, Office and Powers, 1787-1957: History and Analysis of Practice and Opinion* (Fourth Rev. Ed., 1951), p. 302; Clinton Rossiter, *The American Presidency* (Second ed., 1960), p. 169; and R. H. Pear, "The American Presidency under Eisenhower," *The Political Quarterly*, XXVIII (Jan.-March, 1957), pp. 11-12.

30. Richard M. Nixon, in *Six Crises* (1962), p. 141, pointed out that the staff system kept quarrels to a minimum. See also Smith, *Meet Mister Eisenhower*, pp. 128-129.

31. Quoted in Theodore C. Sorensen, *Decision-Making in the White House: The Olive Branch or the Arrows* (1963), p. 13.

32. Eisenhower, *Mandate for Change*, pp. 131, 132.

33. Robert E. Elder, *The Policy Machine: The Department of State and American Foreign Policy* (1960), p. 13.

34. For Allen Dulles's view of this agency, see his *The Craft of Intelligence* (1963).

35. See James L. McCamy, *The Administration of American Foreign Affairs* (1950), p. 171, and Merlo J. Pusey, *Eisenhower the President* (1956), p. 285.

36. Dean Rusk argued that "where an

exaggerated emphasis is placed upon delegation, responsibility, like sediment, sinks to the bottom." In "The President," *Foreign Affairs*, p. 356.

37. Donovan, *Eisenhower*, p. 42, and Hughes, *Ordeal of Power*, p. 79.

38. Rostow, *The United States in the World Arena*, p. 391. The quotation is from Dean Albertson, ed., *Eisenhower as President* (1963), p. xiii.

39. Nixon, *Six Crises*, p. 145.

40. *Ibid.*, p. 150.

41. Corwin, *The President*, p. 304.

42. The New York *Times*, March 11, 1956, p. E7. The quotations are from Eisenhower, *Waging Peace*, p. 632.

43. Quoted in Hughes, *Ordeal of Power*, p. 121.

44. See Marquis Childs, *Eisenhower: Captive Hero. A Critical Study of the General and the President* (1958), p. 188.

45. Quoted in Adams, *Firsthand Report*, p. 89.

46. Richard Goold-Adams, *The Time of Power: A Reappraisal of John Foster Dulles* (London, 1962), p. 70. See also James Reston in The New York *Times*, Nov. 21, 1952, p. 16, Feb. 15, 1959, p. E3, and the Foreword to Eleanor Lansing Dulles, *John Foster Dulles: The Last Year* (1963), where Eisenhower described Dulles as one of "the great Secretaries of State in United States history." ... See also pp. 29 and 31.

47. Quoted in Hughes, *Ordeal of Power*, p. 38. Italics are in the original.

48. Adams, *Firsthand Report*, p. 58.

49. See Eisenhower, *Waging Peace*, p. 365 and Herman Finer, *Dulles Over Suez: The Theory and Practice of His Diplomacy* (1964), p. 71.

50. Quoted in Goldman, *Crucial Decade*, p. 238. See also Rovere, *Affairs of State*, p. 89, for critical reaction to the speech.

51. Adams, *Firsthand Report*, p. 87.

52. Quoted in Gray, *Eighteen Acres Under Glass*, p. 173.

53. For a discussion of this point, with historical examples, see Edward S. Corwin, *The President's Control of Foreign Relations* (1917), pp. 126-163. See also Sidney Hyman, *The American President* (1954), p. 10.

54. Pendleton Herring, *Presidential Leadership: The Political Relations of* *Congress and the Chief Executive* (1940), pp. 15-16.

55. Eisenhower, *Mandate for Change*, p. 181.

56. Quoted in Adams, *Firsthand Report*, p. 99.

57. Eisenhower, *Mandate for Change*, p. 181.

58. "At no time, however, did the President make a formal decision to enlarge the war," according to Donovan, *Eisenhower*, p. 119.

59. The quotations are from Eisenhower, *Mandate for Change*, p. 285, and Hughes, *Ordeal of Power*, p. 144, cabinet meeting of April 3, 1953.

60. The quotations are from Arthur B. Tourtellot, *Presidents on the Presidency* (1964), p. 304, and Donovan, *Eisenhower*, p. 239.

61. C. B. S. Reports, Nov. 23, 1961, quoted in Tourtellot, *Presidents on the Presidency*, p. 306.

62. April 16, 1954, quoted in Graebner, *New Isolationism*, p. 164.

63. Eisenhower, *Mandate for Change*, p. 353.

64. The quotations are from *ibid.*, pp. 351, 373. Almost twelve years later, Lieutenant General James M. Gavin, who had been the Army's Chief of Plans and Operations in 1954, gave another view of Eisenhower's decision on intervention. Gavin recalled that General Matthew B. Ridgway, at that time the Army's Chief of Staff, was the one who had dissuaded President Eisenhower from committing troops to Vietnam. See the *New York Times*, Jan. 17, 1966.

65. Quoted in John R. Beal, *John Foster Dulles* (1957), p. 233.

66. May 25, 1954, quoted in *ibid.*, pp. 234-235.

67. Eisenhower, *Mandate for Change*, pp. 425-426.

68. Quoted in Tourtellot, *Presidents on the Presidency*, p. 343. For the changed role of the Commander-in-Chief, see Rusk, "The President," *Foreign Affairs*, p. 357, and Corwin, *The President*, p. 226.

69. Quoted, with italics, in Hughes, *Ordeal of Power*, p. 248.

70. Eisenhower, *Mandate for Change*, p. 215.

71. Quoted in Graebner, *New Isolationism*, pp. 150-151.

72. Eisenhower, *Mandate for Change*, p. 400.

73. Press conference of Aug. 17, 1954, quoted in Donovan, *Eisenhower*, p. 300.

74. Eisenhower, *Mandate for Change*, p. 459.

75. *Ibid.*, pp. 463-465, and Adams, *Firsthand Report*, p. 127.

76. Eisenhower, *Mandate for Change*, p. 467.

77. Adams, *Firsthand Report*, p. 121, and Pusey, *Eisenhower the President*, p. 203. Compare this with Eisenhower's concern for Congressional support in the crisis of Dien Bien Phu.

78. Quoted in Tourtellot, *Presidents on the Presidency*, p. 303.

79. See, for example, Rovere, *Affairs of State*, pp. 250-251; Wilfred E. Binkley, *The Man in the White House: His Powers and Duties* (1958), p. 240; and Graebner, *New Isolationism*, p. 177.

80. Quoted in Graebner, *New Isolationism*, p. 202.

81. See Eisenhower, *Waging Peace*, p. 295.

82. See James R. Shepley, "How Dulles Averted War," *Life* XL (Jan. 16, 1956), pp. 70-72.

83. Adams, *Firsthand Report*, p. 118.

84. See Dulles to Eisenhower, Sept. 15, 1956, in Eisenhower, *Waging Peace*, p. 33.

85. The speech is printed in Carol A. Fisher and Fred Krinsky, *Middle East in Crisis: A Historical and Documentary Review* (1959), pp. 167-170.

86. Robert Murphy, *Diplomat Among Warriors* (1964), pp. 383-384.

87. Quoted in Adams, *Firsthand Report*, p. 272.

88. *Ibid.*, p. 291.

89. The first instance had occurred early in 1957 when Eisenhower sought, and failed to obtain, Congressional support for a policy of sanctions against Israel because she refused to comply with a United Nations resolution to withdraw from positions her soldiers held in Egypt. For details, see *ibid.*, pp. 279-287; Eisenhower, *Waging Peace*, pp. 183-189; and Finer, *Dulles Over Suez*, pp. 465-490.

90. See Eisenhower, *Waging Peace*, pp. 270, 272.

91. See Adams, *Firsthand Report*, p. 293, and Ernest R. May, ed., *The Ultimate Decision: The President as Commander-in-Chief* (1960), p. 227.

92. Nov. 4, 1956, quoted in Richard P. Stebbins, *The United States in World Affairs, 1956* (1957), p. 348.

93. Nov. 14, 1956, quoted in *ibid.*, p. 306.

94. News conference of Nov. 7, 1958, *Department of State Bulletin*, XXXIX (Nov. 24, 1958), p. 813.

95. Adams, *Firsthand Report*, p. 87.

96. Quoted in Gray, *Eighteen Acres Under Glass*, p. 39.

97. Rossiter, *American Presidency*, p. 167.

98. For details, see Eisenhower, *Waging Peace*, pp. 405-408, and Murphy, *Diplomat Among Warriors*, pp. 438-439.

99. Oct. 28, 1959, quoted in Richard P. Stebbins, *The United States in World Affairs, 1959* (1960), p. 164.

100. Allen Dulles, who pointed out that Khrushchev had known of the U-2 flights before his missile had brought down Powers' plane, defended Eisenhower's departure from tradition in this instance. See *Craft of Intelligence*, pp. 196-197. Eisenhower also defended his action in *Waging Peace*, pp. 550-553, but the men who had handled State Department clearances for U-2 overflights found Eisenhower's "impulsive *mea culpa*" incomprehensible. See Murphy, *Diplomat Among Warriors*, p. 440.

101. The Eisenhower and Khrushchev quotations are from Hughes, *Ordeal of Power*, p. 301.

102. Department of State Bulletin, XLII (Feb. 8, 1960), p. 180.

103. These agreements allowed foreign courts jurisdiction over American service men who committed crimes while stationed in a foreign country. Such agreements fell within the President's powers as Commander-in-Chief. See Corwin, *The President*, p. 224.

104. For details on the Japanese episode, see A. Merriman Smith, *A President's Odyssey* (1961), pp. 209-223; and Eisenhower, *Waging Peace*, pp. 561-563.

105. "The worst periods of our history," one student of the office maintained, "have been when Presidents were weak and Congresses strong." He also argued that in time of crises strong men make great presidents.

106. See George F. Milton, *Use of Presidential Power, 1789-1943* (1944), pp. 311,

323. For a comparison of the presidency with other executive offices, see Koenig, *The Chief Executive* (1964), pp. 386-406.

107. Quoted, including italics, in Hughes, *Ordeal of Power*, p. 124.

108. Rossiter, *American Presidency*, p. 163.

109. Quoted in Johnson, *1600 Pennsylvania Avenue*, p. 318.

110. *Ibid.*, pp. 321-322. The quotations are from Eisenhower, *Waging Peace*, p. 616.

111. Quoted, including italics, in Hughes, *Ordeal of Power*, pp. 105-106.

112. The text of the address, delivered in Washington before The American Society of Newspaper Editors, April 16, 1953, is in Eisenhower, *Peace with Justice*, pp. 34-44.

113. Eisenhower, *Mandate for Change*, p. 458.

114. The quotations are from Graebner, *New Isolationism*, p. 215. See also Elmer E. Cornwell, Jr., *Presidential Leadership of Public Opinion* (1965), p. 249.

115. Quoted from Cabinet meeting of July 17, 1953, including italics, in Hughes, *Ordeal of Power*, p. 151.

116. Quoted from Cabinet meeting of March 6, 1953, in *ibid.*, p. 101.

117. Quoted in Gray, *Eighteen Acres Under Glass*, p. 343.

118. Quoted in Adams, *Firsthand Report*, p. 460.

119. *Ibid.*, p. 124. Eisenhower also believed that events abroad would continue to dominate domestic policies into the foreseeable future. Smith, *Meet Mister Eisenhower*, p. 295. Ike's concept of the presidency in 1955 is summarized on p. 298.

120. The quotations are from Paul Seabury, *Power, Freedom, and Diplomacy: The Foreign Policy of the United States of America* (1963), p. 195 n; Pusey, *Eisenhower the President*, p. 289; and Rostow, *The United States in the World Arena*, p. 386. Eisenhower often spoke of himself as a "Constitutional President," as if there had been another kind. See Donovan, *Eisenhower*, p. 83.

Chapter IV. NOTES (pages 135-195)

1. See Kennedy's address to the Senate prior to his nomination, *Congressional Record*, 86th Congress, 2d Session (Vol. 106, Part 10), pp. 12523-26, June 14, 1960.

This address is an appraisal, on twelve points, of American foreign policy throughout the world.

2. Theodore H. White, *The Making of the President* (Atheneum, 1961), should be read as a partisan (pro Kennedy) study of the election. It slights the consideration of foreign policy under the assumption that it was not an important issue in winning the campaign. Richard M. Nixon, *Six Crises* (Doubleday, 1962), treats the campaign as the sixth crisis, and should be read in conjunction with the White book, to provide a balanced perspective and to give an appreciation of the substantive issues. The texts of the debates and speeches upon which Nixon builds his analysis should be referred to.

3. See *Freedom of Communications*— Parts I-III (87th Congress, First session, Senate report 994, GPO, 1961) Part I, the speeches, remarks, press conferences, and statements of Senator John F. Kennedy, August 1 through November 7, 1960. Part II, the speeches, remarks, press conferences and study papers of Vice President Richard M. Nixon, August 1 through November 7, 1960. Part III, the joint appearances of Senator John F. Kennedy and Vice President Richard M. Nixon and others, 1960 campaign.

4. The leading article on the subject, P. E. Converse et al., "Stability and Change in 1960: A Reinstating Eelection," *American Political Science Review*, Vol. 55 (June, 1961) pp. 269-280, concludes that while the authors could not measure the effect of foreign policy issues on the election, they were confident that it did not compare in importance with the religious issue (which hurt Kennedy). Sidney Kraus, *The Great Debates* (University of Indiana, 1962), chapter by E. Katz and J. J. Seldman, "Debates in the Light of Research," likewise concluded that issues were not important and that the effect of the debates was to strengthen already existing partisan support. N. W. Polsby and A. W. Wildavsky, *Presidential Elections* (Scribners, 1964) agreed with the other assessments regarding substantive foreign policy and gave their estimate that the determining factor of the campaign was the perceived ability of the respective candidates.

5. The story of the election would be in-

complete without fulsome reference to periodical reports. The New York Council on Foreign Relations provided four bulging files of clippings which were taken from U. S. and foreign "elite" press, and periodicals. Those files found most useful for the 1960 campaign included:

U.S. Presidential Campaign, 1960—general

Presidential campaign, 1960—Democratic

Presidential campaign, 1960—Republican

Presidential campaign, 1960—foreign attitudes.

6. Sorensen's father had been the campaign manager for George Norris, had sailed to Europe on Henry Ford's peace ship, and was counsel to the women's suffrage movement.

7. Henry Brandon's interview, "Schlesinger at the White House," *Harper's* (July, 1964), pp. 55-60, confirms and illustrates many of the conclusions found elsewhere (e.g., Cater, Sorensen) relating to the predominant role of the White House staff in policy-making. Once again the Council on Foreign Relations files were found invaluable, especially the three files on U. S. Politics and Government listed under "The Kennedy Administration," "Appointments," and "Reorganization." A few conclusions, not otherwise documented, were reached from off-the-record remarks of decision-makers in the Kennedy administration. While written in the petulant style of a rejected suitor, and entirely untrustworthy in terms of his substantive analysis, Victor Laski's, *JFK: Man and Myth* cannot be ignored. The last two chapters cover the period under review here (including the 1960 campaign), but the earlier chapters provide revealing insights into the Kennedy family and his White House staff.

8. A critical analysis of the Kennedy administration may be found in Douglass Cater's *Power in Washington*. Especially useful is his development of Kennedy's view of leadership. Cater reserves judgment on President Kennedy—his tenure was too brief and his program had not been accepted by Congress. Cater's short summary of Theodore C. Sorensen's *Decision-Making in the White House* is entirely inadequate. The Sorensen book represents the reflections of an experienced adminis-

tration on the complex decision-making process. Richard E. Neustadt, *Presidential Power*, which was so influential in shaping the early oragnization of the Kennedy years, is brilliantly analyzed by Cater, but should be read in its entirety for an adequate understanding of the philosophy of government which was guiding the new administration.

9. For an account of the CIA, the intelligence community, and the personality of its leaders, see David Wise and Thomas B. Ross, *The Invisible Government* (Random House, 1964).

10. The story of the Bay of Pigs has been told by Haynes Johnson, *The Bay of Pigs* (Norton, 1964), but it is preoccupied with the actual execution of the decision and not with the decision-making itself. Wise and Ross, *Invisible Government,* is another recent account, as is Hugh Sidey, *John F. Kennedy, President* (Atheneum, 1964). The Sidey book provides an intimate picture of the inner circle of decision-makers, as does the best single account of this episode—Arthur M. Schlesinger, Jr., *A Thousand Days* (Houghton Mifflin, 1965).

11. The appraisal of the Alliance for Progress was drawn from materials published during the last four years and digested annually for the article "Inter-American Affairs" in the *Americana Annual,* 1961, 1962, 1963, 1964.

12. No account of the Cuban missile story compares in accuracy, completeness, and dramatic impact with Elie Abel, *The Missile Crisis* (Lippincott, 1966).

13. See Theodore C. Sorensen, *Kennedy,* p. 702, for an account of the President's meeting with congressional leaders, some of whom advocated strong measures. "The President, however, was adamant. He was acting by Executive Order, Presidential Proclamation, and inherent powers, not under any resolution or act of the Congress. He had earlier rejected all suggestions of reconvening Congress or requesting a formal declaration of war, and he had summoned the leaders only when hard evidence and a fixed policy were ready."

14. David L. Larson (ed.), *The Cuban Crisis of 1962* (Houghton Mifflin, 1963), p. 41. President Kennedy, in answering questions on a televised press conference following the announcement of this deci-

sion, said that the details of the discussion that led to the decision might "best be left to the historians who will have all the evidence." It was thought that this referred to the Presidential Papers of his administration. For a preview of what they may someday reveal, see Sorensen, *Kennedy,* Chapter XXIV, "The Confrontation in Cuba," pp. 667-718; also Arthur M. Schlesinger, *A Thousand Days,* Chapter XXX, "Again Cuba," pp. 794-819.

15. Measuring Affect and Action in International Reaction Models: Empirical Materials from the 1962 Cuban Crisis—Ole R. Holsti, Richard A. Brody, and Robert C. North. The Holsti study measures the escalation of the crisis from Kennedy's public announcement on October 28, by counting and weighing (they make use of a computer) hostility phases in speeches from both sides. They emphasize the role of "images" each side has of the other's actions which stimulates each with a response which may mean something different to each. Holsti shows how tensions of one side follow those of the other and indicates that lower tensions by Friday, October 26, paved the way for settlement.

16. Roger Hilsman, "The Cuban Crisis: How Close We Were to War," *Look* (August 25, 1964), pp. 17-21, relates the important role of ABC journalist, John Scali. Hilsman hints at a larger role for Stevenson and Rusk than heretofore has been noted. The Hilsman article demonstrates the importance of accurate communications between adversaries in a conflict situation.

17. After Two Years of the Kennedy Administration, Who Determines Foreign Policy?—Charles A. McClelland, *Proceedings,* Institute of World Affairs, December, 1962.

18. Sidey, op. cit., p. 368.

19. *United States in World Affairs,* for 1961, 1962, and 1963 were the chief references for this section on the trade expansion act and Kennedy's grand design for Europe. Disenchantment with the possibilities of an Atlantic Alliance becomes evident only in the 1963 volume. The author was clearly NATO-oriented and seemed to relinquish his point of view most reluctantly.

20. Joseph Kraft, "Kennedy's Working Staff," *Harpers* (Dec., 1962), pp. 29-37, provided some insight as to the allocation of responsibilities of the White House staff.

21. In addition to the sources cited earlier —especially Wise and Ross, Sidey and Schlesinger—the annual volumes published by the Council on Foreign Relations for 1961, 1962, and 1963, Richard P. Stebbins, *The United States in World Affairs,* were useful.

22. Wise and Ross, *The Invisible Government,* p. 150.

23. Claude A. Buss, *The Arc of Crisis,* p. 82.

24. Wise and Ross, op. cit., p. 159. The authors emphasize that the build-up was in violation of the Geneva Accords (of 1954 *and* 1962?).

25. For factual material, heavy reliance was placed on the *United States in World Affairs, 1963.* Other references have been noted earlier. Off-the-record meetings with various principals involved in Russian-American relations held at the Council on Foreign Relations during 1963 provided useful background material.

26. James M. Burns, *Presidential Government, The Crucible of Leadership* (Houghton Mifflin, 1966), p. 217, and Sorensen, *op. cit.,* p. 740, note that Kennedy himself considered this treaty as a "first step." But because it was the direct result of presidential initiative—using all the presidential resources by sounding out the Russians, pressing the negotiations, and pushing the treaty through the Senate, and because it contributed to changing the whole world situation rather than merely responding to a single incident, it deserves the highest accolade of the brief Kennedy administration.

27. "One of John Kennedy's most important contributions to the human spirit was his concept of the office of the Presidency. His philosophy of government was keyed to power, not as a matter of personal ambition but of national obligation: the primacy of the White House within the Executive Branch and of the Executive Branch within the Federal Government, the leadership of the Federal Government within the United States and of the United States within the community of nations." Sorensen, *Kennedy,* p. 389.

28. "And yet he almost never spoke of 'power.' Power was not a goal he sought for its own sake. It was there, in the White House, to be used, without any sense of

263

guilt or greed, as a means of getting things done. He felt neither uplifted nor weighted down by power. He enjoyed the Presidency, thinking not of its power but its opportunities, and he was sobered by the Presidency, thinking not of its power but its obligations. He was a strong President primarily because he was a strong person." *Ibid*, p. 389.

Chapter V. NOTES (pages 199-242)

1. See pp. 100-101 of this volume.
2. See pp. 181-186 of this volume.
3. Commentators at this time called attention to the fact that the President had given heed, more and more, to the advisers on his staff, particularly McGeorge Bundy and C.I.A. Director John A. McCone. The public knew little of the activities of the C.I.A. in South Vietnam.
4. See Lyndon B. Johnson, *My Hope for America* (1964), pp. 99-109.
5. Commentators early in Johnson's service as President noted his tendency to use "we" in discussing the problems of the administration. What was meant is seen in his address at Fort McNair on August 21, 1964, when he spoke of the relationship between military men and civilian political leaders as "one team." He commented on his more than thirty years' knowledge of this as he served on congressional committees, saw action daily in World War II and as a member of the National Security Council during the Kennedy administration. "Today as Commander-in-Chief," he said, "nothing" was more gratifying and reassuring.
6. In raising the question of control of potential use of nuclear power, presidential candidate Goldwater perhaps served to emphasize the fact that as Commander-in-Chief of the nation's armed forces the President's *is* the final decision in the matter. See in particular Senator (sic) Barry Goldwater, *Where I Stand* (1964).
7. See Senator Barry Goldwater, *The Conscience of a Conservative* (1960).
8. Any doubt as to the influence of the commentator in interpreting the actions and words of the President to the public (at the time and often in advance of a decision) will be dispelled by reading the columns of Walter Lippmann and of James Reston. The most complete and exciting, as well as accurate survey of such work is seen in David Brinkley's article, "Leading from Strength: LBJ in Action," in *The Atlantic Monthly* (February, 1965), Vol. 215, No. 2, pp. 49-54.

9. For an excellent summary of the style and value of Johnson's press conferences, see E. E. Cornwell, *Presidential Leadership of Public Opinion* (1965), pp. 201-2; 297-8.
10. "When the late President Kennedy was senator from Massachusetts he said: 'What we must offer them (the people of Asia) is a revolution, a political, economic and social revolution, far superior to anything the Communists can offer, (and) far more democratic." Claude A. Buss, *Asia in the Modern World: A History of China, Japan, South and Southeast Asia* (1964), p. 740.
11. "His (Kennedy's) essential contribution ... was both to raise our commitment and to keep it limited. He neither permitted the war's escalation into a general war nor bargained away Vietnam's security at the conference table, despite being pressed along both lines by those impatient to win or withdraw. His strategy essentially was to avoid escalation, retreat or a choice limited to those two, while seeking to buy time—time to make the policies and programs of both the American and Vietnamese governments more appealing to the villagers—time to build an antiguerrilla capability sufficient to convince the Communists that they could not seize the country militarily—and time to put the Vietnamese themselves in a position to achieve the settlement only they could achieve by bringing terrorism under control." Theodore C. Sorensen, *Kennedy* (1965), pp. 651-652.
12. A declaration of war is not so simple in manner and result as it may seem to be. The reasons why a president might not wish to have this step taken by the Congress include the following, as summarized by C. L. Sulzberger in The New York Times, March 4, 1966: (1) "The Chief Executive (who is also Commander in Chief) does not need *a posteriori* Congressional ratification of a decision to protect national interests.... (2) Congressional approval of existing hostilities is not a constitutional requisite.... (3) Mr. Johnson sees a consecutive legal pattern for his conduct of current military operations.

.... (4) Although it would bring into play certain latent Presidential powers, it would make it far more difficult for both sides to control the situation and thus keep it from exploding more dangerously. Formalization of the conflict could be interpreted by our opponents as a doctrinal challenge that would have to be met on a still greater scale.... (5) The Administration doesn't know if any secret military compacts exist between the Vietcong, Hanoi, Peking and possibly Moscow. It doesn't wish to test its ignorance by formal declaration of war. .... (6) There is an additional problem: Against whom would war be declared? Against the Vietcong or its National Liberation Front 'government' which we don't recognize? .... (7) in the nuclear-missile-age, the Administration insists we must do away with the very concept of *casus belli*. The idea of formalized war declarations has vastly changed.... The Administration considers the existing legal position on Vietnam more than adequate and the commitment irrevocable. The White House sees a clear and long line of precedent for the existing situation—dating right back to the Founding Fathers— and that it would be feckless and foolish to further formalize a bloody confrontation."

Chapter VI. NOTES (pages 245-251)

1. See H. H. Ransom, *Can American Democracy Survive Cold War?* (1963), especially Chapters II, VII. See also Douglass Cater, *Power in Washington*.

2. "Without any consultation with the men of the Senate who had been his colleagues, he (President Johnson in a telecast in the fall of 1964) announced: 'The nations which do not seek nuclear weapons can be sure that if they need our strong support against some threat of nuclear blackmail, they will have it.' Here was the strong President making foreign policy on his own. Perhaps this commitment would be embarrassing in the future." Jack Bell, *The Johnson Treatment*, p. 293.

3. How carefully President Johnson proceeded in August, 1964, when a crisis developed in the Gulf of Tonkin off the shores of South Vietnam, has later become evident. By resolution, the Congress granted the President authority to take "all necessary measures to repel any armed attack against the forces of the United States and to prevent further aggression," referring to the attack of the North Vietnam PT boats upon two U. S. destroyers in international waters. The resolution, which had been prepared by the President, further declared that "the maintenance of international peace and security in Southeast Asia" was "vital" to America's "national interest and to world peace." Also included was the sober statement that "The United States is ... prepared, as the President determines, to take all necessary steps, including the use of armed force, to assist any member or protocol state of the Southeast Asia collective defense treaty requesting assistance in defense of its freedom." Yet as Commander-in-Chief the President would seem to have no restraint upon his decisions in the military position established in South Vietnam.

4. "U.S. Policy on Vietnam," Address by Vice-President Hubert Humphrey on June 1, 1965, quoted in *Congressional Record*, 89th Congress, First Session, June 8, 1965, Vol. III, No. 103, p. 12344. See also George A. Carver, Jr., "The Faceless Viet Cong," in *Foreign Affairs*, Vol. 44, No. 3 (April, 1966).

5. Theodore C. Sorensen, *Kennedy*, p. 389.

6. Two contrasting streams of thought as to the destiny of this nation have revealed themselves in the public mind. One of these is conditioned by the assumption that the United States is involved in the world revolution in the social and economic structure of society that is now under way. Extremists who express this view—not all of them Communists—call for "a complete turnover of American society." The other stream of thought reflects a view long held by a majority of the American people. We have already had our revolution, according to this view, and we should maintain an economic structure that is a result of our unique development and support it by a social structure and political methods that have produced the Americn way of life. The argument between protagonists of these two views has divided the nation in thought and emotion more emphatically than any other issue in the past hundred years. In such a climate of opinion, the President's power to shape relations with other nations in the best interests of the United States is seriously endangered.

7. "On hundreds of occasions during the nineteenth and twentieth centuries, American Presidents or military forces acting under presidential authority, engaged in combat operations abroad with no specific sanction from Congress." Paul Seabury, *Power, Freedom and Diplomacy* (1963), p. 208.

8. "The power of the Secretary of State depends on his relations with the President and hence is personal more than institutional." Alexander De Conde, *The American Secretary of State*, p. viii. "It is of course in the field of foreign relations that the personalization of the presidency has appeared the most strikingly in the past, and that Presidents have the most frequently disported themselves uncontrolled by responsible counselors." E. S. Corwin, *The President—Office and Powers*, p. 494.

The most complete presentation of the actual work of the State Department officials and in particular of their relations with the members of the Congress and the committees of the Congress is to be found in *The Secretary of State and the Ambassador;* Jackson sub-committee *Papers* on Conduct of American Foreign Policy, edited by Henry M. Jackson (1965).

9. See pp. 98-100 (involving notes 59-60) of this volume.

10. This is the problem that is faced by those members of the Senate who, in March, 1966, were attempting, through a continuation of public hearings and by debate on the floor of the Senate to develop a possible course of action. See the State Department Report filed with the Committee on Foreign Relations on March 8, 1966.

BIBLIOGRAPHY

The Presidential Papers

The records accumulated by the presidents during their tenure in office have often provided the historian with invaluable data for an understanding of the various policies adopted by the administrations. The largest single collection of these papers, beginning with those of George Washington and ending with those of Calvin Coolidge, are housed in the Manuscript Division of the Library of Congress. Among the notable exceptions are the papers of John Adams and John Quincy Adams, which are kept at the Massachusetts Historical Society.

The first of the presidential libraries was established to house the papers of Franklin Delano Roosevelt. Erected on the President's estate at Hyde Park, New York, by private funds, the Library was placed under the jurisdiction of the federal government. Following this example, Harry S. Truman placed his records in a special library at his home town of Independence, Missouri, and Dwight D. Eisenhower's files are now located at Abilene, Kansas. In the meantime Herbert Hoover moved his presidential papers from the Hoover Institution at Stanford University to West Branch, Iowa, and those of the late John F. Kennedy will eventually rest at Cambridge, Massachusetts. In each case the Roosevelt precedent has been followed, namely, the erection of a building by private subscription to be placed under the jurisdiction of the General Services Administration with a director who is a government employee.

The value of these collections to the researcher depends on the nature of the materials and their point of time in the past. Some of the files are far from complete, either because they were poorly maintained or because potentially embarrassing items have been culled. Also, certain restrictions have been placed on researchers for a variety of reasons. At no time did Mr. Hoover grant access to his papers and few scholars have had the opportunity to see any portion of them. The majority of the Franklin Roosevelt papers are available to bona fide researchers but many of the files containing material pertaining to foreign policy and military affairs are still closed, especially those relating to World War II. Since most of these items are highly classified they must be read and declassified by authorized representatives of the government agency concerned, and this process is time-consuming and costly. Even though a few scholars have been granted security clearance and allowed to consult some materials under the stipulation that the notes be screened, papers labeled TOP SECRET still remain closed. Obviously, papers in this category are the most valuable for illuminating the mysteries of wartime diplomacy.

In the Truman collection most of the significant material on the foreign policy of the administration remains closed. Again it is a matter of sensitivity and declassification, though information concerning certain aspects of foreign affairs, such as public reaction to specific developments, can be found in some of the open files. The Eisenhower papers, although presently housed in the Library at Abilene, will not be available for some time, and the use of the Kennedy papers is in the even more distant future.

The type of material sought in the presidential papers by the researcher interested in foreign relations is the type that usually cannot be found in speeches, published documents, or even in the files of the State Department. He is usually aware of what the President did, and, to a lesser extent, how he did it. What he is most anxious to know is why a particular policy was adopted rather than any of the alternatives. Occasionally clues may be found in correspondence, in a brief note to a high official, in observations scrawled on a memorandum from the Secretary of State, or in the record of a conversation. Personal diaries, notably those maintained by John Quincy Adams and James K. Polk, have been invaluable in helping subsequent generations to understand the diplomacy of earlier administrations. In more recent times, beginning with Franklin Roosevelt, so much top-level negotiation has been conducted by the President that a reasonably complete account will be impossible without access to his papers.

Perhaps the most striking example is the diplomacy of World War II, about which so much has been written. Almost all significant decisions were made by the heads of state representing Great Britain, the Soviet Union, and the United States. Winston Churchill has presented his version in great detail based on the complete files of the British government. Yet these materials will be denied the researcher for a period of fifty years, which is the restriction placed on Foreign Office records. The Soviet Union has never opened its diplomatic files to scholars and probably never will in the foreseeable future. The State Department files are obviously incomplete for this period because the Secretary of State was not involved in much of the negotiation. Thus a truly satisfactory account of America's wartime diplomacy must await a perusal of Roosevelt's so-called "Map-Room" papers.

Recently the Library of Congress has begun to place on microfilm the papers of the presidents. This is a laudable though expensive project, and it will enable students and scholars to consult this material in their local libraries. With the President the focal point of the American government and the director of foreign policy, the value of this project is incalculable.

But the scholar—like all others—must remain forever in doubt as to the content of conversations and the agreements reached even by telephone. Here it is that memory of participants recorded in "oral history" projects is important, but often inconclusive.

Documents

In addition to Presidential Papers and notes on personal interviews with participants, the sources used in this study have included in particular the following government publications:

POSTWAR FOREIGN POLICY PREPARATION 1939-1945, Department of State Publication 3580, General Foreign Policy Series 15, Released February 1950. Division of Publications, Office of Public Affairs.

IN QUEST OF PEACE AND SECURITY: SELECTED DOCUMENTS ON AMERICAN FOREIGN POLICY 1941-1951, Department of State Publication 4245, General Foreign Policy Series 53, Released October 1951.

COMMAND DECISIONS, Edited with Introductory Essay by Kent Roberts Greenfield, Office of the Chief of Military History, Department of the Army, Washington, D.C., 1960.

ORGANIZING FOR NATIONAL SECURITY: Studies and Background Materials Submitted to the Committee on Government Operations, United States Senate, by its Committee on National Policy Machinery (Pursuant to S. Res. 115, 86th Cong., and S. Res. 20, 87th Cong.). Volume 2 (1961).

THE AMBASSADOR AND THE PROBLEM OF COORDINATION: A Study Submitted by the Subcommittee on National Security Staffing and Operations (Pursuant to S. Res. 13, 88th Cong.) to the Committee on Government Operations, United States Senate (1963).

THE SECRETARY OF STATE AND THE AMBASSADOR. Jackson Subcommittee Papers on the Conduct of American Foreign Policy. Edited by Senator Henry M. Jackson (Praeger, 1964).

The record of discussion and action in the Congress, especially in the Senate, concerning the situation in Southeast Asia is available in the *Congressional Record*. The following government publications on this subject may also be of interest:

A THREAT TO THE PEACE: NORTH VIET-NAM'S EFFORT TO CONQUER SOUTH VIETNAM, Department of State Publication 7308 (1961).

Aggression from the North: The Record of North Viet-Nam's Campaign to Conquer South Viet-Nam, Department of State Publication 7839 (1965).

Background Information Relating to Southeast Asia and Viet-nam, Committee on Foreign Relations, United States Senate, January 14, 1965, 89th Congress, 1st Session (1965).

"Communist China: A Problem in U.S. Policymaking," by Marshall Green, Deputy Assistant Secretary for Far Eastern Affairs, Bureau of Public Affairs, Department of State, Far Eastern Series 131, May 1965, No. 11. Department of State Publication 7870.

"The U.S. Stake in Southeast Asia," by Leonard Unger, Deputy Assistant Secretary for Far Eastern Affairs, Bureau of Public Affairs, Department of State, Far Eastern Series 133, June 1965, No. 13. Department of State Publication 7885.

Why Vietnam, Foreword by Lyndon B. Johnson, August 20, 1965, U. S. Government Printing Office, Washington, D.C.

Atlhough not a government publication, Foreign Affairs, an American Quarterly Review published by the Council on Foreign Relations, especially Vols. 18-43, provides important sections on Source Materials. Also of interest is the series Documents on American Foreign Relations, a yearly publication of the Council on Foreign Relations.

Selected Studies

Elie Abel, The Missile Crisis (Lippincott, 1965).

Sherman Adams, Firsthand Report: The Story of the Eisenhower Administration (Harper, 1961).

Dean Albertson, ed·, Eisenhower As President (American Century, 1963).

Gar Alperovitz, Atomic Diplomacy: Hiroshima and Potsdam (Simon and Schuster, 1965).

John R. Beal, John Foster Dulles: 1888-1957 (Harper, 1957).

Jack Bell, The Johnson Treatment: How Lyndon B. Johnson Took Over the Presidency and Made It His Own (Harper & Row, 1965).

Wilfred E. Binkley, The Man in the White House: His Powers and Duties (Johns Hopkins University Press, 1958).

Robert R. Bowie, Shaping the Futrue (Columbia University Press, 1963).

David Braybrook and Charles E. Lindblom, A Strategy of Decision (Collier-Macmillan, 1963).

Louis W. Brownlow, The President and the Presidency (University of Chicago, 1949).

James M. Burns, PRESIDENTIAL GOVERNMENT: THE CRUCIBLE OF LEADERSHIP (Houghton Mifflin, 1965).

Claude A. Buss, THE ARC OF CRISIS, NATIONALISM AND NEUTRALISM IN ASIA TODAY (Doubleday, 1961; and ASIA IN THE MODERN WORLD (Macmillan, 1964).

James F. Byrnes, SPEAKING FRANKLY (Harper, 1947); and ALL IN ONE LIFETIME (Harper, 1958).

William G. Carleton, THE REVOLUTION IN AMERICAN FOREIGN POLICY: ITS GLOBAL RANGE (Random House, 1963).

Douglass Cater, POWER IN WASHINGTON (Random House, 1964).

Marquis Childs, EISENHOWER: CAPTIVE HERO. A CRITICAL STUDY OF THE GENERAL AND THE PRSIDENT (Harcourt, 1958).

Winston Churchill, TRIUMPH AND TRAGEDY (Houghton Mifflin, 1953).

Bernard C. Cohen, THE PRESS AND FOREIGN POLICY (Princeton University Press, 1963).

Elmer E. Cornwell, Jr., PRESIDENTIAL LEADERSHIP OF PUBLIC OPINION, (Indiana University Press, 1965).

Edward S. Corwin, THE PRESIDENT'S CONTROL OF FOREIGN RELATIONS (Princeton University Press, 1917); THE PRESIDENT, OFFICE AND POWERS, 1787-1957: HISTORY AND ANALYSIS OF PRACTICE AND OPINION (Fourth rev. ed., New York University Press, 1957).

Edward S. Corwin and Louis W. Koenig, THE PRESIDENCY TODAY (New York University Press, 1956).

Robert A. Dahl, CONGRESS AND FOREIGN POLICY (Norton, 1964).

Jonathan Daniels, THE MAN OF INDEPENDENCE (Lippincott, 1950).

W. Phillips Davison, THE BERLIN BLOCKADE: A STUDY IN COLD WAR POLITICS (Princeton University Press, 1958).

Alexander De Conde, THE AMERICAN SECRETARY OF STATE (Praeger, 1962); and HISTORY OF AMERICAN FOREIGN POLICY (Scribner's 1963).

Robert J. Donovan, EISENHOWER: THE INSIDE STORY (Harper, 1956).

Eleanor Lansing Dulles, JOHN FOSTER DULLES: THE LAST YEAR (Harcourt, 1963).

Dwight D. Eisenhower, PEACE WITH JUSTICE: SELECTED ADDRESSES OF DWIGHT D. EISENHOWER (Columbia University Press, 1961).

Dwight D. Eisenhower, THE WHITE HOUSE YEARS: MANDATE FOR CHANGE 1953-1956; and WAGING PEACE 1956-1961 (Doubleday, 1963-65).

Herbert Feis, BETWEEN WAR AND PEACE: THE POTSDAM CONFERENCE (Princeton University Press, 1960).

Richard F. Fenno, Jr., THE PRESIDENT'S CABINET: AN ANALYSIS IN THE PERIOD FROM WILSON TO EISENHOWER (Harvard University Press, 1959).

Herman Finer, THE PRESIDENCY: CRISIS AND REGENERATION, AN ESSAY IN POSSIBILITIES (University of Chicago Press, 1960); and DULLES OVER SUEZ: THE THEORY AND PRACTICE OF HIS DIPLOMACY (Quadrangle Books, Chicago, 1964).

Joseph Frankel, THE MAKING OF FOREIGN POLICY (Oxford University Press, 1963).

Robert Gilpin and Christopher Wright (eds.), SCIENTISTS AND NATIONAL POLICY-MAKING (Columbia University Press, 1964).

Len Giovannitti and Fred Freed, THE DECISION TO DROP THE BOMB (Coward-McCann, 1965).

Eric F. Goldman, THE CRUCIAL DECADE—AND AFTER: AMERICA, 1945-1960 (Vintage edition, 1961).

Barry Goldwater, THE CONSCIENCE OF A CONSERVATIVE (Victory Publishing Company, 1960); and WHERE I STAND (McGraw-Hill, 1964).

Richard Goold-Adams, JOHN FOSTER DULLES: A REAPPRAISAL (American edition, Appleton-Century-Crofts, 1962).

Norman A. Graebner, THE NEW ISOLATIONISM: A STUDY IN POLITICS AND FOREIGN POLICY SINCE 1950 (Ronald, 1956).

Laurin L. Henry, PRESIDENTIAL TRANSITIONS (Brookings, 1960).

Arthur Herzog, THE WAR-PEACE ESTABLISHMENT (Harper & Row, 1964).

William Hillman, MR. PRESIDENT (Farrar, Straus and Young, 1952).

Emmet John Hughes, THE ORDEAL OF POWER: A POLITICAL MEMOIR OF THE EISENHOWER YEARS (Atheneum, 1963).

Samuel P. Huntington, THE COMMON DEFENSE: STRATEGIC PROGRAMS IN NATIONAL POLITICS (Columbia University Press, 1961).

Sidney Hyman, THE AMERICAN PRESIDENT (Harper, 1954).

Malcolm E. Jewell, SENATORIAL POLITICS AND FOREIGN POLICY (University of Kentucky Press, 1962).

Donald B. Johnson and Jack L. Walker (eds.), THE DYNAMICS OF THE AMERICAN PRESIDENCY (Wiley, 1964).

Haynes Johnson, THE BAY OF PIGS (Norton, 1964).

Lyndon B. Johnson, MY HOPE FOR AMERICA (Random House, 1964).

Walter Johnson, 1600 PENNSYLVANIA AVENUE: PRESIDENTS AND THE PEOPLE, 1929-1959 (Little, 1960).

George F. Kennan, ON DEALING WITH THE COMMUNIST WORLD (for the Council on Foreign Relations), (Harper & Row, 1964).

John F. Kennedy, THE BURDEN AND THE GLORY (Harper & Row, 1964).

Stephen D. Kertesz and M. A. Fitzsimons (eds.), AMERICAN DIPLOMACY IN A NEW ERA (University of Notre Dame, 1961).

Louis W. Koenig, THE CHIEF EXECUTIVE (Harcourt, 1964); and Louis W. Koenig (ed), THE TRUMAN ADMINISTRATION: ITS PRINCIPLES AND PRACTICE (New York University, 1956).

Sidney Kraus, THE GREAT DEBATES (Indiana University Press, 1962).

David L. Larson (ed.), THE CUBAN CRISIS OF 1962 (Houghton Mifflin, 1963).

Harold J. Laski, THE AMERICAN PRESIDENCY, AN INTERPRETATION (Harper, 1940).

Sidney Lens, THE FUTILE CRUSADE (Quadrangle Books, Chicago, 1964).

Walter Lippmann, ESSAYS IN THE PUBLIC PHILOSOPHY (Little, 1955).

James L. McCamy, THE ADMINISTRATION OF AMERICAN FOREIGN AFFAIRS (Knopf, 1950).

Ernest R. May, ed., THE ULTIMATE DECISION: THE PRESIDENT AS COMMANDER IN CHIEF (Braziller, 1960).

George F. Milton, THE USE OF PRESIDENTIAL POWER, 1789-1943 (Octagon, 1965).

Robert Murphy, DIPLOMAT AMONG WARRIORS (Doubleday, 1964).

Richard E. Neustadt, PRESIDENTIAL POWER: THE POLITICS OF LEADERSHIP (Wiley, 1960).

Wiliam J. Newman, LIBERALISM AND THE RETREAT FROM POLITICS (Braziller, 1964).

Richard M. Nixon, SIX CRISES (Doubleday, 1962).

Raymond G. O'Connor, ed., AMERICAN DEFENSE POLICY IN PERSPECTIVE: FROM COLONIAL TIMES TO THE PRESENT (Wiley, 1965).

N. W. Polsby and A. W. Wildavsky, PRESIDENTIAL ELECTIONS (Scribner's 1964).

Merlo J. Pusey, EISENHOWER, THE PRESIDENT (Macmillan, 1956).

Harry H. Ransom, CAN AMERICAN DEMOCRACY SURVIVE COLD WAR? (Doubleday, 1963).

Jack Raymond, POWER AT THE PENTAGON (Harper & Row, 1964).

David Rees, KOREA: THE LIMITED WAR (St. Martin's Press, 1964).

Edgar E. Robinson, THE ROOSEVELT LEADERSHIP 1933-1945 (Lippincott, 1955).

Clinton Rossiter, THE AMERICAN PRESIDENCY (Rev. ed., Harcourt, 1960).

W. W. Rostow, THE UNITED STATES IN THE WORLD ARENA (Harper, 1960); and VIEW FROM THE SEVENTH FLOOR (Harper & Row, 1964).

Richard H. Rovere, THE EISENHOWER YEARS: AFFAIRS OF STATE (Farrar, Straus and Cudahy, 1956).

Richard H. Rovere and Arthur M. Schlesinger, Jr., THE GENERAL AND THE PRESIDENT (Rev. ed., Farrar, Straus and Young, 1965).

Warner R. Schilling, Paul Y. Hammond, and Glenn H. Synder, STRATEGY, POLITICS, AND DEFENSE BUDGETS (Columbia University Press, 1962).

Arthur M. Schlesinger, Jr., A THOUSAND DAYS: JOHN F. KENNEDY IN THE WHITE HOUSE (Houghton Mifflin, 1965).

Paul Seabury, POWER, FREEDOM AND DIPLOMACY: THE FOREIGN POLICY OF THE UNITED STATES (Random House, 1963).

Hugh Sidey, JOHN F. KENNEDY, PRESIDENT (Atheneum, 1963).

A. Merriman Smith, MEET MISTER EISENHOWER (Harper, 1955).

Theodore C. Sorensen, DECISION-MAKING IN THE WHITE HOUSE: THE OLIVE BRANCH OR THE ARROWS (Columbia University Press, 1963).

Theodore C. Sorensen, KENNEDY (Harper & Row, 1965).

Harold Stein, ed., AMERICAN CIVIL-MILITARY DECISIONS: A BOOK OF CASE STUDIES (University of Alabama Press, 1963).

Arthur B. Tourtellot, THE PRESIDENTS ON THE PRESIDENCY (Doubleday, 1964).

Martin B. Travis, Jr., "The United States of America" in Philip W. Buck and Martin B. Travis, Jr. (eds.), CONTROL OF FOREIGN RELATIONS IN MODERN NATIONS (Norton, 1957).

David B. Truman, THE GOVERNMENTAL PROCESS: POLITICAL INTERESTS AND PUBLIC OPINION (Knopf, 1958 edition).

Harry S. Truman, MEMOIRS: Vol. 1, YEAR OF DECISIONS; Vol. 2, YEARS OF TRIAL AND HOPE (Doubleday, 1955-56); and MR. CITIZEN (Random House, 1960).

Rexford Guy Tugwell, THE ENLARGEMENT OF THE PRESIDENCY (Doubleday, 1960).

Arthur H. Vandenberg, Jr., ed., THE PRIVATE PAPERS OF SENATOR VANDENBERG (Houghton Mifflin, 1952).

Sidney Warren, THE PRESIDENT AS WORLD LEADER (Lippincott, 1964).

H. Bradford Westerfield, FOREIGN POLICY AND PARTY POLITICS: PEARL HARBOR TO KOREA (Yale University Press, 1955).

Theodore H. White, THE MAKING OF THE PRESIDENT (Atheneum, 1961).

Courtney Whitney, MACARTHUR: HIS RENDEZVOUS WITH HISTORY (Knopf, 1956).

David Wise and Thomas B. Ross, THE INVISIBLE GOVERNMENT (Random House, 1964).

ACKNOWLEDGMENTS

The director of this study has profited greatly from the criticisms and the suggestions of members of the Research Committee of the Commonwealth Club in the preparation of this volume. They read and approved the preliminary draft and succeeding drafts, including the final chapter. The Chairman of the Research Committee, Justice Homer R. Spence, was of aid at every stage of the preparation. Executive Secretary Stuart R. Ward and Associate Executive Secretary William L. Hudson made suggestions and aided in the format, including illustrations. United Press International, the Oakland *Tribune,* and the San Francisco *Examiner* kindly contributed the photographs. For the photographic collection made available, special gratitude is expressed to Cliff McDowell, general manager, U.P. Newspictures, and Richard A. Litfin, Pacific Division general manager, United Press International. Francis A. Knapp of Lederer, Street & Zeus Company, has been of indispensable assistance in the publication of the manuscript.

The director is grateful to each of the authors who, individually and collectively, have contributed vigorous and hearty co-operation throughout the three years in which the study has been in preparation. Their advice and assistance in the presentation of the Notes and Bibliography have been especially noteworthy. The authors are deeply thankful to Lisette E. Fast, Research Secretary of the Institute of American History at Stanford University, who has served as research and editorial secretary throughout the period of the study.

Edgar E. Robinson

NOTES ON THE AUTHORS

Edgar E. Robinson, Margaret Byrne Professor of American History, Emeritus, Stanford University, is the author of *The Evolution of American Political Parties; The Foreign Policy of Woodrow Wilson* (with V. J. West) ; and *The Roosevelt Leadership 1933-1945.* For twenty-three years he was chairman of the Department of History, Stanford University, and Director of the Institute of American History 1942-1952. Since 1956 he has been an advisory editor (American History) for the *Encyclopaedia Britannica.*

Alexander De Conde, Professor of American History and chairman of the Department of History, University of California, Santa Barbara, has published *Herbert Hoover's Latin American Policy; Entangling Alliance: Politics and Diplomacy Under George Washington; The American Secretary of State;* and *A History of American Foreign Policy.* He has been a Guggenheim Fellow and a Fulbright Scholar.

Raymond G. O'Connor, Professor of American History and chairman of the Department of History at Temple University, has published *Perilous Equilibrium: A Study of Naval Disarmament;* and edited *Readings in the History of American Military Policy;* and is editor and co-author of *American Defense Policy in Perspective.* Under contract with the Arms Control and Disarmament Agency, he has prepared a number of studies on treaty making, the use of sanctions in treaties, and the steps taken when treaties are violated.

Martin B. Travis, Jr., Professor of Political Science and chairman of the Department of Political Science, State University of New York, Stony Brook, has co-edited *Foreign Relations in Modern Nations,* for which he contributed the section on "The United States"; has provided articles on Latin America in *Americana Annual, 1948-1965;* and is co-author of a forthcoming sixth edition of the *United States and Latin America.* He served as historian for the Air Transport Command, Alaskan Division, 1942-45.

INDEX